First published in Great Britain in 2024 by
Michael O'Mara Books Limited
9 Lion Yard
Tremadoc Road
London SW4 7NQ

Copyright © The History Gossip 2024

All rights reserved. You may not copy, store, distribute, transmit, reproduce or otherwise make available this publication (or any part of it) in any form, or by any means (electronic, digital, optical, mechanical, photocopying, recording or otherwise), without the prior written permission of the publisher. Any person who does any unauthorized act in relation to this publication may be liable to criminal prosecution and civil claims for damages.

A CIP catalogue record for this book is available from the British Library.

This product is made of material from well-managed, FSC®-certified forests and other controlled sources. The manufacturing processes conform to the environmental regulations of the country of origin.

ISBN: 978-1-78929-754-6 in hardback print format
ISBN: 978-1-78929-765-2 in trade paperback format
ISBN: 978-1-78929-766-9 in ebook format

1 2 3 4 5 6 7 8 9 10

Cover design by Natasha Le Coultre
Cover illustrations © The Trustees of the British Museum
Author photograph © Kate Lgotina
Illustrations by Andrew Pinder

Printed and bound by CPI Group (UK) Ltd, Croydon, CR0 4YY

www.mombooks.com

THE HISTORY GOSSIP

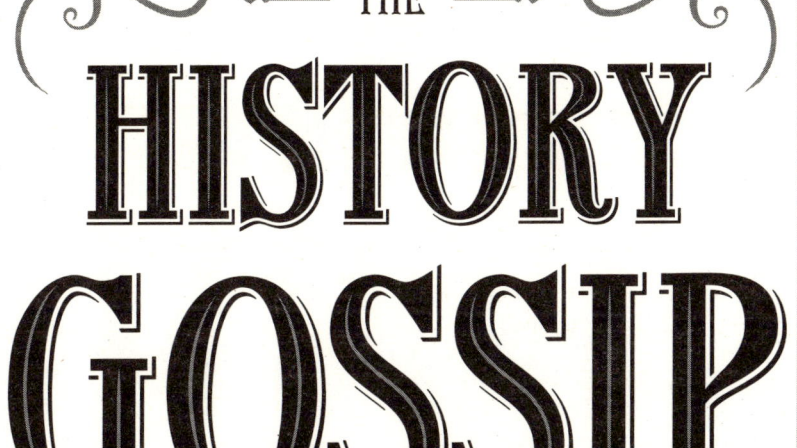

Was Anne of Cleves a Minger?

and *365* other **historical curiosities**

Michael O'Mara Books Limited

Contents

Acknowledgements 6
Introduction 8

January 11

February 29

March 43

April 59

May 77

June 93

July 109

AUGUST	125
SEPTEMBER	143
OCTOBER	157
NOVEMBER	173
DECEMBER	187
Glossary	204
Recommended Reading	221
Sources	222
Index	251

Acknowledgements

To Nicki, Millen and Rachel and the rest of the MOM team for truly listening to my ideas, taking them on board and being so patient. Thanks also to Tash for the beautiful cover, Gabby, Babs and Lizzy for bringing the book together so quickly and Andrew for the illustrations. I'm over the moon with how this book has turned out and I'm so grateful for everyone's incredible work.

Emily. Without you this wouldn't have happened. Thank you for sliding into my DMs and for being my cheerleader. You are so wonderful, and I feel so lucky to have you as my lovely agent!

Charlotte and the Belle PR team for helping alongside the MOM team to get my book out there!

To Durham University, especially the Archaeology and Classics department. My time at Durham has shaped me so much, and I treasure every moment I spent there. Thank you for instilling academic confidence in me.

To the wonderful creators I have connected with on social media over this past year. I love the history community so much, thank you for making me feel so welcome.

To the people who have liked, commented and shared my videos. This is because of you! I love being able to connect with you all, you're all so funny and amazing. Love you lots always.

To my beautiful, sexy, amazing support network that are my friends. Whether you came into my uni room at 2 a.m. with a bloodied head or told me about your shit-filled work woes, I love you all dearly. Thank you, Beth and Molly, for letting me vent to you both about the stress that was putting this together in such a short amount of time in between graduating uni and starting another degree. Ollie for always encouraging me to push myself, I appreciate you more than words can say. To Harriet for being super smart and amazing and helping out when my research made me want to throw my laptop down the stairs.

To my brother, Matthew, for always making me absolutely crease all the time, I'm so proud of you (sometimes) and will miss you so much when you go off to uni. To my dad for helping to build my confidence from a young age by sitting and very patiently listening to me practise my guitar and loop-station skills for hours on end. I will cherish those memories always.

This is for my mam. You are my best friend and I love you so much. Thank you for everything you do for me and Matthew, your emotional support is so invaluable to me. You really are amazing, and right about everything ...

I hope you enjoy it!

Introduction

Have you ever sat back and thought, I wonder what the Victorians were doing on this day, hundreds of years ago? Were they going to society balls? Courting and writing copious letters to their beloved? Getting blown up down the coal mines? And what about the Tudors? Fiddling and diddling their cousins, perchance? Day and night, I have been searching restlessly for answers. Painstakingly, I have scoured sources, transcribing them as accurately as I can. I have been the first to uncover mindblowing diary entries from the likes of Elizabeth I, who noted, 'Proper hate using Aquafresh. Fucking rank stuff, that. Also, Robert Dudley keeps trying to get in my pants. I've told him no, the only thing I'm shagging is England,' word for word. Incredibly poetic stuff. And finally, I have it all written up in the Holy Oracle™ I present before you now.

But in all seriousness, I really wanted to write a book that made history easily digestible, and I thought that an 'on this day' format was a great way to do that. Historical accuracy is at the heart of what I do (it really is, I promise!). There's always so much misinformation circulating online these days, which is very frustrating, so I strive to get things right. Also, if you stumble across a word or phrase that leaves you puzzled, flip over to the glossary at the back of the book.

I only started my TikTok account at the end of 2023, partly as a distraction from my final-year uni exams. If I'm being completely honest, I was so embarrassed about it, initially, that I didn't tell anyone, and blocked everyone I knew in real life. There's just something about talking about Henry VIII's penis online that you don't really want your immediate family seeing. But my confidence grew and I started to show more personality, and I feel so grateful that people have taken a liking to that. All the comments, likes and shares mean so much to me. So, this is for you, as a thank you. I love what I do, and I love that you have given me the platform to do that. Thank you a million times over.

Why did *Georgian rahs* do a striptease in a hot-air balloon, and why did *Robbie Burns* proper love pubes?

January

The new year arrives, dragging behind it the corpse of your resolutions like a cholera-ridden street urchin. You're cold, miserable, and trying to convince yourself that this year will be different, as you down gin in a pub famous for its stabbings next to the bins. Your greatest accomplishment this month? Not dying. And you should celebrate that: twelve is a splendid age to reach. In fact, you're probably getting on a bit now.

— 1ST —

1540 – Alleged minger Anne of Cleves arrives in England to meet her fiancé, Henry VIll, otherwise known as King Henry VIII. Keen to run her through so much that she'd end up resembling a butcher's bin, he decided to disguise himself and meet her at Rochester Castle before the actual wedding.

He believed that if Anne recognized him despite the costume, it would signify true love or some shite. So, after Henry VIII burst into Anne's room with five of his mates, the next thing Anne knew was that some podgy bugger had his tongue down her throat. It was reported that she said, 'Aw, thanks for putting your slaver all over my chops, that's really kind but unfortunately I don't get with randoms as I am engaged and that, all the best though x', as she didn't recognize Henners.

Absolutely mortifying for Henry, he then proceeded to declare her a butters anyway, who looked nothing like her portrait. For when it came to choosing his next conquest, Henry hadn't just relied on his ambassadors' word. He had sent his court painter, Hans Holbein, to create a portrait of Anne in 1539. Holbein must have nailed it, as Henry's ambassador in Cleves raved about how lifelike the portrait was. Even after Henry and Anne

annulled their marriage, Holbein stayed in the King's good graces, so it sounds like maybe Henry was telling porky pies.

— 2ND —

1890 – Alice Sanger proves that the girlies can do more than mop floors and open their legs. She became the first female staffer in the White House, as an assistant secretary to President Benjamin Harrison. She shattered that glass ceiling – and then probably polished it a bit from underneath, as she was a woman. Around the same time, in 1890, the American Woman Suffrage Association and the National Woman Suffrage Association merged into the National American Woman Suffrage Association (NAWSA). But what did Alice think of the suffrage movement? Was she a token hire by Harrison so he could go, 'Look! Diversity!' Though Sanger's stance on suffrage is unclear, her appointment by Harrison indicated a cautious step towards increasing female representation in government.

— 3RD —

1987 – Aretha Franklin becomes the first woman to be inducted into the Rock and Roll Hall of Fame. That's because, before 1987, women didn't exist. But from 1987, they appeared out of the sky. Men were astounded, 'Whomst are these creatures? How are they so good at making my dinner? It's a shame none of them can drive.' They then realized that not all of them had a sole purpose of making shepherd's pie, and some could even sing. 'That's actually really good,' they thought, 'so maybe let's put one woman in the Hall of Fame for doing an all right job. Not all of them, though, you don't want to push it and give them thoughts and ambition, so we'll just stick to one.' And thus, Aretha Franklin was immortalized.

— 4TH —

1656 – Sharks are wined, dined, and probably sixty-nined.
The Spanish ship *Nuestra Señora de las Maravillas* sank, carrying about six hundred people onboard, only forty-five of whom survived. The ship contained lots of jewellery and treasures, both as royal tax and private property, and was making its way to Seville. But because some pillock messed up the navigational route, the ship collided with another, then smacked into a coral reef and sank. People weren't stressed, though, because they'd watched *Titanic* and knew that all you had to do was lie on floating debris and hold some povo's hand, telling them you won't let go, but as soon as they die they are absolutely getting hoyed back into the ocean. But this time, DIY *Titanic* didn't really make the cut, so most died from exposure or became a morsel on the menu for the shark buffet.

— 5TH —

1531 – Henry VIII punches a hole in the wall and calls Pope Clement VII slurs on PlayStation, after being forbidden to remarry. The Pope had written Henry VIII a letter saying, 'Listen son, you're already married to Catherine. I don't really want to hear you telling me in graphic detail that it's like feeding a Tic Tac to a whale. Maybe that's more of a reflection on you. Throwing hot dogs in hallways isn't really a wise use of your time neither. And if you do try to marry this Anne, I'll excommunicate you, and that'll be really embarrassing. Chin up though, you'll get a son soon enough. Lukewarm regards, The Pope.'

— 6TH —

1066 – Harold Godwinson holds a funeral for his brother-in-law and King of England, Edward the Confessor. Harry thinks it's shit craic as everyone's just moping about and getting

January

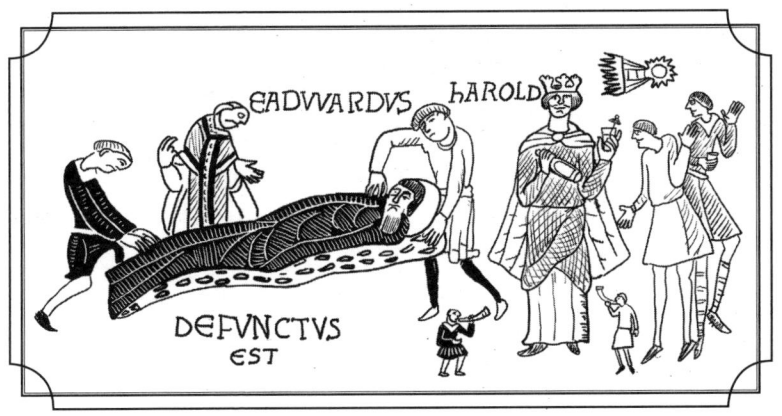

emosh. So, quoting his idol, Gemma Collins, he said, 'Do you know what, fuck this, no more being down. Let's crank the tunes up, everyone', and crowned himself king the same day. Although some say, when Edward died, the crown was allegedly passed to Harold, others say he was meant to act as regent until someone better came along. Whatever the case, having a coronation/funeral party was odd behaviour, as it was customary for kings to wait a few months before they took the throne.

— 7TH —

1785 – Jean-Pierre Blanchard and John Jeffries cross the English Channel in a gas balloon. Blanchard started stripping off, to which John said, 'Woah there, sunshine, I know we enjoy playing international cock or ball from time to time, but no homo mate, no homo.' But Blanchy was only doing a striptease to remove extra weight from the balloon so they wouldn't crash. By the time they were three quarters of the way through the journey they had started going down, and, to Blanchy's disappointment, not on each other. After throwing out food, equipment, and trousers, they were still descending to the ground. Their last stroke of luck was pissing themselves to further lighten the load. According to their

◆◆ The History Gossip ◆◆

own accounts, about six pounds of urine drained out of them both helped to save the day, landing them, pretty much intact, in France.

— 8TH —

1992 – US President George H. W. Bush vomits on the Prime Minister of Japan. 'Bushy boy' was one of a 135 attendees at a state dinner in Japan, but between the second and third courses, he suddenly felt like he'd just done four Jägerbombs in a row. When Kiichi Miyazawa, the Japanese prime minister, noticed Bush looking a bit green, he kindly suggested Bush 'tacky-chun in a pint glass' to avoid embarrassment. Unfortunately, it was too late, as Bush decided to share his dinner in Miyazawa's lap before fainting, dramatically – perhaps hoping that Kiichi wouldn't quite understand what just happened due to the language barrier. The next day, the White House announced that the president had a mild case of 'the liquid shits', a.k.a. acute gastroenteritis.

— 9TH —

2007 – Sales for turtlenecks spike as the iPhone is announced to the public. An iPod Touch with the ability to receive phone calls – people went mental over this device. The possibilities of this new iPhone are endless, life-changing: romantic date nights where neither person speaks, ignoring calls and texts while clocking up an impressive screen time of twelve hours a day, and messaging someone in the same room.

— 10TH —

1863 – The world's first underground railway opens, between Paddington and Farringdon Street. If you are fucked off with little chimney sweeps in training doing jazz hands saying, 'Please sir, can I have some more?' when you're walking around London town, then today is your lucky day. The underground gives you the ultimate high-end London experience. This includes being next to daily commuters who look at you like you've shanked their nan, and American tourists who loudly exclaim everything is like Harry Potter, complete with backpacks on their front which, not to be a cow, screams 'rob me'.

— 11TH —

1569 – Could it be ye? England's first lottery takes place. The nation's favourite frigid ginge, Queen Elizabeth I, needed to raise money for England's harbours and coastal defences. Even though every ticket was guaranteed a prize, people were scared of getting done diddled, so only 10 per cent of the 40,000 tickets were sold.

Your lottery ticket was just a blank piece of paper where you'd write your name and a little verse or prayer. Keen to let everyone know they were Biggus Dickus reincarnate, a 1569 ticket read, 'God send a good lot for my children and me, which have had twenty by one wife truly.' A child, sometimes blindfolded, picked tickets from an urn and matched them with prize slips from another. The winner's verse was read out, but not their name, keeping it secret. Every ticket won something, from a silver plate to a £5,000 jackpot. The money helped England's defences just in time for the Spanish Armada in 1588, but due to lack of interest, the lottery was shelved in 1571.

— 12TH —

1896 – Three neeks in North Carolina decide to bribe a cleaner and sneak into a lab. Instead of doing the normal things university students do of an evening, like drink each other's piss on initiations then pass out in the club toilets, this lot were the first to produce X-rays. The objects they wanted to see through included an eggshell with a button in it, pins, cartridges, and a rubber-covered magnifying glass, after German physicist Wilhelm Röntgen discovered the new form of radiation just six days earlier.

— 13TH —

1404 – King Henry IV bans the times tables with his Act Against Multiplying. The thickies who were made to do Kumon after school are jumping for joy, but it turns out that this was actually to deal with the rise of alchemy: the false belief that you'd be able to turn base metals into gold with the right formula. But for those whose teeth match their horses', also known as posh people, this was catastrophic, as if anyone could make gold at their will, there'd be white Audis and Louis Vuitton bags everywhere. So, from that moment on, alchemists needed a licence.

✦✦ January ✦✦

— 14TH —

1697 – The General Court of Massachusetts declares a day of fasting, in honour of the falsely accused witches during the Salem Witch Trials. After calling Susan next door a witch because your husband keeps looking down her top when she bends over to water the plants, you realize you've probably gone too far when she's executed for witchcraft. But don't worry, love, we've all been there, and even judge Samuel Sewall and accuser Ann Putnam apologized and admitted guilt. Luckily, Ann's words have been found in surviving manuscripts:

> *Hey guys, it's been a while. I never expected to have to hop on here to address my wrongdoings, so this is going to be a really difficult time for me. First off, I just want to say even though I did accuse Susan of witchcraft because she's a whore, that was never my intention and I would never do anything like falsely accuse someone because my bread didn't rise, even though it's been proven that I did indeed do that. All the negative backlash I have since received, probably sent by the devil and his workers, and Susan, has really impacted my mental health. I am the victim. I've decided to take a long and well-needed two-day break from the Town Crier message forums, but you can still buy my merch below.*

— 15TH —

1797 – John Hetherington was the first to sport the top hat in public. Children screamed, women fainted at the sight, and dogs yelped. No, Prince Andrew didn't enter a playground, but the man in a top hat was fined £500 for disturbing the peace, as a crowd had gathered to see it, and a boy broke his arm after being thrown down by them.

— 16TH —

27 BC – Octopus, oh sorry, Octavian, gets sick of people mispronouncing his name. Octoman decided to rebrand as 'Augustus' and became the first Roman emperor. And, just like that, the Roman Republic was dead. With Augustus in charge, the Roman Empire officially kicked off, sparking two thousand years of men everywhere thinking of it a bit too often, and how much they 'miss it'. Yet each of the men in question, such as Brandon, 23, from Leeds, probably would've been one of the ones the Romans chucked in arenas with lions for fun. So it's hard to say exactly what they're yearning for – maybe they just like the idea of having a strong chin and a sword.

For Augustus, the answer to 'How often do you think of the Roman Empire?' was clearly 'all the time', because he was a man with a vision. While the Senate tried to pretend they still had a say in things, Augustus flexed his power, filling Rome with grand monuments and a lot of statues of himself, just in case anyone forgot who was in charge.

— 17TH —

1912 – Captain Robert Falcon Scott sets off on a race against Norwegian explorers to see who could be first to reach the South Pole. Before fidget spinners were invented, people were bored shitless, with nowt to do apart from shagging arsenic and dying of mysterious illnesses. It was Captain Scott's lifelong mission to sit on Father Christmas's lap and, using sledges and ponies to get there, he went so far as to try and cosplay him, not realizing he looked like an absolute tit.

The Norwegians used expert dog teams and skiers, resulting in them getting there thirty-three days before the English. When Scott and the lads arrived on 17th January, the Norwegians had long since departed. Knowing he'd been beaten by a country whose only contribution was being next to one that produced flatpack furniture and Abba, he was mortified. Worse yet, it turned out Father Christmas lives in the North Pole, not the South. Disappointed that there were no chunky lads' laps to sit on, the next day, they set off home, but died from the cold on their way back.

— 18TH —

1644 – Ancient aliens spaff themselves as a group of pilgrims report one of the first UFO sightings in America. John Winthrop recorded in his diary that he saw two explosions and flashing lights in the water, then, the following week, various people heard a voice calling, 'Boy! Boy! Come away! Come away!'

The voice saying, 'Boy! Come away!' was heard about twenty times by various 'godly folk', and many saw the sparkling lights, too. The eerie phenomenon turned out to be near where Captain John Chaddock's ship had spectacularly exploded, killing five crew members. Among the casualties was a sailor who was suspected of murder and liked to go around saying he saw dead people, thinking that was a perfect chat-up line. With many believing it was his vengeful ghost, and the ye olde aliens added to the mix, people were left clutching their pearls and prayer books.

— 19TH —

1511 – Henry VIII and his og ting, Catherine of Aragon, give a ruby collar to a statue of the Virgin Mary. This was their way of saying 'Cheers, love,' to Mary, as Catherine gave birth to a baby boy. Giving a statue a ruby collar was also Henners' and Cathy's good deed of the day, so they didn't have to feel bad walking past the Tudor povos, such as the five-year-old on his way to plough some fields or tarmac drives, or whatever such povos did. A few weeks later, Catherine and Henry's baby passed away. During Henry's dissolution of the monasteries in 1538, the statue was taken to Chelsea in London and publicly burned.

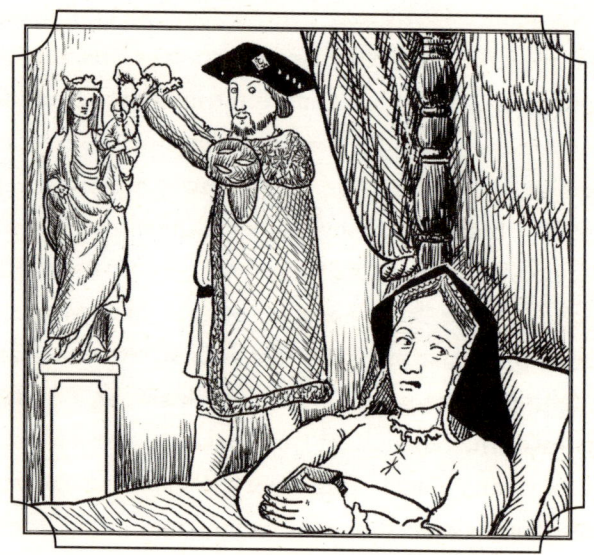

— 20TH —

1649 – Charles I is put on trial for treason. But you couldn't really put a king on trial, as he was effectively above the law and could only answer to God. I mean, like you could, because these blokes did, but you couldn't really, because of the Divine Right of Kings, essentially meaning that Charles was God's gift. Any parliamentarian who didn't agree with the trial was booted out or arrested. Charlie boy was accused of being an enemy of the public and being a murderer. He denied any wrongdoing, refusing to acknowledge the legitimacy of parliament, speaking only to say that it was not him. One may accuse him of acting like a wasteman, but henceforth, that is not him. To lips any maiden, that might be him, perchance. But alas, it was not him.

— 21ST —

1908 – New York City bans anyone who owns a 'public place' from letting women light one up, saying it makes them look rough. Women reassured New York by saying, 'Omg no, we're not smoking in a "Pat Butcher" way, sat on the swings after school. We're smoking in a "Lana Del Rey, Old Hollywood, Bond girl, Monica Bellucci in *Malèna*" way.' The mayor of New York, George Brinton McClellan Jr, grasped their vision straightaway, and two weeks later vetoed the ban, branding the authorities as uncultured snowflakes.

— 22ND —

1973 – Lead pills and flinging yourself down the stairs are made a thing of the past, for now at least, as Roe v. Wade becomes law. The outcome of this trial meant that women had the right to get an abortion legally. In the Victorian era, you'd get mysterious 'female monthly' pills, or you'd go to the back alleys where the midwives secretly operated. 'Now get yourself on that table and spread those legs, don't be shy we know you've done that before', and she'd use some needles or other spiky tools. Women in Newcastle in the late eighteenth and early nineteenth centuries took lead pills like birth control, just to make sure there were no surprises. If that didn't tickle your pickle, you could try boiling some copper coins and swigging that.

The History Gossip

— 23RD —

1789 – He loved writing smut for his readers to bust a nut: novelist John Cleland dies. He was the first to write English prose pornography, titled *Fanny Hill: Memoirs of a Woman of Pleasure*. The book explored the life of Fanny, a prozzie, and her quest to get her pasty smashed. Despite no vulgar or explicit language used throughout the whole novel, Cleland was arrested for 'corrupting the King's subjects', a year after its publication in 1749. George II and his subjects – such as his many mistresses, including his very own prozzie – would not stand for such vulgarities.

— 24TH —

1972 – Shoichi Yokoi, the Japanese solider who hid in the jungle and refused to surrender for nearly thirty years after World War Two ended, is found and brought back to his hometown. The winner of the Sorest Loser award, Yokoi was hiding in the jungles of Guam, and was adamant that his comrades would return for him. Living on a gourmet diet of venomous toads, rats and eels, he also weaved clothes out of tree bark. Yokoi stayed in occasional touch with two other Japanese soldiers who also remained in hiding, but, after they died in a flood in 1964, he spent his final eight years in hiding completely alone. When he returned to civilization, the copious amounts of disco dancing made him cringe, and he preferred to look back on his days in Guam.

— 25TH —

1759 – Scottish poet Robert Burns exits his mother's foof. This is great news for Robbie, as he can't get enough of them, especially hairy ones, but I don't think he went so far as to pine for his mother's. He'd go on to write the famous poem 'Nae Hair O'nt'. Written from Robbie's heart, the masterpiece expresses his grievances about marrying a lass with no pubic hair and his vexations that her fru fru was 'out o' fashion'. How he coped with the lack of a licey jungle, scholars still struggle to understand to this day.

—— 26TH ——

1926 – Scottish inventor John Logie Baird gives the first formal demonstration of a television. He sat forty neeks from the Royal Institution down and said, 'Listen, fellas, be ready to jizz in those pantaloons because I've got some science to show you.' He transmitted the television picture, using an image of the head of a ventriloquist's dummy. The images produced were faint and blurry, with many people confused and frustrated, as they were unable to watch contestants in a villa on an island, sitting around having beige conversations about looking for love and needing nothing more than a lad with top qualities such as 'banter'.

—— 27TH ——

1832 – Alleged kiddie fiddler Lewis Carroll, the author of *Alice in Wonderland*, is born. He was probs in his element being a kid, as he was rumoured to be partial to one. He befriended a man called Henry Liddell while at Oxford, but his real passion lay in taking pictures of Liddell's kids, including Alice, who was the muse behind his famous story. But instead of getting the photographer on the register and the nonce patrol on their way, in the Victorian era photos of naked children were a symbol of innocence. Photos of children posing as nymphs, cupids or cherubs were all the rage, and weren't seen as pornographic. It was only thirty-five years after Carroll's death that the rumours started. In 1933, a Freud wannabe, A. M. E. Goldschmidt, published an essay called *'Alice in Wonderland Psycho-Analysed'*. He believed the well wasn't the only hole Lewis wanted to trip and fall into, writing that Alice falling down the rabbit hole was a metaphor for creepy kiddie fiddling escapades. But Goldschmidt had no psychology qualifications whatsoever, so I'm not being funny but out of all things how did he manage to come to this conclusion? Actually, I don't even want to know.

— 28TH —

1896 – The world's first boy racer hits the road. Walter Arnold had just pimped out his newly financed Ford Fiesta, complete with spoiler, backfiring exhaust and a small peen. As he whizzed past the local coffin dodgers, people couldn't believe the speed he was going at – an astonishing 8 mph. Not only that, but Walter was tear-arsing in a 2-mph zone and was given a speeding ticket.

— 29TH —

1737 – English-born American Founding Father Thomas Paine is born. According to the Old-Style calendar, anyway – if we're going off the Gregorian Calendar, he was born 9th February. Paine wrote *The Rights of Man*, published in 1791, which defended the early stages of the French Revolution, including liberty, property, security and resistance to oppression. Other staunch defenders of men's rights also chipped in with their intellectual prowess, including academic Joseph Donald Essex, from the hit TV show *The Only Way is Essexeth*. He noted, 'The government should give away free holidays to Marbella. It's like, what, £150 there and back? Government can afford that.' This sparked an emotional response from the public, who nodded in agreement, 'Why aren't we getting free holidays to Marbs?' Thus the French Revolution catapulted into history.

January

— 30TH —

1661 – Warty munter Oliver Cromwell rises from the dead. Twelve years after he played a part in deleting Charles I by chopping block, Cromwell's body was dug up and beheaded, to teach him a lesson. Cromwell's head was put on a spike, beside other disembodied heads, including that of the judge at Charles I's trial, for everyone to see at Westminster Hall. It was rated the top attraction of 1661, with many saying it came a close second to dodging airborne chamber pots.

— 31ST —

1835 – An unemployed house painter, convinced he was the King of England rather than the King of the Job Centre, decides to shoot US President Andrew Jackson. But misses. Twice. Richard Lawrence was convinced Andrew stood in the way of him claiming his crown, but as he pulled the trigger, the powder failed to ignite. With all that free time on his hands, you'd think he'd have spent some time learning how to aim. Bless his cotton socks. This was the first US assassination attempt on a president, and Andrew Jackson, being used to fighting duels, only did a light piss in his pants, nothing drastic.

Why did *Mary Queen of Scots* get the chop, and was *Voltaire* into incest?

February

This is the twenty-eight-day reminder (sometimes twenty-nine) that no one loves you. Such joys. The singleness really hits home when you're sat knitting alone by the fire with only the rats to keep you company. But the fleas seem to take a liking to you, so at least you're getting some action. Is that a hickey? No, it's buboes from the plague.
You then die, of the plague.

◆• The History Gossip •◆

— 1ST —

1887 – A devout Christian called Harvey Wilcox registers his newly acquired land: Hollywood. He wanted a spiritual settlement, free from anything he deemed had morally questionable vibes, such as 2-4-1 strawberry woo woos and the cast of *Selling Sunset*. This worked out really well for him! Yet people weren't exactly itching to numb their bums on church pews every Sunday, so by 1900 the population was only five hundred. In 1910, Hollywood then became part of LA, because they couldn't manage something as basic as a proper water supply.

— 2ND —

1901 – Queen Victoria has her funeral. Unfortunately, she wasn't there to see it, so we'll never know if she enjoyed the day or not. By August 1900, she'd had enough practice with funerals after burying three of her nine kids, losing a favourite grandson, and waiting around for her eldest to kick the bucket from cancer. By November, she was mega-emosh, big time – but that's no surprise there.

— 3RD —

1637 – People in Holland realize that tulips are not in fact bottles of Prime. The mugs finally stopped paying 1,000 lbs of cheese or four fat oxen for a single bulb, like they had been doing for the previous three years.

— 4TH —

2004 – Zuckerburg creates 'The Facebook'. This enabled us all to stalk our exes and see how awful their lives had become, as well as the mother's brother's niece's sister of the person you'd been in a talking phase with.

❖❖ February ❖❖

— 5TH —

1626 – A famous writer is born and, unfortunately, she is a woman. Marie de Rabutin-Chantal was widowed by age twenty-four, but she wasn't too sad about that because the girlies told her that her she'd definitely find her Mr Big at some point. They said your twenties were all about finding yourself and cutting out toxic people, like her (now dead) husband, who died from a wound he got in a duel over his mistress. Marie didn't remarry, and instead spent her days bitching about French society via letters to her daughter.

— 6TH —

1952 – Queen Elizabeth II ascends to the throne and spends the next seventy years cutting ribbons. Luckily, she did have one wild night out: back in 1945, on the day World War Two ended, she celebrated by hitting the town incognito with Vanessa Kirby, linking arms with strangers and walking down Whitehall. We also can't forget that time she skydived out of a helicopter for the 2012 London Olympics. Classic.

— 7TH —

1845 – Some bloke called William Lloyd wanders into the British Museum absolutely trollied, mistaking it for his local Spoons. Enraged that they refused to put the Beethoven techno remixes on, he retaliated by throwing a sculpted stone exhibit at a glass cabinet which contained the priceless Roman Portland vase. He spent the next two months in prison, with a severe hangover.

— 8TH —

1587 – Mary, Queen of Scots, is beheaded. During her lifetime, she was never to beat the nepo-baby allegations, as she became queen at only six days old. After debating different career choices, she eventually decided on 'queen', keeping her place in the family business. But people knew deep down there was no way she would've got the job without her parents' connections. Mary got the chop because she was found to be complicit in a plot to murder her cousin, Elizabeth I, which is a good lesson for all the nepo babies out there as to how far their privilege can take them.

— 9TH —

c. 200 BC – Happy St Apollonia's Day! Apollonia is the patron saint of dentistry. When the Pagans seized her, she asked for a quick scale and polish, but instead they ripped out her teeth. She threatened to leave a bad Tripadvisor review for the shit service, and to add insult to no teeth they kept asking her to commit blasphemy

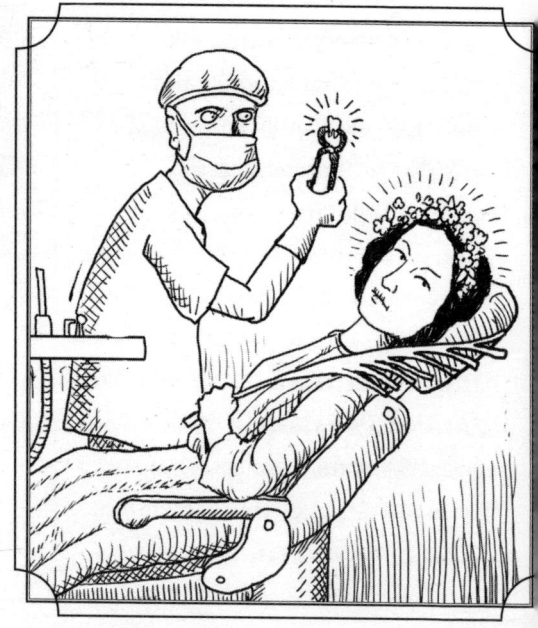

against Christ. They said they didn't do refunds, so she hopped into a fire and burned to death instead.

— 10TH —

1355 – Oxford students Walter and Roger go for a St Scholastica Day drink in the Swindlestock Tavern and complain that their wine tastes of poverty. This really put a dampener on their day, as they were on the lash to try to find a fellow trust-fund baby with a wanky name like Pistachio or Arabella Mozzarella or something. There were already tensions between locals and students, with many previous fights breaking out, but this complaint trumped those by turning into a three-day riot, which resulted in up to sixty students and locals suffering a violent death.

— 11TH —

1778 – Notorious quill-warrior Voltaire is allowed to return to Paris after twenty-eight years of exile. He had kept taking the piss out of the government with his satirical writing so they went in a rage and banned him from France. As one of the top shaggers of the Enlightenment, he liked being Enlightened about many things. Incest wasn't one of them, though, as he basically married his niece – even adopting a child with her.

— 12TH —

1909 – The National Association for the Advancement of Colored People (NAACP) is formed in the USA. Had you asked the average Joe about the concept of civil rights for everyone back then, they'd have looked at you as if you'd gone into their living room and pissed on their kids, so this was a necessary first step. The Springfield riot in 1908 was the final tipping point in the NAACP's formation, as numerous lynchings had taken place. Outraged by the unchecked chaos and violence, white liberals, including Mary White Ovington and Oswald Garrison Villard, sent out a call for action, which was met with the enthusiastic support of around sixty people. Seven of these were African Americans, including W. E. B. Du Bois, Ida B. Wells-Barnett, and Mary Church Terrell.

— 13TH —

1542 – Middle-aged Henry VIII gets stroppy because he finds out his teenage wife, Catherine Howard, has been involved with other men before their marriage. Then Henry realized the men in question were way older than his wife and these relationships had been abuses of authority. Just kidding! Henners couldn't get over that her fields had already been ploughed. Her head was subsequently ploughed via chopping block.

— 14TH —

Happy Vinegar Valentine's Day! If you didn't have the nerve to tell your ex that they're a bint in person, you could just send them an anonymous Vinegar Valentine card instead. During the Victorian era, these were the opposite of Valentine's Day cards, complete with illustrations and a few insulting lines about their recipient. They'd say things like 'your face is aesthetically deficient' – or take an aim at the lad who started playing and singing 'Wonderwall', by writing things such as:

> *If someone would choke you, and thus end their pain, Hearty thanks from your poor distressed neighbours he'd gain.*

Given the Victorians would self-combust if they saw an elbow on a table, are we even surprised that these anonymous personality-bashers flew off the shelves? It's unconfirmed whether they were sent as light-hearted banter or if givers genuinely had it in for their receivers, but not everyone took to the trolling. In 1885, the *Pall Mall Gazette* reported that a woman was shot by her husband for sending him an insulting card. You've been warned.

— 15TH —

1804 – New Jersey becomes the last Northern US state to pass a law to grant 'gradual emancipation' of slaves. The law generously allowed children of enslaved Blacks, born after 1804, to be free – once they'd put in a good 12 a.m.–12 a.m. shift of twenty-one years for women and twenty-five for men. As for their families and friends, they had to stick with the old-fashioned method of either waiting for death or making a break for it. But at least Jersey got around to it, just like they eventually realized walking around colour-matching their skin to a cheesy puff was also not the one.

— 16TH —

1923 – Howard Carter enters King Tut's burial chamber. Back in the 1920s, no one had cared to find and raid King Tutankhamun's tomb because he was one of the lesser-known indie kings. But that didn't bother archaeologist Howard Carter, because he only listened to not-yet-discovered grunge artists on Spotify and stopped liking them as soon as they went mainstream.

After spending five years trying to find a tomb – with the financial backing of his sugar daddy, Lord Carnarvon – Carter was getting a bit tired of trekking through the sand. But all was not lost – after one final push he found the tomb in the Valley of the Kings, entering

Tut's burial chamber on this day in 1923. It was found decked out with a chariot, golden shrines, jewellery, and Tutankhamun tucked away in a solid gold coffin. There weren't any curses on Tut's tomb, but rumours still circulated that the people who'd entered it were cursed. Lord Carnarvon thought it was bollocks. (He died from an infected mosquito bite two months later.)

— 17TH —

1936 – The first skintight-bodysuit-wearing fictional hero, The Phantom, is born. In this adventure comic strip created by American Lee Falk, The Phantom didn't have any superpowers, but still loved giving his enemies a good left, right, goodnight, with pants so tight you could see his religion.

— 18TH —

1478 – George, Duke of Clarence is executed by his brother King Edward. 'Why' was your classic reason of treason, so Edward tried to mix things up with the 'How': rumour has it that he had his brother drowned in a big vat of wine. Maybe Ed thought it was better to spill grape juice than royal blood, or maybe Georgie was an avid sesh-head and Ed was considerately helping him go out in style.

— 19TH —

1600 – Peruvian volcano Huaynaputina spouts off big time. Estate agents hadn't admitted on Rightmove that the closest local attraction was a ticking timebomb, so the masses of lava and ginormous ash clouds came as something of a surprise to the locals. Over a thousand people died, and the eruption was so massive it caused a volcanic winter in the northern hemisphere. Don't worry, though, it hasn't erupted again. Yet.

Top 5 Power Couples

5. Tutankhamun and Ankhesenamun. When eight-year-old King Tutankhamun's teenage sister Ankhesenamun started giving him the eye, he was confused and said, 'What are you doing? We're related!' Ankhesenamun then replied, 'Yeah? Only by blood.' And thus, they had a long and prosperous marriage, until Tut died at eighteen. As his parents, his duncle and mauntie, were also related, he didn't have much of a chance from the start.

4. Katie Price and Peter Andre. They met on *I'm a Celebrity* in 2004 and the world hasn't been the same since. The couple went from strength to strength, from filming reality shows where Peter, unprovoked, would call Katie an 'arrogant bitch', to releasing a cover of 'A Whole New World', taking the UK Charts by storm. It was even believed that Walt Disney himself rang up the pair to ask if he could use their version in the film instead.

3. Gandhi and his Flip-flop. Nothing could part Gandhi from the love of his life – no, not his wife, as he thought she was a right cow. Not even his grand-niece, who, among other women, would sleep naked in his bed so that Gandhi could prove the strength of his commitment to celibacy. His flop was his ride or die. Never seen without it. No matter the state of the flop – manky, dishevelled – his love for it lasted a lifetime.

2. Kanye West and Kanye West. Kanye has been in a committed relationship with his own ego for years, and they're inseparable. From interrupting award shows to launching presidential campaigns, this duo has been unstoppable. Kanye never misses a chance to praise his own brilliance, sometimes even breaking into spontaneous monologues about his misunderstood genius, which Kanye really appreciates.

1. Caligula and his Horse. The Roman emperor Caligula was known for his eccentricities, but his most famous love was for his horse, Incitatus. While most people had advisors, Caligula had a stallion. He loved his horse so much that he planned to make it a consul of Rome, reasoning that Incitatus had more sense than most of his senators. Whether dining with his horse or building it a marble stable, Caligula's love knew no bounds. It wasn't just about the companionship – Caligula genuinely believed Incitatus would make better decisions than half of his court.

— 20TH —

1824 – William Buckland announces to the Geological Society of London the name of the dinosaur species he's discovered. This was the first time a dinosaur had been called anything other than chunky lizard. The name? Megalosaurus. Despite his supposedly high IQ, he couldn't think of any other adjective to describe it.

— 21ST —

1804 – The world's first railway journey takes place in Wales. With not much to see other than the locals playing smash or pass with the sheep, it's a good job this wasn't a commercial journey. That wouldn't happen for a few years yet, when quiet-coach passengers would be mesmerized by classic on-board entertainment such as 'screaming child' or 'If you see something that doesn't look right, call the British Transport Police. See it. Say it. Sorted.'

— 22ND —

1935 – *The Little Colonel* premieres, featuring Hollywood's first interracial dance couple. The American South quaked in their cowboy boots, declaring a Black man dancing with a white girl the most heinous of crimes. They deemed themselves too respectable to watch something so horrific.

— 23RD —

1954 – A group of children from Pittsburgh, Pennsylvania, begins the time-honoured tradition of thumping each other on the arm where they'd just been injected. They say whatever doesn't kill you makes you stronger. Except for polio. This was the first time the polio vaccine was administered, which by now has prevented nearly 30 million cases of paralysis.

— 24TH —

1981 – Prince Charles and Diana Spencer announce their engagement. After initially going for her sister, Charles settled on the young Diana, partly because his family appreciated her innocence – like thinking 'missionary' was just about spreading the good word of Jesus in far-off lands. Diana soon found out that Charles and Camilla's definition was not the same.

— 25TH —

1956 – Sylvia Plath meets her future husband, Ted Hughes, at a party in Cambridge. Sylvia thought the best way to pull was to re-enact *Twilight* scenes, so she bit Ted's cheek to the point where she drew blood. They soon got married. Shockingly, it didn't go as well as Bella and Edward's story, although at least neither of Ted and Sylvia's kids were forced to suffer the indignity of the name 'Renesmee'.

— 26TH —

1802 – Victor Hugo is born. Some years later, he put his blood, sweat and tears into writing the 1,500-page novel, *Les Misérables*. He said his greatest accomplishment was that, even though the whole plot was centred in France, his characters still somehow sported thick cockney accents.

❖• February •❖

— 27TH —

1693 – *The Ladies' Mercury*, the first magazine in England marketed to women, is published. It consisted of advice columns on the most pressing issues of a woman's life, such as 'Why does my husband keep eyeing up the maid even though she's financially challenged?' and 'My husband tells me I'm past my prime, what do I do? – Anon, 21'. Only four editions were published.

— 28TH —

1953 – Scientists Watson and Crick discover the structure of DNA. The duo were listening to their favourite pop girls, Little Mix, when the groundbreaking lyrics about DNA taking their breath away really struck an emotional chord. This led to them discovering that the DNA molecule exists in the form of a three-dimensional double helix.

— 29TH —

Happy leap day! Julius Caesar introduced the first leap year in 46 BC and it's had some strange superstitions surrounding it ever since. In some cultures, women are encouraged to propose to men on 29th February. In Denmark, a man who refuses a woman's proposal must give her a dozen pairs of gloves.

Some cultures consider 29th February to be an unlucky day. In Italy, people say 'Anno bisesto, anno funesto,' which translates to 'Leap year, doom year.' In Scotland, there's a saying that 'Leap year was never a good sheep year'. But as leap-day babies only celebrate their birthday every four years, you'll only be sixteen when you're actually a pensioner so it's not all bad.

Was *Charles II* a boy racer, and why did *Thomas Cranmer* drop a remix on *Mary Tudor*?

March

Have you ever heard anyone go, 'Yes, lads, pure buzzing for March!' No? Exactly. This is the month no one really cares about. You thought spring might be near, but, instead, you get a month of misery and false hope. St Patrick's Day is just another excuse for the riffraff to drink themselves into oblivion and do swapsies for STIs.

✦✦ The History Gossip ✦✦

— 1ST —

AD 589 – Happy St David's Day! Davi-boy is the patron saint of Wales, and he served as a bishop, though today joyfully commemorates the year of his death. The Gwyneth Paltrow of his time, he was so committed to clean eating he made vegans look like they should be on Fat Fighters. Because he preferred a strict diet of bread, leeks and water, he missed out on the joys of British tapas (turkey twizzlers, beans and potato smiley faces). The only thing missing was a candle that smelled like his bits.

— 2ND —

1882 – Roderick Maclean attempts to assassinate Queen Victoria in Windsor. Unfortunately, Queen Vicky was not clued up on boundaries and thought this meant that he fancied her big time, writing to her daughter, 'it is worth being shot at to see how much one is loved'. This was the eighth and final attempt on the queen.

— 3RD —

1875 – As the first ever game of indoor ice hockey takes place in Montreal, Canada, a group of little shits in the audience decid to hop on the ice rink. The young boys decided to show everyone that they no longer needed a penguin skating aid and could go off all by themselves. One was struck across the head, with the *Daily Witness* reporting that 'the man who did so was called to account, a regular fight taking place in which a bench was broken and other damage caused'.

— 4TH —

1966 – John Lennon calls The Beatles 'more popular than Jesus' in an interview with the *Evening Standard*. There was a massive backlash and confusion over this statement in the USA.

'It's simply not true,' people would utter. 'Does he not know the impact "Shine, Jesus, Shine" had? Children yearned for this song. You couldn't step foot in a primary school without it gracing every morning assembly. If the teacher played something different, kids would be screaming, crying, and throwing up. Nothing can beat the cultural phenomenon that was "Shine, Jesus, Shine".' Due to the outrage, The Beatles never toured the USA again. Lots of radios banned their music and people burned their records.

— 5TH —

1973 – The late-stage consequences of putting keys in a bowl: Yankees players Fritz Peterson and Mike Kekich announce they've swapped wives. While Kekich's marriage swap eventually went tits up – perhaps as they were the couple that was left having to sit in the corner and watch – the foursome initially remained civil. They even toyed with the idea of a double divorce and wedding, with the wives particularly delighted by having a new set of balls to play with. Meanwhile, Matt Damon and Ben Affleck have been trying to turn this into a movie for quite some time now.

— 6TH —

1945 – George Nissen gets a patent for the trampoline, after building a prototype in the 1930s. Trampolines really took off during World War Two as the US used them as training tools for pilots. It is said Nissen was buzzing about this because it now meant he could have an obnoxiously large trampoline in his garden and make his mum watch him do forward rolls for hours.

— 7TH —

AD 321 – Roman emperor Constantine declares that Sunday should be a day of rest. This was purposefully chosen to appease Christians, who regarded Sundays as the day of worship, and non-Christians, as that was usually the day workers were paid. Concern was voiced by older generations, who claimed that Generation XVII had it so much easier than they did, and not only could young Romans not afford to buy a house because they kept spending it on avocado focaccia, but that the empire was now plagued by unproductivity.

— 8TH —

1699 – Blitzing about London in his horse and Corsa, King Charles II has 50 Shilling's music on max and an orange Year Nine in the front seat. Life was good. That was until he reached Holborn, where his carriage overturned in the dark. According to Samuel Pepys, a famous London diarist, the king was 'All dirty, but no hurt'.

March

— 9TH —

1959 – Barbie debuts at the New York Toy Fair. Ruth Handler, the creator, noticed that girls only had the choice to play as a mother or caregiver with baby dolls and decided to change things up. She thought girls could be anything they wanted to be, so created Barbie dolls to reflect that. So now, girls can be: Space Barbie, President Barbie, Twist My Arms and Grow Some Pointy Boobies Barbie, Pooper Scooper Barbie and the classic Spawn A Child Then Shove It Back In Barbie.

— 10TH —

1876 – The first telephone call is made. The call was made by Alexander Graham Bell to his assistant Thomas Watson. He said, 'Mr Watson, come here – I want to see you.' Watson said, 'That's mega stalker Ghostface vibes, so no.' Watson then used the advice from the Year Six 'stranger danger' assembly talk and proceeded to block his number.

— 11TH —

1708 – Queen Anne refuses to sign the Scottish Militia Bill. The bill was aimed to provide Scotland with arms, but when there was news that the French had plans to invade Scotland, people were sus that the Scots would be disloyal, which would've meant an overthrow of the monarchy. So it wasn't her being an arsey cow, she just didn't trust people who thought deep-fried Mars Bars were a cultural delicacy as they were, according to her, 'fucking rank'.

This was the last time a British monarch vetoed a bill passed by parliament. If she wasn't vetoing a bill, she was getting busy in the bedroom as she was pregnant over seventeen times. Tragically, she experienced at least twelve miscarriages or stillbirths; of the five live children she gave birth to, four died before reaching the age of two.

— 12TH —

1836 – Mrs Isabella Beeton is born. Married to an ambitious publisher, Mrs Beeton wrote *Mrs Beeton's Book of Household Management* at twenty-one. It contained sections on etiquette, cooking and cleaning. She'd give advice such as, 'If your husband is ill, just starve him.' Or other gems such as, 'You don't actually need to clean your baby's bottle that much, tbh,' which led to quite a few of them dying. Other sound advice included: 'If your milk has gone off, just put some boric acid in it,' and, 'If your kid ends up seeing Jesus, then that's just a coincidence.' She also loved a bit of meat, with recipes for 'beef tea and egg' and 'beef juice', although she probs didn't enjoy her husband's too much, because he had syphilis.

◆◆ March ◆◆

— 13TH —

1781 – Uranus is discovered, the first planet to be found since ancient times. They kept putting off the discovery, knowing full well the endless jokes that would follow. Oracles predict that in the year 2620, a petition will be started to change its name because people will be exhausted by the jokes. But what will they change it to, you ask? Urrectum.

— 14TH —

1950 – The FBI's 'Ten Most Wanted' fugitive list begins. The most notorious criminals included robbers, murderers and escaped convicts. They all had a New York accent and a fedora, and clicked their fingers in sync. Adding thousands of eyes to these investigations proved to be integral, with nine of the first twenty 'Top Tenners' arrested due to public cooperation. But the criminals weren't too fussed. Despite their deep-seated mummy issues, each found solace knowing that they had finally made someone's top ten.

— 15TH —

44 BC – Julius Caesar Salad's reign ends dramatically with the infamous Senate stabbing. Brutus, forever in Caesar's shadow, whispered to the other senators, 'Brutus is just as hot as Caesar. We should totally just stab Caesar,' an important line in history that was directly echoed by Gretchen Wieners thousands of years later. Cassius, ever the loyal sidekick, nodded along while touching his breasts in hopes of rain, slightly confused but fully on board.

— 16TH —

1792 – King Gustav III of Sweden is shot at a masked ball in Stockholm. Although he had been warned not to go to the ball, he went anyway, dressed as a monk, as monks are harmless and their bald patches are sick, so no one would want to bang bang him. He died thirteen days later.

— 17TH —

AD 461 – Happy St Patrick's Day! This day commemorates the traditional date that St Patrick, the Patron Saint of Ireland, died. Everyone was absolutely devo and really struggled with his sudden and untimely passing at seventy-eight. So, to commemorate this, Ireland drinks in his honour, living up to the age-old saying, 'Get that stomach pumped for Patrick.' However, in 1927 they vowed to pump no more, as a law was passed that stopped pubs from opening on St Patrick's Day. I can't imagine that lasted very long.

— 18TH —

AD 978 – Sixteen-year-old King Edward the Martyr is murdered in Dorset, England. The story goes that he was murdered by his stepmother, Queen Elfthryth, so that her son could become king. Sadly, subtlety wasn't her forte, and common tales relate that she poisoned him, then one of her servants stabbed him, then he was dragged around on his horse.

— 19TH —

1931 – To help the masses of newly converted and long-time brokies during the Great Depression, the US state of Nevada, unable to read the room, thinks that giving everyone a gambling addiction might be the move. As citizens were abandoning Nevada in increasing numbers, disappointed they were unable to smell the spirit of teens, the state took the drastic measure of legalizing gambling and, later on, divorce. Founded in 1905, Las Vegas has since become the gambling capital of the world.

✦• March •✦

— 20TH —

1345 – The Black Death is unleashed, according to fourteenth-century scholars. Despite these weapons walking round smelling like the back of an earring and living in conditions reminiscent of the aftermath of Leeds Fest, many wondered why they were dying of the plague. Scholars from the University of Paris blamed the disease on the 'conjunction of Saturn, Mars, and Jupiter in Aquarius', which allegedly happened on this day. They tried almost everything to cure it: bloodletting with leeches, rubbing buboes (painful swellings in the thighs, neck, groin or armpits spread by the fleas on rats) with chopped-up pigeons, quarantining (maybe they did have some sense) and ingesting arsenic (never mind).

If that didn't work, they could always proceed to bathe in piss or drink it down in one, echoing sacred spiritual chants such as, 'We like to drink with Bartholomew Geoffrey de Percy Mortimer Percival Thistlethwaite III because Bartholomew Geoffrey de Percy Mortimer Percival Thistlethwaite III is our mate. And when we drink with Bartholomew Geoffrey de Percy Mortimer Percival Thistlethwaite III he gets it down in eight.' But unfortunately, when the lads got to three, Bartie's tongue was turning white, his lymph nodes had swollen, black and purple spots appeared on his skin, and by one he was knocked clean out.

— 21ST —

1556 – After being Billy Big Bollocks under Henry VIII as the architect of the English Reformation, Thomas Cranmer is tried for treason and heresy, and sentenced to death by Mary Tudor. With Mary determined to make an example of him and Cranmer even more determined to show people he was an absolute lad, he asked to do a final speech at Oxford University Church. Although he was made to give a sermon that blew smoke up Mary's

◆◆ The History Gossip ◆◆

backside, he decided to drop a remix. He said that Catholicism didn't fit well with him as he would always hear them chat about the smell of burning incest during services, and that wasn't something he was morally OK with. Cranmer was then dragged to the stake, where he put his hand into the flames first, exclaiming, 'This hand hath offended.' As the flames engulfed him, he remained calm and collected, straight-faced and doing the Darlo finger.

— 22ND —

1888 – Plans for the world's first football league are announced, the teams include Aston Villa, Preston, Blackburn Rovers, Bolton Wanderers and Wolverhampton. Suddenly, players were being bought for record-breaking numbers of four shillings and sixpence with a side of gruel, some even going for five. The public couldn't believe the astronomical figures these players were going for. They agreed that these sorts of wages should have been going to respected members of the community, such as the armed forces or doctors, not lads who dropped out of being chimney sweeps at twelve to chase dreams of kicking balls and having girls bounce on theirs. It didn't help that the lads kept losing games.

— 23RD —

1839 – The yutes of the 1830s enjoy their slang. In educated circles, many words were intentionally misspelt, just for shits and giggles, such as OW for 'Oll Wright' (All Rright). But OK was thrust into the limelight when published by the *Boston Morning Post* on this day for the lols, as an abbreviation for 'Oll Korrect' (All Correct).

— 24TH —

1458 – After they finally heal from their toxic relationship, leaders from the Yorkist and Lancastrian factions stroll together through London's streets toward St Paul's Cathedral, for a reconciliation service known as the 'Loveday'. This was to prove that division caused by the 1455 Battle of St Albans, which had been fought by Waitrose shoppers and yummy mummies, was well and truly healed.

The Duke of York made a speech saying, 'I'm sorry I said that your dad sells Avon.' The Duke of Somerset was moved to tears by this heartfelt apology, as although those words brought up some traumatic flashbacks, he truly believed they could move past this. The Lancastrian Duke of Exeter also chimed in, stating, 'I'm sorry I said that your mum drops 50p down the radiator and goes, "Zone 3, please", but tensions rose again, as talking about the Duke of York's mum was off limits. Just eighteen months later, the two sides went to war once more.

— 25TH —

c. 1180 – The annual Tichborne Dole is inaugurated in Tichborne, Hampshire. Just before Lady Tichborne's clogs were popped, on her deathbed, she told her husband, 'If you don't give the soap deprived some scran after I die, I'll watch you at the end of your bed at night and whisper things like, "I'm a ghost," and that, and then I'll tap the table and make you shart.'

As she didn't trust her husband, Lady Tichborne added that, if they ever stopped the handouts, there would be seven sons born, followed by seven daughters, then the family would die out, leaving the house in ruin. In 1796, the tradition briefly paused, due to vagabonds taking the piss. In 1803, part of the house went into ruin and subsided, with the heir, Sir Henry Tichborne, one of seven brothers, having fathered seven daughters. So today the residents are still given some flour, but get a bit pissy if it's not organic.

— 26TH —

1839 – The Henley Royal Regatta is born. In a moment of sheer brilliance, a public meeting in Henley-on-Thames town hall proposed that the town would greatly benefit from an influx of red trousers and very obvious physical signs of family inbreeding. The annual race lasts from Tuesday to Sunday, ending on the first weekend in July.

— 27TH —

1915 – Mary Mallon, infamously known as Typhoid Mary, achieves worldwide fame for coughing loudly with her mouth open, like a five-year-old. An Irish immigrant, she was fond of her mornings being top, and the occasional scrap. As a teen, Mary left for the USA, where she started working as a cook. As a woman, she slaved away in those kitchens, where she belonged, chopping those Guinnesses and making her signature peach ice cream for New York's wealthy households. But she left a trail of death wherever she went, with all seven families she worked for falling ill or dying.

Then, George Soper, a sanitation engineer, was hired by the family of one of the victims, to investigate the mysterious deaths. When he first tracked Mary down, she chased him out of her kitchen with a carving fork. Eventually, Mary was quarantined from 1907 to 1910. When she was released, she was strictly forbidden from working as a cook. Mary, however, believed everyone was chatting absolute shite, since she never had typhoid herself and occasionally did use Dettol on the bench in between chopping raw chicken and making apple pies. Stubborn as ever, after being released from another stint of solitary confinement, she tried working as a laundry maid but eventually returned to cooking under a string of fake names. She even, in a spectacular display of poor judgement, took a job in a hospital kitchen. This landed her back in solitary confinement for twenty-three years, until she died.

Why was Mary's peach ice cream so crucial to her story? It turns out the typhoid bacterium can live in cold food but is destroyed by cooking. Maybe if she'd made a cracking corned-beef pie, she could've kept under the radar.

— 28TH —

1881 – P. T. Barnum and James Bailey decide to join forces and create a three-ring circus in Madison Square Garden. They ambitiously named it 'The Greatest Show on Earth', serving up overpriced popcorn, animal acts that would have given PETA a menty-b, and clowns who'd seen better days. And thus, the American public was treated to the finest blend of chaos and spectacle that two men could dream up, all under one roof.

Tudor Insults

Feeling bland for just calling people fucking munters? Time to throw it back a few centuries and spice up your slurs, Tudor-style.

1. 'A Plague Upon You!' The catch-all curse for when you really, really want the universe to rain down misery on someone. Use it liberally for things such as: catching the clap from your missus, even though she swore she popped her cherry with you, or when your small child barges into your room at 3 a.m. to tell you they've been sick.

2. 'Zounds!' (from God's Wounds) This is the Tudor equivalent to dropping an F-bomb in church. The go-to expletive for everyone from furious monarchs to exasperated peasants, it was so overused that King James had to step in and play the fun police with some heavy-duty laws.

3. 'I Don't Give a Fart' In 1595, Elizabeth Wheeler made a bold proclamation in a Stratford-upon-Avon courtroom: 'Goodes woonds, a plague of God on you all, a fart of ons ars for you.' She was quickly removed from court.

4. 'Knave!' Henry VIII loved this one – it's medieval for 'idiot', but with a royal seal of disapproval. Perfect for those moments when 'tosser' just doesn't cut it.

5. 'Bull's Pizzle' Shakespeare's version of calling someone a tool, but with more livestock involved.

March

— 29TH —

1848 – For about thirty hours, Niagara Falls becomes drier than a nun's vagina. Some were convinced it was the end of the world, but legend has it that Niagara was chatting to this lad and all seemed well until she got told that not only did he wear tracksuits with socks pulled up around them, but was also a SoundCloud rapper, which resulted in the dry spell. Others say that, after a harsh winter, ice from Lake Erie broke up in March and strong winds pushed it into the Niagara River, creating a dam that blocked the water.

— 30TH —

1811 – In Gottingen, Saxony, chemist Robert Bunsen is born. He revolutionized spectroscopy, and co-discovered big-dick science things like caesium and rubidium. Most notably, he became immortalized with the invention of the Bunsen burner, around which students gather in science each year, wafting their hands through the flames and almost setting themselves alight in the name of being hard.

— 31ST —

1889 – The Eiffel Tower is finally finished, after two years, two months and five days. To celebrate, French couples everywhere got creative in the bedroom, re-enacting its iconic shape with their favourite third wheel. A truly landmark achievement, 'La dame de fer' (French for 'Iron Lady') was built for the 1889 World's Fair to celebrate the hundredth anniversary of the French Revolution and to showcase France's industrial strength to the world.

Why did **Dick Turpin** strive to be reem, and to whom did **Jane Austen** give the middle finger?

April

This month brings the showers that make everything wetter than Catherine the Great going into the stables, and mud that clings to your boots like the stink of the Thames. Meanwhile, April Fools' Day is just a sadistic reminder that everyone in your life is a conniving bastard. And let's not forget the taxes, a legal form of robbery where you're fleeced like a sheep by the Crown, with no choice but to grin and bear it.

— 1ST —

1816 – Jane Austen politely tells the Royal Librarian to do one after he asks her to write a historical romance. Austen's chats with the Prince Regent's librarian, Reverend James Stanier Clarke, came after her commercial success from works such as *Sense and Sensibility* (1811) and *Pride and Prejudice* (1813). Jane was disapproving of the Prince of Wales (later George IV), believing that being notorious for pulling nines and doing lines should be reserved for the cast of *Geordie Shore*, not the Royal Family. Nonetheless, after Stainer Clarke's request, she dedicated her novel *Emma* to the prince. On 1 April 1816, Jane replied to James's letter in which he asked her to write a 'historical romance illustrative of the history of the august House of Cobourg'. Jane then tactfully replied, 'I'm not being funny, but I'd rather guide my dad into my mum. That sounds wank.' She then went on to say that although that could be more of a bestseller than her 'pictures of domestic life in country villages' she 'must keep to her own style'.

— 2ND —

1647 – German scientific illustrator Maria Sibylla Merian is born. After a childhood of eating worms, one day Merian thought to herself, 'Where do these forbidden strawberry laces actually come from?' She lived during a time where people thought insects just magically appeared from the mud – a phenomenon known as 'spontaneous generation'. Merian had a hunch that it was bollocks, and was one of the first to record the process of insect metamorphosis. Her contributions were noticed by the Royal Academy, although women were still forbidden to join for another two hundred and fifty years.

April

— 3RD —

1954 – Oxford wins the hundredth boat race, beating Cambridge. These races have been going on since 1829 and show just how long the River Thames really is. This is also known as the posh way of seeing who has the biggest schlong, with normal folk just resorting to putting each other in headlocks in the smoking area.

— 4TH —

1975 – Microsoft is founded. Hippies were getting fed up with typewriters – and just couldn't type 'peace, love, and STIs' fast enough. They ended up finding Microsoft a bit slow, so decided to wait for Apple to be invented anyway.

— 5TH —

1614 – Pocahontas, whose real name was Matoaka, is forced to marry and gets stuck in one of history's worst cultural exchanges. She was from the Powhatan tribe, who kindly gave the colonizers gifts and food – probably thinking that would prevent the English from acting like total savages, after there'd been a few accidental fires. But, naturally, things went downhill, and Captain Samuel Argall came up with the genius plan to do a non-consensual cultural exchange, the one-sided edition.

During her captivity, Matoaka was abused and then made to marry John Rolfe. She was baptized, given the name Lady Rebecca, and was then forced into the ways of the Caucasian customs – like saying, 'Well, it seems everyone had the same idea,' when going to a busy place, or taking up veganism. In a bid to make her feel at home, the English spoke to her slowly and loudly, asking her where she was 'really from'.

— 6TH —

1896 – After skipping PE for 1,500 years, the first modern Olympics was held in Athens, Greece. The Victorians really felt like they missed out on being shouted at during rounders before being gassed by the vanilla aroma of the girls' changing rooms. So, they brought it back with a bang, including fourteen nations from around the world.

— 7TH —

1793 – Bad boy Dick Turpin is hanged in York. A notorious highwayman, he was known for hijacking and looting people's carriages as they were travelling. The snickers at him announcing himself as 'Dick' were soon put to a halt when he whipped those guns out, giving you a good 'left, right, goodnight' if you didn't hand over those gunky pearl earrings that had never seen an anti-bac wipe. Big Dick was an Essex boy, so it was his lifelong quest to have enough saved up to pay for a veneers and lipo two-for-one deal in Turkey. 'I just want to look reem,' he sighed, as he strived to make a living by stealing and selling horses after going on the run for killing a man.

Unfortunately, after shooting his landlord's cockerel, he was imprisoned and gave his name as John Palmer. After being moved to York Castle, he wrote to his brother asking for help. But his brother was a bit of a tight-arse, refusing to pay the postman sixpence to receive the letter, which was then returned to the post office. Big Dicky's handwriting was recognized by his old schoolmaster, and he was sentenced to death. But our lad wanted to go out with a bang, so he hired five professional mourners to put on a show for the crowd as they followed him onto the scaffold. They were said to have chanted comforting sentiments, such as 'Free up my man' and 'Big Dicky did nothing wrong'.

April

— 8TH —

563 BC – If you're in Japan, you'll likely be celebrating Buddha's birthday. If you're in England, though, it's likely that the closest you'll get is contemplating your life choices on the toilet after last night's spicy curry from The Fat Buddha.

— 9TH —

1963 – Winston Churchill becomes the first honorary citizen of the USA. John F. Kennedy made various brown-nosing remarks about Churchill when presenting him with the honour, in which Winston replied, 'Cheers, mate, but shouldn't you be focusing on more serious concerns, like the fact that your supermarkets have entire aisles dedicated to different Oreo flavours?' But Churchill wasn't exactly the pinnacle of health, either. The founder of the Smirnoff Ice strawpedo, he downed a pint of champers or wine for lunch and another for dinner. He'd also imbibe whisky sodas for breakfast, and brandy in between. Churchill actually wrangled a doctor's note that allowed him to drink unlimited booze on a trip to the USA during Prohibition.

— 10TH —

1633 – A crowd gathers outside a shop in Holborn, London. People were dying to see what no one in this era had seen before. Soap? No, it was a banana. The shop owner, Thomas Johnson, thought it was mint that if you 'turned it up, it looked like a boat'. It's lovely to see how men are entertained by the simple pleasures of life. He was so enthralled by it, he didn't even eat it, just kept it on display, noting that it became ripe in May and then went manky in June. Even towards the end of the Victorian era, most people hadn't seen a banana, so it's no surprise how amazed they were to see one.

— 11TH —

1814 – Napoleon Bonaparte signs the 'Treaty of Fontainebleau'. After a lifetime of fighting battles with Prussians, his small-man complex, and (false) rumours that he preferred his wife's punani unwashed, he was signing his assent to be exiled from France. 'Oh no, this is mega sad,' he replied, as he was told he'd get full sovereignty and ownership of his own island, Elba, on the Mediterranean. 'How will I ever survive this?' he sobbed, as he unveiled the grand opening of Ocean Beach Elba with a special DJ set from Wayne Lineker, as well as balls, theatre performances and organizing a small court. Unfortunately, necking pints of vodka with a dash of orange just didn't hit the spot anymore, so less than a year later, he fucked off back to France.

— 12TH —

1709 – The first edition of *The Tatler* hits the streets, offering London's elite a thrice-weekly dose of gossip and self-importance. Edited by Richard Steele, under the pen name Isaac Bickerstaff Esq., the paper quickly became a must-read for anyone who thought discussing the latest bonnet trends was the pinnacle of intellectual conversation. It featured hard-hitting articles for Jontys and Montys alike, such as, 'How to Complain About the Poor Without Looking at Them Directly', an essential skill for any gentleman or lady who wanted to express disdain while maintaining a safe distance. But we can't forget the classic, 'Secrets to Perfect Posture: Tips from People Who've Never Had to Work'. *The Tatler* was a triumph, finally giving posh people something to do between fox hunts and wondering why the help keep asking for more wages.

— 13TH —

1870 – The Metropolitan Museum of Art opens to the public.
The Victorians, always ahead of their time, envisioned it as the perfect backdrop for people to sit on the steps and take painfully posed pictures of themselves unironically mewing into the distance, captioned 'xoxo Gossip Girl' for social media. Not only that, they also needed a grand stage for the annual spectacle of extravagance and questionable fashion choices known as the Met Gala, where billionaires compete in a high-stakes game of 'Who Looked Like the Biggest Bellend?'

— 14TH —

1896 – Have you ever spaffed while eating Kelloggs? John Harvey Kellogg submits a patent for cornflakes, originally created by the Kellogg brothers to combat stomach problems in sick patients. Myths have persisted that cornflakes were invented to stop people from having solo sexy times. But this isn't true! John Kellogg was a super-strict Christian and believed that foods with any ounce of flavour were a gateway to sin, so he did encourage people to eat bland food, but this had no link to the invention of cornflakes.

— 15TH —

1912 – The *Titanic*, the world's most famously overhyped cruise ship, sinks into the chilly embrace of the North Atlantic at 2.27 a.m., taking with it 1,500 people. With 2,224 passengers on board, it turned out that 'unsinkable' was less of a fact and more of a misguided marketing slogan. The *Carpathia*, arriving fashionably late by about two hours, managed to rescue 700 lucky souls.

— 16TH —

1705 – Queen Anne is so impressed with Isaac Newton's passion for watching apples being launched onto the ground, she honours him with a knighthood at Cambridge. As she tapped his shoulder with the sword, she reportedly whispered, 'Imagine what you could do with a whole fruit basket,' while others watched, longingly. 'All it took was one apple,' they sighed, 'and here I am, eating oranges and still irrelevant.'

— 17TH —

1524 – Present-day New York Harbor is discovered by Italian explorer Giovanni da Verrazzano. This guy wrote interesting, though sometimes erroneous, accounts of his encounters with new lands and inhabitants. Stumbling upon New York Harbor, he found many of the great things the city had to offer, such as rats, people talking about apples that were big, and pizza-slice vendors with a one-star hygiene rating on every corner. With tears of happiness streaming down his face, he immediately signed a contract for a $4,500-a-month box studio flat, whispering to himself, 'I'm home.'

— 18TH —

1918 – Clifton Keith Hillegass, founder of the study guides known as CliffsNotes, is born. Thanks to him, every GCSE student now has a fighting chance to scrape together at least a solid three. By cramming quotes the night before the exam, they can desperately clutch at straws to link those quotes to whatever curveball question is hurled at them (the curveball question being something their teacher discussed in class many times).

— 19TH —

1897 – An unidentified flying object throws itself into a windmill in a town called Aurora in Texas. After getting absolutely done in, the alleged aircraft exploded, leaving nothing but a dead and badly toasted pilot inside. A US signal service officer named Mr T. J. Weems loudly declared that this UFO must be from Mars. He knew this for definite because he said so. Coincidentally enough, boll weevils had decimated Aurora's cotton crop and a fever outbreak wasn't exactly driving up tourism, either. So was this an actual UFO, or a ploy to drive up tourism in the area? Don't be thick, you know which one it actually is.

— 20TH —

1912 – Dublin-born writer Bram Stoker, famed for his literary masterpiece *Dracula*, expires at his London residence at the age of sixty-five. Despite his best efforts to avoid a vampire's fate, it seems even this master of the macabre couldn't escape the inevitable. Stoker's passing marked the end of a life that, while rich in gothic fiction, lacked the dramatic flair of his own creations.

— 21ST —

1590 – Henry VIII becomes King of England, following the death of his father, Henry VII. The living definition of gout was known mainly for pumping then dumping his six wives. But in 1509 he had been a strapping fella, charming and physically active. He soured and became horizontally challenged as he aged, adopting the motto "Ate Catholics, 'ate the French, luv me pints, simple as.' Suffering from a terrible jousting accident in 1536, when he was knocked unconscious for two hours after his horse fell on him, didn't help. It was alleged that he wasn't the same after that.

— 22ND —

1945 – Moustache-man Adolf Hitler admits defeat in his bunker. Chaos ensued, apple strudels were thrown and the yodelling ground to a steady halt. He didn't quite know what to do with himself – was promising every German citizen affordable Volkswagens and ethnic cleansing not enough to win the people's hearts?

— 23RD —

1564 – William Shakespeare is born. He goes on to make it his lifelong quest to bore kids shitless in English class by writing passages such as:

The knave turns fool that runs away;
The fool no knave, perdy.

Those poor sods. How people read that without feeling like they're having a stroke is beyond me.

April

24TH

1558 – Fifteen-year-old Mary, Queen of Scots, marries fourteen-year-old Francis, the Dauphin of France. She'd originally been set to marry Henry VIII's son, Edward VI, but Catholics opposed this and broke off the match, preferring to return to Scotland's original alliance with France. Henry had an absolute dicky fit and raided Scotland, which is known as 'The Rough Wooing'. Mary was a little pissed at this because she was barely a year old, but it was noted that one of the first phrases she said was, 'Not to be a cow and that, but why the fuck would I want a sickly, speccy git as a husband? I could literally knock him out and I'm not even two.' But anyway, she was shipped off to France where she was brought up in the royal court and at six years old got engaged at playtime via Haribo ring, as Francis decided to look past Mary's antics of swinging upside down on the monkey bars next to the lads playing football.

Would you survive a Tudor marriage?

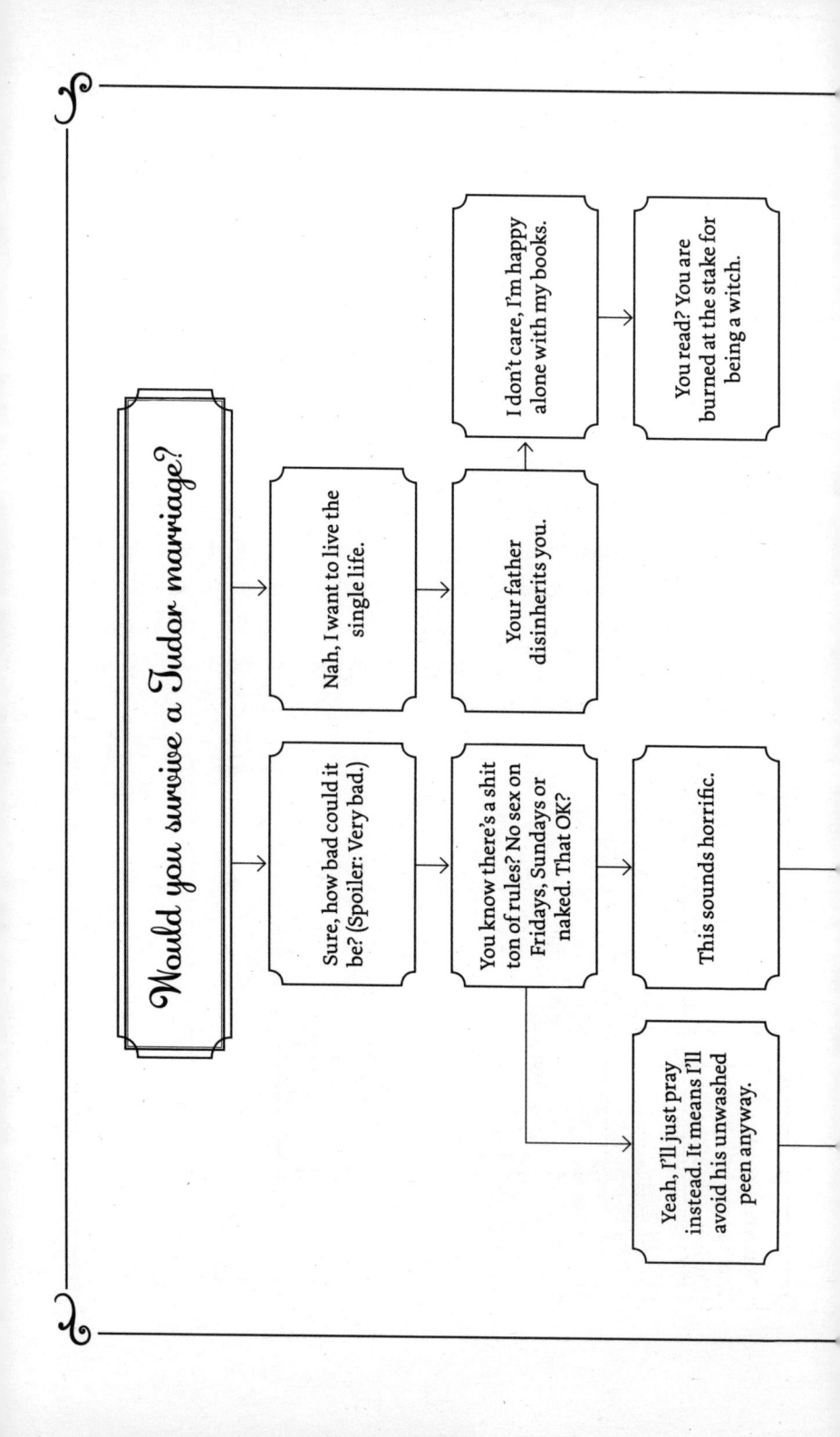

- **Sure, how bad could it be? (Spoiler: Very bad.)**
  - **You know there's a shit ton of rules? No sex on Fridays, Sundays or naked. That OK?**
    - **This sounds horrific.**
    - **Yeah, I'll just pray instead. It means I'll avoid his unwashed peen anyway.**

- **Nah, I want to live the single life.**
  - **Your father disinherits you.**
    - **I don't care, I'm happy alone with my books.**
      - **You read? You are burned at the stake for being a witch.**

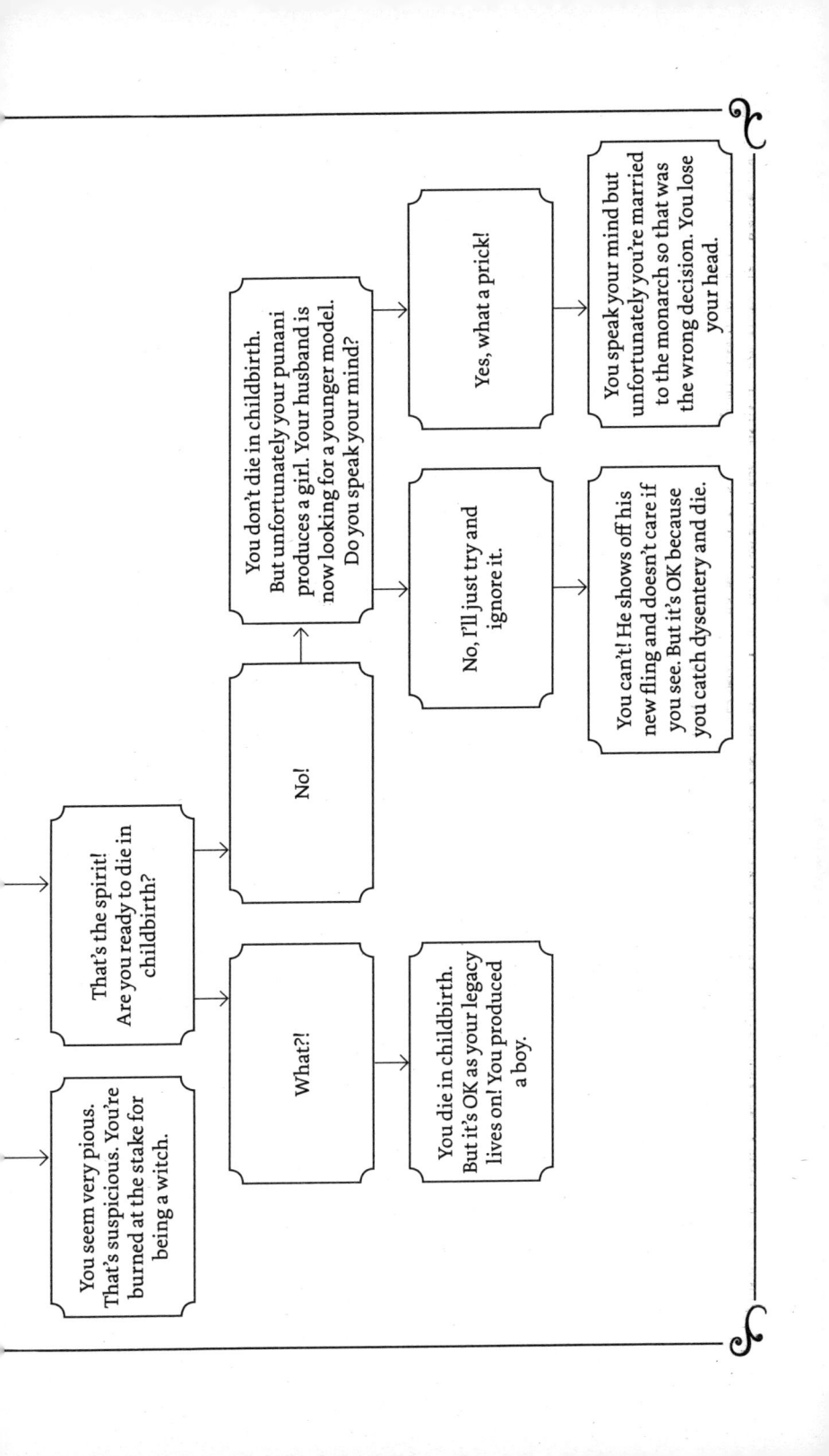

- You seem very pious. That's suspicious. You're burned at the stake for being a witch.

- That's the spirit! Are you ready to die in childbirth?
  - What?!
    - You die in childbirth. But it's OK as your legacy lives on! You produced a boy.
  - No!
    - You don't die in childbirth. But unfortunately your punani produces a girl. Your husband is now looking for a younger model. Do you speak your mind?
      - No, I'll just try and ignore it.
        - You can't! He shows off his new fling and doesn't care if you see. But it's OK because you catch dysentery and die.
      - Yes, what a prick!
        - You speak your mind but unfortunately you're married to the monarch so that was the wrong decision. You lose your head.

— 25TH —

1792 – The guillotine claims its first victim. Nicolas-Jacques Pelletier, a violent criminal in his thirties, was the lab rat for the new high-tech invention. After being awarded Executer of the Year many a time, Charles-Henri Sanson's passion was the guillotine, but not so much that'd give it a go himself. Pelletier's head was chopped off, with the audience only giving the performance three stars, declaring it anticlimactic, and preferring the suspense of the wooden gallows.

— 26TH —

1478 – Murder is committed in Florence's cathedral. Lorenzo and Giuliano de' Medici were attending church. Everyone was jealous of the Medicis, including two rival families who hatched a conspiracy to remove them from power. The pope was also in on it, which is not very Jesus-y of him. Bernardo Baroncelli stabbed Giuliano until his white shirt ran red, to which Giuliano replied, 'Can you at least pay for dry cleaning? This is brand new, man.' Although Lorenzo got partially guillotined by some priests with a knife, he survived. The city guard and townsfolk then turned against the conspirators. Some conspirators were stripped naked and beaten to death; reports detail people sinking their teeth into the corpses, probs because they hadn't had anything to eat.

— 27TH —

1889 – *Tit-Bits*, **the Victorian magazine that unfortunately contains neither tits nor bits, asks the all-important question of their female readers.** That is, 'If you're a spinster, why? Does one frequent the hobby of muff-diving instead?'

April

Here are some of the answers:

Because men, like three-cornered tarts, are deceitful. They are very pleasing to the eye, but on closer acquaintanceship prove hollow and stale, consisting chiefly of puff, with a minimum of sweetness and an unconquerable propensity to disagree with one.
– Miss Emaline Lawrence, 8 Abbey Gardens, St John's Wood, N.W.8

Because I do not care to enlarge my menagerie of pets, and I find the animal man less docile than a dog, less affectionate than a cat, and less amusing than a monkey.
– Miss Sparrow, 9 Manor Place, Paddington, W.2

Miss Sparrow cleverly communicates to the reader that she is in fact not running an animal shelter, and is saddened to hear that a man is for life, not just for Christmas.

Because matrimony is like an electric battery: once you join hands, you can't let go, however much it hurts; and, as when embarking upon a toboggan slide, you must go to the bitter end, however much it bumps.
– Miss Laura Bax, 29 Pelham Road, Wood Green, London, N.15

Miss Laura shows off her deep affection for Central Cee and effortlessly writes about her commitment issues, and how she's not trying to fix them for you.

— 28TH —

1926 – Harper Lee is born. She's best known for writing *To Kill a Mockingbird*. Sadly, this is a misleading title as the book contains very little information about avian techniques. Instead, readers are treated to a deep dive into the complexities of justice, morality and the challenges of growing up in the American South (plot twist: life is a lot harder when you're Black). The novel became a sensation, mainly because people were too polite to ask where the actual guide to mockingbird extermination was.

❖• April •❖

— 29TH —

1770 – Captain Cook enters Australia, landing in Botany Bay. He thought he'd be welcomed with a pint of Foster's and the traditional greeting of being called a 'C U Next Tuesday', but the indigenous people weren't so keen on interacting with him. So instead of setting up a land-based camp, he wrote back to England to say that the land was unoccupied, and he and his crew remained on board the ship. If only that were the end of the story, but many aborigines were slaughtered and would be mistreated for years to come.

— 30TH —

1859 – The first instalment of Charles Dickens' *A Tale of Two Cities* **is published.** I grew up thinking this book was a wholesome story about two mice, one a country mouse and one a city mouse, and they both have separate lives but get along really well. But it's not! It's about the French Revolution and getting guillotined.

Why did *Anne Boleyn* get accused of doing backshots, and how did **Amelia Earhart** prove that women aren't thick?

May

May arrives and the summer is nigh. (Not that you would get a day off, so get yourself back to scrubbing Lord Fauntleroy's skiddies.) Everyone is supposedly thrilled by the blooming flowers, but in reality, you're just thrilled that you haven't been dumped in the workhouse. Yet. The sun may shine, but don't be fooled – it's just bright enough to illuminate the grime on your windows and the futility of your existence.

— 1ST —

1967 – Supreme champion of dodging a case, Elvis Presley marries Priscilla. He loved a girl fresh out the womb and had been eyeing her up since she was fourteen. He waited until she was twenty-one, and he was thirty-two, to marry – the epitome of romance, some may say. It's said that people came up to him during their wedding and asked why he kept doing an Austin Butler impression.

— 2ND —

1536 – Anne Boleyn is arrested. After spending seven years chasing Anne and calling his wife Catherine a cockblock, Henry VIII repeatedly tried to convince the pope he should be allowed to divorce. He'd write, 'Yeah, I do think wine and bread is class, love a Holy Communion, but if you google "Anne Boleyn in Nike Pros" then you'll understand, hope that's OK x'. And although he upheaved England's religion to marry Anne, he eventually got fucked off that she only popped out one daughter. He knew third time lucky would do the trick, so called Anne a tart, got her head chopped off and married Jane Seymour very soon after.

May

— 3RD —

1937 – *Gone With the Wind* receives a Pulitzer Prize. The 1,000-page book is reminiscent of the bygone days of the old American South: the gowns, the chivalry, the polite society, the days of looking out of your window to the beautiful fields and tens of slaves working away, without feeling one ounce of remorse. A golden era. The film adaptation faced protests when it premiered in 1940, due to its portrayal of African Americans as passive and supportive of the South's slave system, which persisted until the Civil War ended in 1865. Hattie McDaniel, who plays Mammy, was the first Black person to win an Oscar. However, she wasn't actually allowed to attend the premiere in Atlanta as it was a whites-only cinema, and her table at the Oscars was segregated.

— 4TH —

1942 – The USA introduces food rationing, starting with sugar. In November, coffee was added, followed by meats, fats, canned fish, cheese, and canned milk the following March. This caused a catastrophe for Americans. No one could fathom how to eat their deep-fried sugar pop tart cheeto waffle (chopped-up bananas on the side for health) without sugar. This left many questioning the very foundation of their existence.

— 5TH —

1864 – It's Nellie Bly's birthday – she's one of the first female undercover reporters. After editors laughed her out of the office, shocked that women could read more than microwave-meal instructions, Nellie was determined to pursue journalism. She one-upped Jules Verne's famous novel *Around the World in Eighty Days*, managing to do it in seventy-two by threatening to slit her throat when the oceanic crew mentioned a bureaucratic delay. But the ultimate banger she published was *Ten Days in a Madhouse*. Working for *The New York World*, she had herself committed to an asylum to expose its poor conditions. She practised looking 'crazed' in her mirror, wandered the streets, refused to sleep, and ranted incoherently until the boarding-house owners summoned the police. Bly, then pretending to be a Cuban immigrant with amnesia, was sent to Bellevue Hospital, then on to the asylum, where she dropped the act but was still treated horrifically.

Nellie Bly's report on the asylum shocked the public and led to increased funding to improve conditions. Her hands-on approach developed into what's now known as investigative journalism. A grand-jury panel visited the asylum a month after Bly's articles, but the staff had been tipped off, and it had been cleaned up. Despite this, the grand jury agreed with Bly, pushing through a bill that added nearly $1 million (about $24 million today) to the budget. Abusive staff were fired, translators were hired for immigrant patients, and changes were made to prevent the wrongful commitment of those without mental illness.

— 6TH —

1840 – Penny Black stamps are introduced. Before stamps, you had to pay the postman to receive your letters, which worked out great if you wanted to piss someone off: just spam them with relentless hate mail. And although stamps are a far better idea, initially people weren't really keen on using their mouths as a gluepot to lick Queen Vicky's arse, excepting Prince Albert, of course.

— 7TH —

1824 – Beethoven's final symphony premieres in Vienna. The crowd took their seats after willingly paying £125 on concert merch. Beethoven announced that he wanted people to live in the moment to fully experience his concert, suggesting that attendees put away their canvases and easels. He began to play, going absolutely ham with his conducting skills, thinking he'd done a class job. But he wouldn't have known, as he was so deaf at this point that the musicians were told to ignore his conducting.

— 8TH —

1373 – Thirty-year-old Julian of Norwich claims to have received a vision from Christ. On what was almost surely her deathbed, she said she received visions from Jesus and was suddenly cured. It was twenty years before she wrote it all down in *Revelations of Divine Love*, the first book published in English known to have been written by a woman.

— 9TH —

1671 – A newsletter is written to inform that Thomas Blood and his associates tried to steal the Crown Jewels. A few months later, they are pardoned. Maybe the king feared an uprising, or maybe he just said, 'Look Charlie, I'm gonna be real. I am sorry and that but I just wanted to make some quick cash off Depop. I've been struggling for a while now, as I've been absolutely rinsed by these girls who sold me some vintage garms for like £80. It turns out it's just from Ye Olde Primarni so that's like really pissed me off, so I wanted to make the money back but nws, hope you're well.' Charles II may have then said, 'We've all been there, love,' and pardoned him.

— 10TH —

1872 – Victoria Woodhull becomes the first woman to run for US president. Born in 1838, she married at fifteen, ditched an alcoholic husband, and after deciding the tradwife life wasn't for her, became a 'medical clairvoyant' – which was basically just vintage MLM. Her presidential run wasn't exactly taken seriously, especially as she was very vocal about free love, and had tits.

— 11TH —

1708 – The architect for Versailles, Jules Hardouin Mansart, dies. He pulled out all the stops when designing iconic rooms in the palace, such as the Hall of Mirrors, with gold leaf spaffed about like it was going out of fashion. Unfortunately, Mansart's finer details did not include designing a shitter. But that didn't mean that people were constantly defecating behind curtains, then laughing at the poor for being scuddy. Maybe it happened on occasion, but it wasn't the norm. There are anecdotes about servants pissing in the courtyard or in the corner of public rooms and getting screamed at for it. But if you were a courtier at Versailles, you would've had access to chamber pots and public latrines, at the very least. Or if you were noble, you could've had a chamber pot built into a seat: in other words, a commode.

— 12TH —

1820 – Florence Nightingale is born. Although her parents expected her to think of England while she spread her legs for her husband, Flo decided that being a nurse was her calling. This was much to her family's dismay, as they thought that she'd stick to more respectable pursuits, like complaining about the struggle to understand the help because they couldn't pronounce their

Ts. Nonetheless, in 1854, Florence led a group of thirty-eight nurses to care for wounded British soldiers in the Crimean War. When arriving, Florence was startled to not find a single bottle of hand gel. When she found out there weren't even any Baylis and Harding shower scrubs, she broke down in tears. 'These men have gone through war. You can't just let them leave their bollocks unwashed. It'll get cheesy. The lack of lily and magnolia blossom scented shower gel is a hate crime,' she sobbed. It was time for a change. Low hygiene standards and widespread infections were rampant. Nightingale and her team immediately began to clean every room and she insisted that her nurses wash their hands frequently. Her focus on cleanliness and handwashing significantly improved conditions, and we now understand that these practices are among the best ways to prevent the spread of disease.

— 13TH —

1857 – Ronald Ross is born in India. He discovered the malarial parasite in mosquitoes and we have this man to thank, because without him we'd never have experienced the full joys of having Cheryl Cole tell us, 'Weak? Limp? Lifeless? Pure fugly? Then try this conditioner. Your hair will still look fucking shite. But maybe you can look like me, Cheryl Cole Fernandez-Versini Houdini Zucchini Linguini Bellini, the nation's sweetheart, even though I clearly have hair extensions in.'

— 14TH —

1080 – Walcher, Bishop of Durham and Earl of Northumberland, gets himself murdered. So, heeding the motto, 'Don't let a good thing go to waste', William the Conqueror decided to send an army to ravage the region again. While he was at it, he invaded Scotland too. But he didn't stop there. He thought, 'Why not build a castle in Newcastle? I mean, it's called Newcastle for a reason.' But deep down, he knew the real reason was because he wanted to go to Bigg Market to watch absolute munters getting in 2 a.m. kebab-shop scraps.

— 15TH —

1536 – Anne Boleyn is accused of doing backshots with her brother, Lord Rochford. Although the aristocracy of Europe did love a family wreath, they wouldn't go this far. Henry VIII just fabricated that excuse because Anne's time was up – she'd not produced a male heir. Apparently, Henry decided that accusing his wife of incest was a more elegant solution than simply pieing her off, as a prelude to condemning her to death.

— 16TH —

1929 – The first Oscars are held. Stars lined up to receive their Academy Awards, and winners were told about their awards three months in advance, unlike today. *Wings* won Best Picture, the only silent film to do so, probably because it couldn't give an acceptance speech. Nowadays, actors waltz up on stage to give compelling speeches about saving the environment and standing up to the creeps in the industry. They then hop on their private jets, right after making sure to congratulate their directors, each boasting four pending allegations.

— 17TH —

1824 – Notorious daughter-pounder Lord Byron has his diaries burned by friends and family. He spent his years writing poems and chanting 'any hole is a goal' with the hole in question being that of his sister, Augusta Leigh. She was only his half-sister, but unfortunately that's one half too much. Although he wanted his diaries to be published because he was proud of his exploits, his family and friends wanted to salvage his reputation, and destroyed them instead.

— 18TH —

AD 332 – Roman emperor Constantine the Great decides to win some brownie points with the locals in Constantinople by giving out free daily bread rations. The citizens were like, 'Cheers Constantine, you've done us a solid, but we can't exactly live off carbs. Or if you could just fix the roads, or stop hoying slaves into arenas to be noshed on by lions?'

— 19TH —

1897 – After spending two years observing soap being dropped in the communal showers, Oscar Wilde is released from Reading Gaol. Wilde was charged with gross indecency, which essentially meant being gay, as in court he never even denied topping his lover, Lord Alfred Douglas.

— 20TH —

1932 – Amelia Earhart flies across the Atlantic, proving that women can drive. She then UNO reverses herself by flying across the ocean and never finding her way back. Earhart's groundbreaking achievements include being the second person to fly solo and nonstop across the Atlantic and the first person to fly solo and nonstop across the United States. However, she still hasn't managed to find her way home from flying across the Pacific Ocean, which her mum is well pissed off at because she'd already made her tea, and she may as well put it in the bin at this point because it's gone cold now.

— 21ST —

AD 996 – Sixteen-year-old Otto III is crowned Roman emperor. While most lads his age would be asking girls for nudes, Otto preferred the exhilarating life of being cooped up in a monastery, or daydreaming about secular power from Rome. He was dead set on recreating the glory of the old Roman Empire, with himself as the top shagger of Christianity, bossing around a subservient pope. Sadly, his grand plans were cut short when he decided to be a fun sponge and die from fever at twenty-one.

— 22ND —

1882 – The United States finally gets around to formally recognizing Korea. After years of awkwardly pretending to not see it at all, the yanks engaged Korea in its first diplomatic interaction with a Western nation.

— 23RD —

1701 – Scottish privateer Captain William Kidd gets a two-for-one special at Execution Dock, Wapping, when his hanging for piracy and murder turns into an unexpected encore. The rope broke mid-execution, giving him a brief reprieve before they strung him up again for a more successful second act. Because apparently, even executions sometimes need a practice run.

— 24TH —

1809 – The first French prisoners from the Napoleonic Wars arrive at Dartmoor Prison, purpose-built to house them. Britain had been at war with France on and off since 1789, and French prisoners were initially crammed into old warships known as 'prison hulks'. These hulks were riddled with all sorts of disease and mank. To improve things slightly and for security reasons, the admiralty moved prisoners from the hulks to inland war prisons such as Dartmoor, which was built between 1806 and 1809, due to the risk of Napoleon invading ports. As the conditions were just unliveable, they rented it out as student accommodation, advertising it as: 'Rustic rooms with an authentic "lived-in" feel. Each room boasts its own unique stains and marks, telling the stories of countless others who lived there before you. The carpet even tested positive for chlamydia, so you can feel like you're in Nottingham's Ocean nightclub, right in the comfort of your own home.'

— 25TH —

1850 – A hippopotamus named Obaysch arrives in London Zoo, salad dodger Queen Victoria goes to gawk at it shortly afterwards. It was the first one to be in Britain since prehistoric times as they're pretty fucking useless, so there wasn't much point in them being here. Queen Victoria was allegedly thoroughly impressed by Obaysch's massive arse, which inspired a quest for her to grow her own to that size.

— 26TH —

1651 – Jeane Gardiner is executed for witchcraft at St George, Bermuda. During her trial, she was thrown into the sea twice. Their logic was that if she sank and drowned she was innocent – a risk they were willing to take, as they didn't want some lass cursing people and giving them veruccas, or whatever witches supposedly did. According to a contemporary account 'she did swyme like a corke and could not sinke', so was very clearly a witch.

— 27TH —

1657 – Lord Protector Oliver Cromwell refuses parliament's offer of the title King of England and parliament has a debate.

He went, 'Lads, I am too humble to accept this. I want not only to keep it lemon, I also want to keep it super cushty. So I'll just be Lord Protector.' Lord Protector was just another fancy way of saying 'Head of State'. But what was the difference between that and a king? The first has four syllables and the latter only has one. He said, 'I even think we should do a little remix and take out the letters K-I-N-G from the alphabet because of my humbleness.'

— 28TH —

1908 – Ian Fleming is born. He's best known for creating the iconic character James Bond. But did you know he also enjoyed creating characters that had noncy tendencies? Yes, he also wrote the novel *Chitty Chitty Bang Bang*. It's about a car that flies or something, but a pivotal plot point is the absolute weapon who tries to catch kiddies in a net. Kids would fear him, yet only the bravest would say, 'If you come near me, I'll tell Childline you fondled my arse, so you better nick off.'

— 29TH —

1660 – Charles II comes back to the throne. He lifted the ban on Christmas, reopened theatres, and people were allowed to walk around without having the face of a slapped arse. He was also a lover of the popular toy spaniel, then renamed the 'King Charles Spaniel'. He loved the pups so much he was known to have joined a 'Cavalier Lovers' Facebook page, where many would post delightful pics of their pooch. But you'd also get the odd one posting a status such as: 'Our fluffy girl crossed the rainbow bridge today, only nine. Absolutely gutted.' Alongside a picture of the fattest bong-eyed dog known to man. Like yeah, no wonder.

— 30TH —

1667 – Margaret Cavendish is the first woman to attend a meeting of the Royal Society, which is basically a neek convention. It was pretty much full of scientists doing experiments, and she watched science demonstrations by Robert Boyle and Robert Hooke. None of the men were able to look her in the eye, as this was the closest they'd come to a vagina since they were birthed out of one.

— 31ST —

1669 – Samuel Pepys writes his last diary entry. He wrote the diary in Thomas Shelton's shorthand, which was probably for the best as he described his side hoes, so definitely wouldn't have wanted his wife reading that. He kept a diary detailing various everyday aspects of seventeenth-century life, including the Great Fire of London, the Plague and bitching about people in the royal court. But he had to stop due to his deteriorating eyesight.

Smash or Pass

Genghis Khan – Smash. He ploughed his way through half of Asia, so his 'dominant energy' can smash its way through you.

Rasputin – Pass. He may have looked like he didn't wash, but it's probably no worse than what you managed to pull in Freshers' week. He had a reputation for sleeping with other men's wives in order to 'spiritually save them', and got women to lick jam off his fingers.

Women in Green Dresses – Smash. The ladies were glowing in their green gowns. (You'll have to ignore the fact she's absolutely done in by the arsenic poisoning from the green fabric, of course.)

Sigmund Freud – Pass. He'd spend the entire time psychoanalyzing you, telling you that by ordering calamari it means you want to intimately caress your mum.

Chimney Sweeps – Hard Pass. It's all fun and games until your romantic candlelit dinner is interrupted by coughing fits and you find soot in places you didn't know existed. Plus, they're likely minors, and we're not trying to get on a watchlist today.

Two Lads Who Murdered People and Sold Them to Edinburgh Uni – Pass. These gents might know how to handle a stiff, but messages might get mixed when they're taking about 'taking someone out'. In 1827, William Hare's lodger died and his mate, William Burke, sold the corpse to an anatomist at Edinburgh Uni. After realizing they'd be able to make a bit of quick cash, they started suffocating people, so as not to show any obvious signs of murder.

Ada Lovelace – Smash. The original tech girl, Ada was a mathematician and the first computer programmer. Intelligent, pioneering and probably the only person in the room who could calculate how to maximize your mutual pleasure coefficients. Just be prepared for pillow talk that involves algorithms and the occasional debugging session.

Boudica – Smash. The Celtic warrior led a rebellion against the Roman Empire and didn't take any shit. You're in for a wild ride with a queen who knows exactly what she wants.

Did *Mozart* piss off his music teacher by pressing the DJ button on the keyboard? Why didn't *Alexander* do a tacky-chun?

June

Ah, June, the so-called start of summer. The nobility parade around in their frilly outfits, pretending the sun isn't making them sweat under all those layers of fabric like a dyslexic on *Countdown*. Everyone around you is as irritable as King George IV when he's told 'no more pies'. The sun rises earlier, as if mocking you with more daylight hours to suffer in, and everyone pretends to enjoy it, while praying for a swift rainstorm to drown their misery.

— 1ST —

1712 – The Duke of Marlborough, John Churchill, starts screaming, crying, and pissing on the floor in distress. He'd only gone and fallen from royal favour. Not only had his wife, Sarah Churchill, been publicly munching the royal carpet, but she'd been doing a shite job lately and had fallen out with Queen Anne, who had begun to instead favour Sarah's cousin, Abigail. That, and she was a bit of a straight-talking cow. The drastic demotion meant that the treasury stopped funding the construction of the Churchills' home Blenheim Palace in Oxford. Distraught, they were forced to spend £50,000 of their own money to finish it, like ordinary working people.

— 2ND —

1953 – Queen Elizabeth II is crowned Queen of Great Britain and the Commonwealth at twenty-seven years old. The coronation was aired on radio and was the first to be televised. The TV edition was produced by Bravo, with the queen's tagline being, 'People say I have resting bitch face, but this bitch never rests'. She ruled for seventy years.

June

— 3RD —

1937 – The marriage no one wanted but people were forced against their will to see anyway. No, not Ben Affleck and Jennifer Lopez's, but Wallis Simpson and King Edward's. Wallis was an American socialite, and was asked to babysit her friend's boyfriend, who happened to be King Edward. Her friend asked her to make sure no one stole him, and Wallis replied, 'My girl Ariana Grande told me that if you break up with your girlfriend, I'll let you hit in the morning. I think that's a really solid foundation to build a relationship, so those lyrics will be taken as gospel.' She shook that inverted arse and he fell to his knees. Edward was in love. Wallis just wanted to get a Birkin bag and a holiday home, but Edward said that if they didn't get married he'd top himself. So, alas, they married and lived happily ever after. Apart from they didn't, and because they were also pro-Nazi, they were shipped off as far away as possible.

— 4TH —

1913 – She went out with a bang, and a hoof – Emily Davison steps in front of a horse for women's suffrage. Educated at Oxford, but unable to be awarded a degree as she had boobies, in 1906 Emily joined the Women's Social and Political Union (WSPU), founded by Emmeline Pankhurst three years previously. After burning postboxes, going on hunger strikes and throwing stones at chancellor David Lloyd George, Emily decided to level up and step in front of the king's horse. But why? Some say it was a deliberate attempt to commit suicide, but she bought a return ticket for the Derby that day. Was it an accident, or did she die trying to pin the suffrage flag to the king's horse?

— 5TH —

1944 – Today was meant to be D-Day, and although the army were there on 4th, the weather was absolute wank over the English Channel and it put a halt to things. President Eisenhower said, 'Fascism is really bad so we want to liberate people from that, but no one's brought their pack-a-mac. So we're going to have to wait it out for another 24 hours.' This delay unsettled the soldiers but when the weather cleared on 6th they were good to go.

— 6TH —

1795 – A fire in Copenhagen ravishes the Navy's old base. Workers had already gone home and clocked out, so if they weren't getting paid, it wasn't their problem. Because everyone in Copenhagen was a scruff, the fire hydrants had previously been removed in case of theft, too. People's mentality was that the military should deal with it. So because people were incompetent shits, thousands were left homeless.

— 7TH —

1811 – James Simpson, the inventor of chloroform, is born. Unfortunately, his mother had to rawdog giving birth, because James hadn't yet had the chance to invent. He went on to revolutionize the way women gave birth and was appointed Queen Victoria's physician when she was in Scotland. Queen Vicky also used chloroform when giving birth, which helped to popularize the anaesthetic. But every small win has some pushbacks, as chloroform has also played a big part in rapes, murder and robbery.

— 8TH —

1929 – In a shocking turn of events, Margaret Bondfield, a former shop worker, becomes Britain's first female cabinet

June

minister. Appointed as the Minister of Labour in Ramsay MacDonald's government, Bondfield was expected to multitask effortlessly, handle crises with a smile, and still have time to bake a corned-beef pie. After all, who better to manage the nation's workforce than someone who's already mastered the art of balancing shopping bags and household chores?

— 9TH —

1873 – London's Alexandra Palace gets commitment issues and makes an early exit, going up in flames only sixteen days after its official opening. Over four thousand pieces of porcelain and pottery were destroyed and three staff members were killed.

— 10TH —

323 BC – At thirty-two, Alexander the Great finds out the hard way that he can't stomach more than two Porn Star Martinis anymore. Usually after a drinking binge, he just did a tacky-chun and was back in business on the dancefloor. But this time ancient sources say his condition worsened to the point where he couldn't speak, and Alexander died a few days later. Many think he was poisoned, but, honestly, that's probably on him because no one likes an insufferable know-it-all. He was a massive overachiever and spent his short life being the king of Macedonia, leader of the Greeks, overlord of Asia Minor and pharaoh of Egypt for the craic.

— 11TH —

1509 – A player from a young age, seventeen-year-old Henry VIII marries his brother's widow, Catherine of Aragon. He was determined to smash that pasty, even if said pasty had already been demolished by his dead brother.

— 12TH —

1942 – Anne Frank is given a diary. She named her diary Kitty, and there she'd confide her deepest thoughts. Such thoughts included telling Kitty that the girl on her maths table was a sket, and that even though her shawty, Peter Schiff, was three years older than her, she was really impressed with the wheelies he did round Aldi carpark. But such whimsical musings and tales of blossoming romance had to grind to a halt as the following month she and her family had to go into hiding. She'd spend the next two years cooped up in an annex, sharing a room with a middle-aged dentist and getting off with another lad called Peter.

— 13TH —

1763 – Mozart's first performance of his family's three-year 'grand tour' of Western Europe. While many his age were trying to invite birds back to their igloo on Club Penguin, this wasn't the case for seven-year-old Mozart. His parents put him on a tech time out, which meant he had to find a hobby outside of media consumption. But all was not lost, as it turns out he was actually pretty class at the piano. The child prodigy stunned audiences in Munich, playing for Elector Maximilian of Bavaria. Music filled the air, not a single note out of place, with only the occasional sound of the DJ button in between stanzas.

— 14TH —

1907 – The Norwegian government announce that, as men, they understand women. They were birthed out of women and had their dinners cooked by them, so they knew a thing or two. They'd also seen the Barbie movie, so were really aware of the complexities of the battle for equal rights. So, the government decided to grant women the vote! But not quite. Let's not get carried away, girl bosses. Only women who were at least twenty-five years old and met certain tax-paying thresholds had the right to vote, with the move being about as empowering as an advert for Vagisil.

— 15TH —

1878 – The world's first moving pictures are caught on camera. Eadweard Muybridge, in between murdering his wife's lover, photographed a horse in different stages of its gallop by lining up multiple cameras and essentially created the first stop-motion film. The 'unsupported transit' controversy had divided science shaggers and non-science shaggers for years. Not only did this settle the age-old debate about whether all four hooves leave the ground at once, it also provided a cracking piece of cinema.

Some thought it was the most moving piece ever made. 'The film may be lacklustre on plot, but it more than compensates with its engaging characters,' gushed one reviewer, calling it one of the best and most well-acted pieces in film history. 'I think the best part was when the guy was on the horse. I wish I could replicate the feeling I got from watching this for the first time. This is cinema at its best.' Not everyone shared the enthusiasm. One critic scathingly remarked, 'The film feels stale. 2/10, just watch *Rick and Morty*.'

— 16TH —

1963 – The Soviet Union, where you were free to say anything you wanted, once, launches the first woman into space. Valentina Tereshkova was buzzin' to do something other than queue for bread and glug vodka for a bit of warmth. The authorities loved her because she was a skydiver and her dad was a dead war hero, so she hopped into the aircraft and away she went. She completed forty-eight orbits in two days, but because this was

Communist Russia and everyone was equal, the rest of the population had to have a go afterwards. To this day, budding babushkas are still being launched into space.

— 17TH —

1631 – Shah Jahan is inspired to build the Taj Mahal after being titmatized by his wife, Mumtaz Mahal. Mumtaz was betrothed to Shah at fourteen, but was so loyal that he didn't 'like' any other girl's portraits, even if they were a fitness influencer.

Mumtaz died on this day after giving birth to her fourteenth child. A year later, the work for the mausoleum began.

— 18TH —

1633 – Charles I rocks up to Edinburgh to collect his cheque, get a crown put on his head and called King of Scots, and then fucks off back down south. He'd already ascended to the throne in 1625, which shows just how much this was on the list of his priorities. After going to get some overpriced cocktails at The Dome to celebrate, but mainly for the 'gram, he did all the touristy staples and called it a day, making this one of the only two visits he made to Scotland.

◆• June •◆

— 19TH —

1917 – World War One is at its peak. The British were fuming that it was called the First World War, as they were all about a cash grab and weren't really keen on a sequel. To make matters worse, their monarchs had the surname of Saxe-Coburg-Gotha. The British hated the fact that foreigners had taken all of their jobs, even the top ones, like monarch. 'Soon every bugger will be walking round with bloody bratwurst. Can't stand it. Come over 'ere and try and change our culture. No wonder I can't get a job,' said Daz, forty-two, just released from prison. To avoid backlash, the royal family decided to change their surname to Windsor instead.

— 20TH —

1837 – Princess Victoria becomes queen. Before her days of sulking about and being a miserable git, she was proclaimed queen at eighteen after the death of her seventy-one-year-old uncle, King William IV. The population weren't used to someone so youthful taking the throne, never mind a woman. In a letter to her other uncle, King Leopold of Belgium, she said that she wasn't stressed and was actually looking forward to her new role. She wrote, 'I am not alarmed at it and yet I do not suppose myself quite equal to all; I trust however that with good will, honesty and courage, I shall not, at all events, fail.' Her governess was actually given ye olde poppers in the form of smelling salts to give to the newly appointed queen in case things got a bit too much.

— 21ST —

1539 – Catherine of Aragon has a tantrum in the courtroom to try to save her marriage. Henry VIII was desperate for an annulment so he could marry Anne Boleyn, but Catherine got the big guns out. She went up to Henry and fell to her knees, not in the way Henry would've liked Anne to, but in a passionate plea. She claimed that she had been 'humble and obedient', like a dog, for twenty years. While Catherine was putting on a show, Henry just sat there checking the football score on his phone, not arsed about any of it. After Catherine exclaimed, 'I will let God be my judge,' and left, she knew she needed more sympathy, so she took to Facebook. There, she wrote compelling statuses such as: 'I'm nothing but nice to people and what do I get! You know exactly who you are, fucking sick man, wolf in sheep's clothing everywhere. No one but me and my kids from now on xxx.'

— 22ND —

1772 – In a landmark case of the anti-slavery movement, James Somerset, an enslaved man, makes an escape from his owner, Charles Stewart. Stewart, a devout Christian man, who enjoyed loving thy neighbour, except the ones with melanin, had Somerset recaptured and imprisoned on a ship bound for Jamaica, intent on reselling him like a second-hand sofa. Somerset's godparents, not exactly thrilled with Stewart's plan, launched a legal challenge. The court, having a rare moment of clarity, ruled that an enslaved person couldn't be shipped out of England against their will. Poor Stewart had to learn the hard way that people aren't cargo, much to his aristocratic dismay.

— 23RD —

1912 – The founding father of AI, Alan Turing, is born in Maida Vale, London. He knew all of his times tables, even his twelve times table. So off he went to Cambridge, then Princeton, and was recruited in World War Two to help crack the Enigma code. It's estimated his work helped to shorten the war by a good few years and saved millions of lives. In 1940, in an attempt to protect his assets from Nazi invasion, Turing converted his savings into silver ingots and buried them in Bletchley Park, but hid them so well that he never managed to find where they were. Even to this day, no one knows where it is. Despite everything he did to help win the war, England had a face on about him preferring a special kind of swordfight. Turin was chemically castrated in 1952 and only pardoned in 2013, well after his death in 1954 from cyanide poisoning (likely suicide by eating an apple he had poisoned).

— 24TH —

1943 – Americans step in to defend human rights. While the infamous moustache man was cutting about dropping bombs and wanking over blue eyes and blonde hair, many people in the USA had come to believe that people had the right to live how they wanted, be they Jewish, non-Jewish, brown haired, blonde haired, white skinned or pale skinned. When stationed in Bamber Bridge, Lancashire, American soldiers were segregated based on skin colour and tensions between US white and Black troops reached boiling point.

Back in the USA, many states had Jim Crow laws to keep segregation alive and well. Britain, however, would proudly exclaim, 'We don't see colour!' to which Black Americans would scratch their heads and go, 'Love the enthusiasm, but also no.' Black American servicemen were often warmly welcomed by the locals, much to the chagrin of white American officers. Terrified that Black soldiers might rizz up the English women, American troops tried to enforce a 'colour bar' in the village. The locals, being British and stubborn, responded by putting up signs at the three pubs in Bamber Bridge saying, 'Black Troops Only'. This led to armed fighting when white US military policemen tried to arrest a Black American soldier for being out without a pass, tragically resulting in the death of Private Crossland.

— 25TH —

1561 – Quack physician Francis Coxe is summoned before the Privy Council and is charged with partaking in sorcery. Although he tried his best to convince the girlies they can be their own boss by selling 'vitamin-infused' carcinogenic fizz sticks, the privy counsellors were not convinced. The Privy Council charged him with sorcery and being a dipshit. Francis Coxe publicly confessed at the pillory in Cheapside to his 'employment of certayne sinistral and divelysh artes', to which the Council then said, 'Mate, what fucking language is that?' and proceeded to make him get a Grammarly subscription.

— 26TH —

1830 – Who ate all the pies? George IV ate all the pies! Georgie takes his final bow and passes away. The cosmetic-wearing prince weighed twenty-four stone and was regularly called the Prince of Whales. Unfortunately, the face-slimming contouring make-up techniques didn't help much. He was known for running up huge debts, banning his wife Caroline of Brunswick from his coronation as he hated her poor personal hygiene, and feuding with his father, George III.

— 27TH —

1880 – Deaf-blind activist Helen Keller is born. Growing up, she got really sulky that she couldn't communicate with people, and her parents weren't sure what to do with her. Luckily her teacher, Miss Sullivan, came along, and helped Helen to communicate by drawing letters on her hands, such as drawing 'W' for water, then pouring water on Helen, to help her understand. Eventually, she knew the whole alphabet and could write letters to her mother, saying things like, 'If you try to marry me off, I'm telling Miss Sullivan in sign language that you're a bint.' She went on to be the first deaf-blind person to be awarded a Bachelor of Arts degree.

— 28TH —

1919 – World War One comes to an end and Germany signs the Treaty of Versailles. The Germans were excited to sign this, as they loved Marie Antoinette. But the terms of the treaty meant that the country had to disarm themselves, lose their territory, give up colonies overseas and pay financial reparations.

— 29TH —

1926 – Italian leader Mussolini announces a nine-hour working day to boost national production and limit imports. To keep productivity and spirits high, Mussolini's government thought it wise to blast Ne-Yo's lyrics, about the importance of working hard but also never forgetting the secret element of playing hard too, like it's your job. However, to stop the workers from getting carried away and thinking they were able to actually do anything leisurely, they cut out the 'play hard, keep partying' part, leaving Ne-Yo to chant 'work hard' on a loop for nine hours straight.

— 30TH —

1660 – English mathematician William Oughtred dies at Albury in Surrey. After he introduced the x symbol for multiplication, he was told to pack it in and stop including letters in maths. Legend has it he was murdered by Year Eights, who had double maths on Friday afternoons.

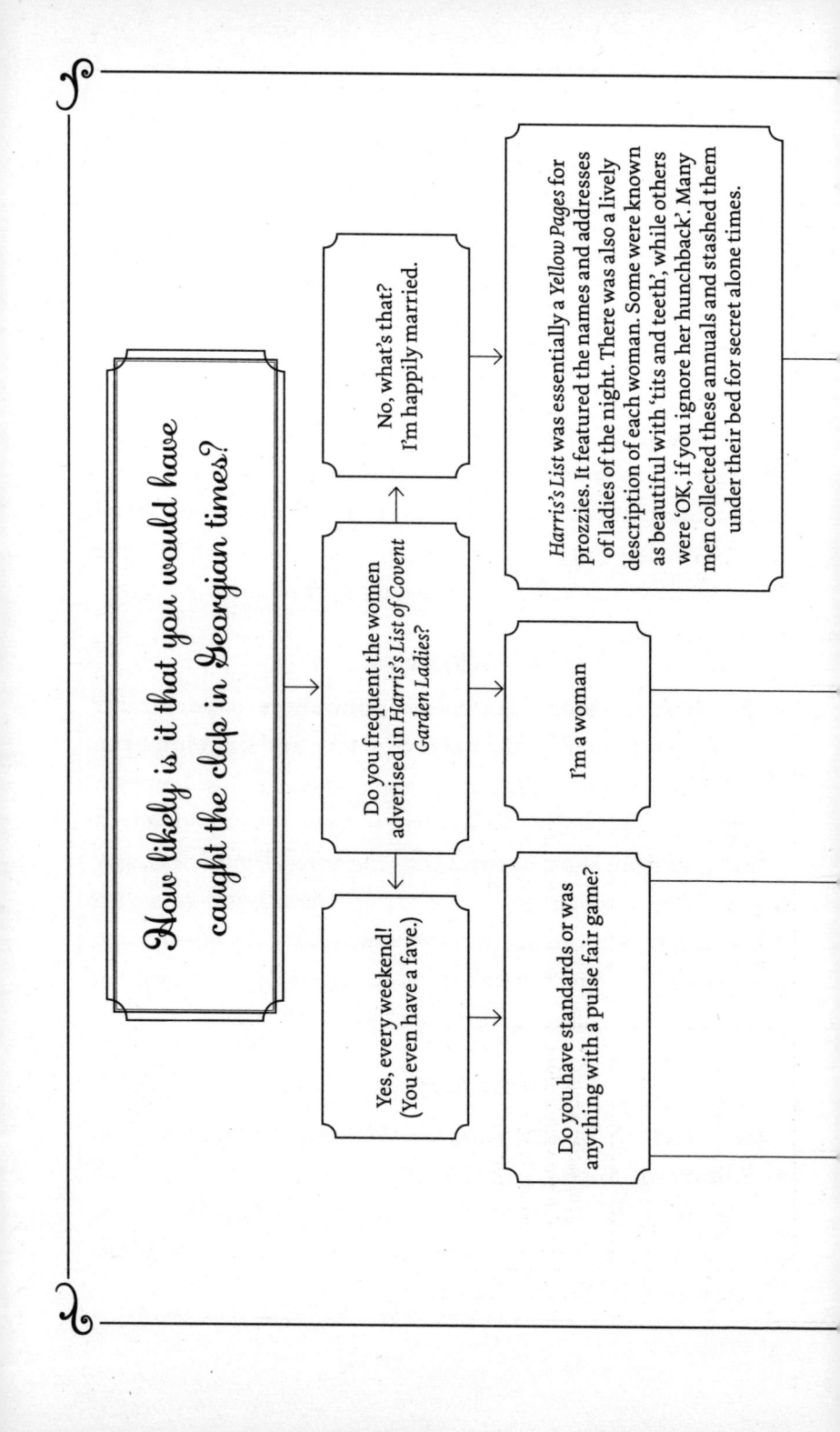

How likely is it that you would have caught the clap in Georgian times?

Do you frequent the women advertised in *Harris's List of Covent Garden Ladies*?

→ **No, what's that? I'm happily married.**

→ *Harris's List* was essentially a *Yellow Pages* for prozzies. It featured the names and addresses of ladies of the night. There was also a lively description of each woman. Some were known as beautiful with 'tits and teeth', while others were 'OK, if you ignore her hunchback'. Many men collected these annuals and stashed them under their bed for secret alone times.

→ **I'm a woman**

→ **Yes, every weekend! (You even have a fave.)**

→ **Do you have standards or was anything with a pulse fair game?**

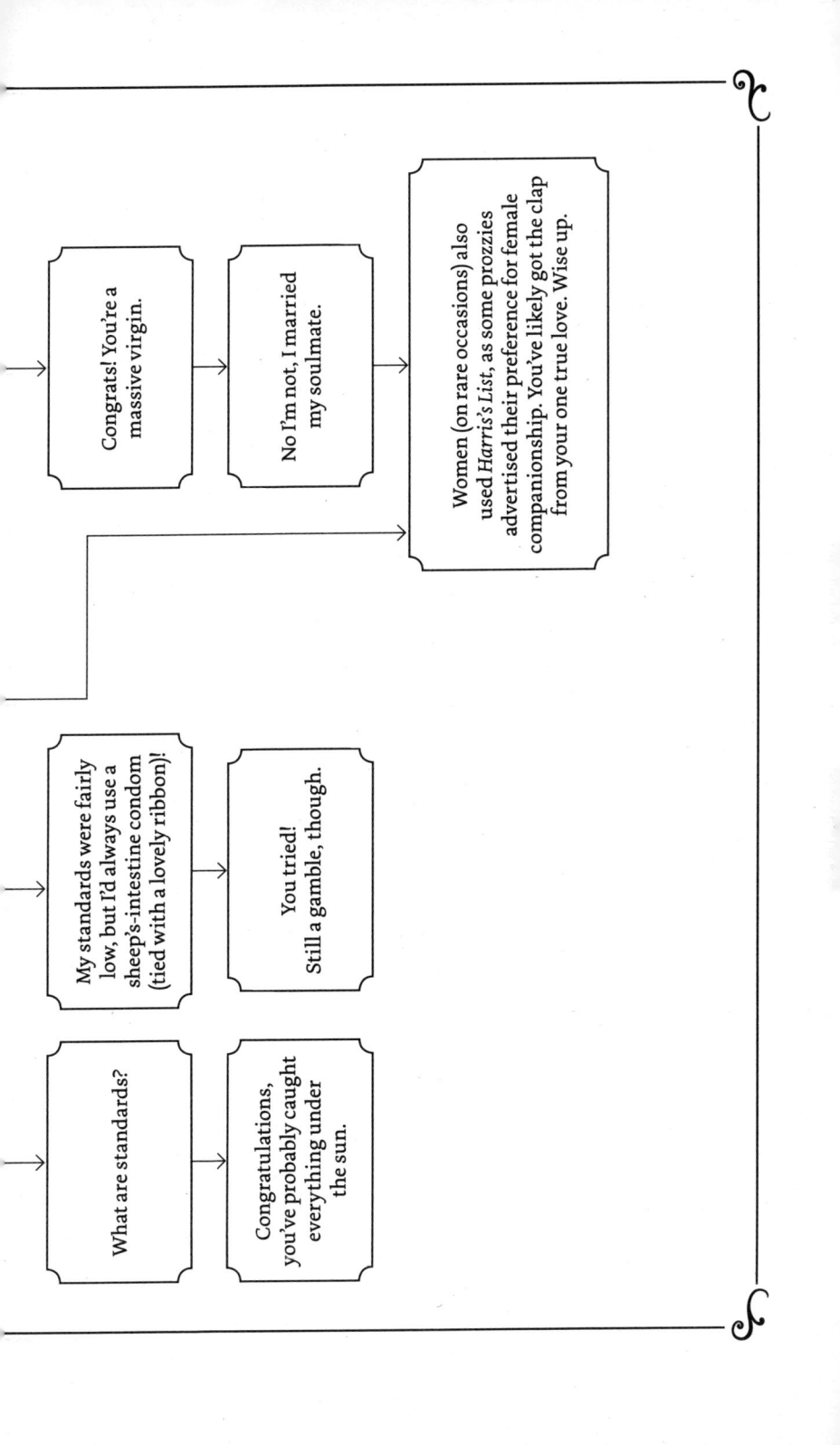

- Congrats! You're a massive virgin.
- No I'm not, I married my soulmate.
- Women (on rare occasions) also used *Harris's List*, as some prozzies advertised their preference for female companionship. You've likely got the clap from your one true love. Wise up.

- My standards were fairly low, but I'd always use a sheep's-intestine condom (tied with a lovely ribbon)!
- You tried! Still a gamble, though.

- What are standards?
- Congratulations, you've probably caught everything under the sun.

Was *Edward IV* a fat slag, and did *Casanova* catch the clap?

July

Ah, the month when everyone's one step away from heatstroke and an even worse case of lice. The rich flee to their country estates, leaving the stench of the city and their unwanted offspring behind. The rest of us are left to rot in the sweltering heat with more BO than the CeX employee of the month. It's also party season, so festivals and fairs abound. You get seshy at the festival to all the top artists, like Chopin or Elgar, and make memories with your mates. Not a phone in sight. Just pure vibes. And diphtheria.

— 1ST —

1961 – Diana Frances Spencer, Princess of Wales, is born. The first to pull your hair back when you were spewing in the loos, but also the first to scrap her lad's bit on the side, Ar Di was the people's princess. When she got mugged off by Charles again in 1994, she'd had enough. She'd been invited to a dinner at the Serpentine Gallery in Kensington Gardens. All she had was next-day delivery and a dream. Ar Di pulled up in new garms, now known as the 'revenge dress', to get back at Charles saying he wanted to be Camilla's tampon. Di also loved a bit of charity work, and was always grafting for good causes. Whether it was hugging bairns with AIDS or shaking hands with landmine victims, she was there, giving it her all, like she was one of us.

— 2ND —

1964 – Americans decide that maybe people should have rights? The Civil Rights Act becomes law. President Lyndon Johnson signed the Act, which would see the integration of white and Black pupils into the same classrooms and other public places, and made employment discrimination illegal. *Shrek 2* is released also on this day in 2004.

— 3RD —

1842 – Pissed off that people kept asking him when he's going back to Santa's workshop, John William Bean, a man barely four feet tall, takes his anger out on Queen Victoria.

July

She was travelling via carriage down The Mall, because even in one's pre-lard-arse days, one was only partial to moving legs horizontally for her cousin. But suddenly, Bean fired a shot at the queen from a pistol found to be loaded with paper and tobacco. Victoria replied, 'That's really cringe that you missed.' He was sentenced to eighteen months in prison for 'high misdemeanour'.

— 4TH —

1776 – The Declaration of Independence is adopted. The Founding Fathers, all dressed up in their finest American-flag bikinis, announced that the Thirteen Colonies were no longer under the rule of King George III and all states were independent. The Founding Fathers celebrated with everything that was American: beer, Katy Perry's *Teenage Dream* album, fuck-off massive trucks and eagles.

— 5TH —

1948 – It's a good day if you've got a dysfunctional muff, as the National Health Service begins. Before then, if you were pissing stones or the likes, the doctor would absolutely rinse you a tenner just to launch some leeches at you and call it a day. But Aneurin Bevan had pioneered a service that would provide tax-funded healthcare for all. There were talks of it before World War Two, with many in government, who had been elected by their people to serve the people, thinking that it wasn't their problem if povos got ill. They should've just done a juice cleanse or something.

— 6TH —

1483 – He took dodgy uncles to unseen highs; Richard III is crowned at Westminster. He strutted in looking like Lord Farquaad with his bob, ecstatic for the vibes and to sit on a chair and wear a hat. After his twelve-year-old nephew inherited the throne, he made sure to call his dad, Edward IV, a fat slag for finger blasting a lass before he got married, making Edward and his sons illegitimate. After Richard III thus crowned himself, his two nephews disappeared, never to be seen again. It all paid off, though, as he ruled for a long two years.

— 7TH —

1456 – Joan of Arc is given a posthumous pardon for her crimes. She believed that holy guidance had come to tell her that shovelling shit was not her destiny. Instead, she was chosen to lead the French army to a victory at Orleans in 1429. Far from being celebrated, she was accused of witchcraft and rejection of Church authority in favour of direct inspiration from God. When Joan was pardoned, she was like, 'Aye, that's solid and that but I am dead now?'

— 8TH —

1796 – The oldest known extant passport is issued to Francis Maria Barrere. Some note that this was the first US passport, but as Barrere sent it in for renewal, it is clearly not the first issued document. But anyway, like many Americans, Francis was yearning to go to Europe. He'd heard so many good things about it, such as baguettes and knife crime. But when asked if the Europe he was referring to meant Marseille or Birmingham, he just replied, 'Europe.'

— 9TH —

1762 – Horse-shagger Catherine the Great overthrows her husband and becomes the ruler of Russia. After mistakenly searching ancestry.com instead of Hinge, she married her second cousin, Peter III. They weren't happy in the marriage and she wrote

◆◆ July ◆◆

that they kept to separate sides of the castle. He was an absolute wet wipe, but they did produce a son. She wanted an aesthetic name like what other famous people do, something like Banana or X Æ A-Xii. She settled on Paul. She then staged a coup with her side piece, Grigory Orlov, and took the throne, and Peter III was killed shortly afterwards. It's still unknown whether she played any part in his death. But rumours about her persisted throughout her life and after her death, including that she shagged a horse, which wasn't true. There was also a rumour that she had a chair with peen and boobs littered about as decoration. Apparently, said chair was destroyed during World War Two, so we can't know for sure.

— 10TH —

1553 – Lady Jane Grey becomes Queen of England. Her cousin, Edward VI, who made lepers look like the pinnacle of health, died after six years on the throne. The fifteen-year-old had a cough, but no one thought of just giving him a Berocca and a pat on the back? Like come on, man. The throne passed to Lady Jane after he declared his half-sisters, Mary (Bloody Mary) and Elizabeth (later Queen Elizabeth I), illegitimate. Lady Jane wasn't like other girls, though. While others preferred to go hunting, Jane simply said, 'I wist all their sport in the park is but a shadow to that pleasure that I find in Plato. Alas, good folk, they never felt what true pleasure meant.' People then proceeded to reply, 'Why are you speaking like that? You sound like a tosser.' Her reign wouldn't last long, though, as after nine days she was executed for treason.

— 11TH —

1804 – Founding Father Alexander Hamilton and Vice President Aaron Burr meet in a dawn duel. The men became frenemies in 1791, when Burr ran for the US Senate against Hamilton's father-in-law, Philip Schuyler, and won. Things reached boiling point when Burr found out Hamilton had been chatting shit about him in the newspapers. But as neither were keen on doing a rap battle to lighten the mood, they instead partook in a duel. But why, though? Was it even that serious? Imagine someone coming up to you and saying, 'I challenge you to a duel,' like, how did the other person not just laugh? Anyway, Hamilton actually took him seriously but sadly died thirty-six hours after being shot by Burr. Burr was indicted but not arrested.

— 12TH —

1543 – The wife that no one really gives a shit about, Katherine Parr, becomes the sixth consort of Henry VIII. They married in Hampton Court Palace, with eighteen people in attendance. Henry, unable to function without fanny, couldn't stand being alone, so picked Kathy to be his wife. But Henners was pretty much past it at this point. As well as being wife, Katherine also took on the unpaid role of carer and nurse, looking after his ulcerated leg, which was oozing and goozing with all sorts. She helped to restore Mary and Elizabeth to the line of succession and ended up outliving the king.

◆• July •◆

— 13TH —

1793 – Jean-Paul Marat, a big fan of the French Revolution, is having a bath to help him relax and to help with his dermatitis. He had the Jo Malone candles lit, and the *Call Her Daddy* podcast playing, when suddenly Charlotte Corday appeared. As she walked in, he went, 'I'm a grower not a shower, it's literally because I'm in water, I'm actually so embarrassed.' Charlotte then replied, 'Aw, kid, don't stress. We all come in different shapes and sizes and if anyone shames you for that then they're not worth being in your life.' Charlotte then proceeded to stab Jean-Paul as she was a Girondin sympathizer, not a Jacobin like him, and therefore believed in a constitutional democracy.

— 14TH —

1930 – A play is aired on television in Britain for the first time. *The Man with a Flower in his Mouth* by the Italian playwright Luigi Pirandello was transmitted on the BBC. People eagerly gather around the TV to watch a one-act dialogue, as a man with a fatal illness talked about himself and his wife to a stranger. Audiences were bored shitless. They decided they'd rather watch groups of students perform their GCSE drama performance, over-acting lines such as, 'Oh no, my throat has been sliced open. This is the consequence of snorting crack cocaine.'

— 15TH —

1381 – English priest John Ball is absolutely done in by a fourteen-year-old, by getting hung, drawn and quartered. His crime was helping povos to not be povo or something, assisting in the Peasants' Revolt. A poll tax had been introduced and, coupled with low pay, the peasants were fuming and decided to revolt. John Ball disagreed with the class system, arguing that God saw everyone as equals, which encouraged the poor to demand change. Such peasants would therefore chant, 'We desireth adequate wages for the fruits of our labours, perchance.' However, the fourteen-year-old King Edward II wasn't taking any shit. He wanted extra money to spend on lairy trainers that he'd outgrow within three months. He decided to take out his anger on John by hanging him, but while he was alive his organs would have been removed. Sometimes, body parts would be placed in different parts of the country. But what about the people who did that for a living? Imagine someone asking you, 'What's your job?' and you reply, 'Oh, I take arms to Grimsby on weekdays.'

— 16TH —

1880 – Dr Emily Stowe becomes the first woman licensed to practise medicine in Canada. After a university in Canada told her it was 'not for girls', Emily was like, 'Are you a fucking Yorkie bar or something?' and packed her bags. She then headed to America for her degree. She practised medicine on the sly for years until, in 1880, the College of Physicians and Surgeons of Ontario finally said, 'They make a Yorkie bar for girls now and that's inspired us,' and gave her a medical licence.

July

— 17TH —

1955 – Disneyland opens to the world, creating a safe space for adults to wear Mickey ears in public without getting battered. Since then, Disney enthusiasts have made the pilgrimage to get blindly rinsed out of a couple of grand, complete with teary-eyed selfies next to a minimum-wage worker in a Simba costume. The theme park in Anaheim, California, cost $17 million to build. Special invites were sent out to celebrate its grand opening. However, passes were counterfeited and thousands of uninvited people rocked up.

— 18TH —

1925 Adolf Hitler's *Mein Kampf* is published. He wrote it in prison, where he was serving a sentence for a failed coup he attempted in 1923. He pioneered the *X Factor* sob story, saying life got really hard for him when he was rejected from art school because it wasn't his fault he was wank at drawing, he's a flat-earther and can't handle the concept of 3D shapes. He talked of his troubled youth, saying his dad put parental controls on the Disney Channel because of his attitude.

— 19TH —

1860 – Parent-murderer Lizzie Borden is born in Massachusetts, USA. Despite her family being pretty well off, her father, a businessman, Lizzie, her sister Emma, and her stepmother were always bickering over money. According to Lizzie's testimony, she strolled in to find her father with an axe lodged in his head and swore down he just 'fell'. When asked if her stepmother, who was also brutally mutilated upstairs, had similarly 'fallen' into multiple stab wounds, Lizzie was like, 'Yeah. Are you accusing me of lying? 'Cos if you are, I'll fuck you up – sorry, I mean I'll be quite cross, but definitely not in a stabby way.'

It was later revealed that Lizzie had tried to buy prussic acid (cyanide) and had allegedly burned a dress in a stove. When questioned again, Lizzie replied, 'What are you going to do? No one has invented DNA testing yet, and I'm a woman. None of you can grasp the possibility of women sharting, never mind chinning their family members.' Thus, she was acquitted and got away with the murder. Her community ostracized her, but hey, at least she was free.

— 20TH —

1969 – Neil Armstrong and Edwin 'Buzz' Aldrin become the first men to 'walk' on the moon. Reality remixers, formally known as conspiracy theorists, or more globally known as thick people, concluded that these leaps were filmed in Hollywood, after scrutinizing photographs of the event and questioning some shadows and what looked like wind that rustled the flag. Meanwhile, NASA engineers who had spent years meticulously planning the mission were like, 'Are you taking the piss? Do you really think we'd spaff money up the wall on this and then mess up on something like the wind?' In the end, whether you believe they walked on the moon or just took a stroll through a Hollywood backlot, Armstrong and Aldrin's 'moon landing' has kept us entertained. And for that we can all thank NASA – or Stanley Kubrick, depending on who you ask.

— 21ST —

1853 – Land is set aside to create New York's Central Park. This offered New Yorkers the chance to look at grass, rather than a drunken flasher, on a Tuesday afternoon. But in the 1850s, New York was a mix of marshlands and farms. The most densely populated area was Seneca Village, with two-thirds of residents being African-American landowners. Could this be some form of civil progress? No! All residents in Seneca Village were displaced by 1857. This was to make way for meandering bridle paths, a zoo, and insufferable millennials taking selfies with the caption: 'I'm such a Rachel!'

— 22ND —

1210 – Alexander II of Scotland scrolls through Tindeth and finds a new option to make pre-orders. 'Sound,' he thought. He decided on Joan of England, and later Queen Consort of Scotland, who was born on this day. She was the eldest daughter of King John, the monarch who issued the Magna Carta. Alexander misheard an infamous phrase about ages and clocks and married her at York Minster when she was ten and he was twenty-three, because, according to his understanding, if her age was on the clock, she was old enough for …

— 23RD —

1745 – Charles Edward Stuart lands in Eriskay, an island in Scotland, as he attempts to invade Great Britain. This is known as the Jacobite Rebellion, an attempt to remove the Hanoverian 'usurper' George II. Charles – or Bonnie Prince Charlie, as he's known, but because it's the 1700s he's probably only called that because he's got some teeth left – originally, in 1744, had the support of the French for an invasion. But due to the bad weather, the plan was abandoned with the French telling him, 'Zer is weather and it iz 'ow you say? Shit? We go cigarette break now.' After getting fucked off with the French being flakey, Charles left Brittany, secretly carrying arms and arrived in Eriskay. He lost the invasion and escaped to France, eventually dying in Rome in 1788, bitter, drunk, and relegated from a bonnie 10 to a 4.

— 24TH —

1851 – The window tax is abolished. Introduced in 1696, the tax was meant to target the wealthy, as the more windows you had, the more you paid. The rich were like, 'You know what, I'm actually sick of seeing lasses cutting about getting pregnant out of wedlock. We've seen enough, let's brick these windows up.' But if you were the said pregnant lass, bricking up windows to avoid paying the window tax absolutely did you over. Fewer windows, in already cramped conditions, meant that the poor struggled with damp, shoddy ventilation.

— 25TH —

1797 – Lord Nelson is in Tenerife with the maritime mandem. He was having a good time, with those all-inclusive cocktails leading to decisions such as getting 'Reef 1797' tattooed on his cheeks. He needed to prove to the lads his banter was on top form. But the reef wasn't all about pulling 4s and chunning on bathroom floors – he had been sent there to take possession of the port city of Santa Cruz, where Spanish treasure ships were reported to be. During the battle, Lord Nelson had to have his right arm amputated, and was gutted because that was his wanking hand. Although his friends told him that he's one down and three to go before he resembles a chicken nugget, he took it in his stride, and within half an hour was issuing orders to his men.

July

— 26TH —

1755 – Casanova is arrested. Known for being the toppest of shaggers – his communal dick would put Hugh Hefner to shame – Casanova went to university at twelve, dabbled in the clergy, and then dabbled in catching the clap. His police record grew, including allegations of religious corruption, blasphemy, sexual assault and public controversy. Casanova was arrested in his lodgings by a force of forty police. Not even aware of what he was being charged with, Casanova was taken to a prison known as the Leads, named after the lead roof it resided under in the doge's palace at Venice.

— 27TH —

1549 – Francis Xavier, a Spanish Jesuit monk, is the first Christian missionary to reach Japan. When he got there, people gave him major side-eye. They're like, 'Hiya pet, what are you selling? Eternal sal-what? Oh sorry, we've just stocked up. Maybe try next door, their bairns are always running about and falling over. Unsupervised too, proper scruffy behaviour isn't it.' With everyone finding him very suspicious and no one wanting to buy into his eternal Savlon, he was forced to wait for weeks before being allowed ashore.

— 28TH —

1540 – If you were a teen, he'd make you ride his peen – Henry VIII of England marries teenage Catherine Howard. By the sounds of things, forty-nine-year-old Henry could barely keep his hands off those training-bra chebs, as he was lusting and thrusting at first sight. Only a few days earlier, he'd announced an annulment to Anne of Cleves. But one couldn't really have expected Miss Howard to have exactly had a wide-on over him, especially as the old git had someone regularly give him enemas. One Tudor recipe for an enema consists of 'combining dill oil, white wine, chicken, and duck grease, butter, egg white and cassia fistula plant, to be inserted into the rectum using an animal bladder'.

— 29TH —

1905 – Clara Bow is born. She was 'It' during the 1920s – not the clown noncing on kids from the gutter kind, but an 'It Girl'. She was dubbed so after her breakout role in the 1927 film *It*, as she embodied the flapper-era's spirit.

But behind the Hollywood sheen, Clara's life was far from a Gatsby party. She clawed her way up from a rough upbringing in Brooklyn, facing poverty, a mentally ill mother, and an absentee father who made Houdini look reliable.

— 30TH —

1818 – Emily Brontë is born in Thornton, West Yorkshire. Painfully shy and living an isolated life, Emily couldn't be arsed with people and preferred to cut about the moors, doing what all women wish to do – screaming into the void while wearing petticoats. An avid Kate Bush fan, Emily was inspired by her music to create the classic novel, *Wuthering Heights*. The book is about people who fancy each other, then hate each other, and are pricks to everyone, with no single character having a redeeming quality. The violent and sexually passionate story shocked readers, originally heralding negative reviews.

— 31ST —

1923 – The fun sponge known as British parliament passes a law that bans giving alcohol to under-eighteens. Ten-year-olds are fuming they can no longer they can no longer grab a pint after a long shift up the chimney.

Top 5 Worst Things in History

5. Poulaines. During the medieval period in Europe, there was a trend for men to walk around town with massive pointy shoes, looking like a right tit to impress Mathilde next door. The impracticality of the shoes was itself a status symbol for the rich, as you weren't going to be seeing a povo clarting about the fields in poulaines anytime soon.

4. The Dancing Plague of 1518. Everyone is flailing their arms around, singing 'Hail, fair Caroline, good times never seemed so good' like they're Mr Tickle on E. The dancing plague occurred in Strasbourg and some people uncontrollably danced for weeks, their feet bloodied and limbs spasming. The Church said it was punishment for taking part in 'sinful' activities, such as sodomy, or using an Android.

3. John F. Kennedy Deciding to Take the Convertible on 22nd November 1963.

2. Being Scared of Water. If you lobbed a bottle of Evian at a peasant, they'd probably cry. Up until the eighteenth century, water was seen as the devil's cocktail, and if you could swim, folk figured you were probably on first-name terms with the lad. And for bathing? Hold your nose. People believed that baths exposed your body to the elements and let infections enter it.

1. Tudor Collar Ruffs. You look like a dog who has to wear a cone after he just had his bollocks clipped.

Why did *Cleopatra* off herself, and did *Mary Shelley* lose her V-card on her mother's grave?

August

August is just July's clapped-out sister – hotter, sweatier and twice as unpleasant. The heat is unbearable, and the air is thick with the stench of unwashed bodies and rotting refuse. The wealthy are still hiding in their summer homes, lounging around while their servants fan them with palm fronds. You're sadly stuck ploughing those fields harder than you ploughed little Mary-Anne last night. The only relief is knowing that September might bring a slight drop in temperature, though not, alas, in your misery.

— 1ST —

1774 – Scientist Joseph Priestley discovers oxygen. Before this monumental discovery, no one knew how to breathe, which would cause many a problem in everyday life, such as being unable to breathe. However, Priestley prepared oxygen by heating mercury oxide with a burning glass. Not sure how you'd even think to do something like that, but henceforth he did, and found that oxygen did not dissolve in water and made combustion stronger. And because of this discovery, everyone now doesn't walk around blue in the face.

— 2ND —

1820 – Irish physicist John Tyndall asks why the sky is blue. He asked his mate who replied, 'Because that's the colour of it.' Unsatisfied with the answer, he decided to find out himself. He started shining beams through different liquids and gases. He then used a glass tube to act as the sky, with the sun representing a white light at one end of the tube. He discovered that as he gradually filled the tube with smoke, the beam of light looked blue from the side but red from the far end. Tyndall realized that the colour of the sky results from sunlight scattering around particles in the upper atmosphere, a phenomenon now known as the 'Tyndall effect'.

— 3RD —

1527 – The first letter in English is sent from North America, by John Rut. He was chosen by Henry VIII to command an expedition to North America. John wrote that it was worth succumbing to scurvy and seasickness over booking a Jet2 flight, as the thought of having Jess Glynne on full blast for eight hours was enough to send him over the edge. Not that Henners gave a shit, as he was busy trying to divorce his first wife, Catherine of Aragon.

August

— 4TH —

1914 – World War One is declared, a month after the assassination of Archduke Franz Ferdinand and his wife Sophie. Queen Victoria's grandchildren were occupying the thrones of Europe, but suddenly got pissy and declared war on each other. People from all over Europe, from Cannes to Bradford, were confused by why a random getting shot was such a massive deal. Couldn't they have just done a 'Gallagher special' and ignored each other for fifteen years? No, Austria-Hungry declared war on Serbia. Russia got involved because of their alliance to Serbia, then Germany piped up and announced they wanted to deck Russia because of their alliance with Austria-Hungary. Then Britain declared war on Germans for not being able to take a joke and because they invaded Belgium, who was neutral.

— 5TH —

1962 – Marilyn Monroe is found dead in her Los Angeles bedroom with a bottle of sleeping pills by her side. Even in death, Monroe couldn't escape the fixation of men, with some even vying for the ultimate 'proximity to fame' by wanting to be buried next to her. Because why let a little thing like mortality stop creepy obsession?

— 6TH —

1888 – Jack the Ripper, the gold medallist of the involuntary celibacy olympics, murders Martha Turner in George Yard, just off Whitechapel High Street. Martha was married to a furniture maker and had two kids, before her husband left her due to her heavy drinking. Martha resorted to the prozzie life. She was last seen going off with a soldier before being found dead in the early hours of the morning. Her death was known as the first strike of Jack the Ripper's serial murders.

— 7TH —

1840 – Parliament makes it illegal for anyone under sixteen to be apprenticed as a sweep, and for anyone under twenty-one to be made or allowed to climb a chimney to clean it. England then gave itself a pat on the back for a good day's work of saving the kiddies, before settling down for the evening and checking the delivery status of their Shein order.

— 8TH —

1963 – £2.6 million is stolen from a train by a gang of robbers. Typically, the items stored would have been worth around £300,000, but thanks to a Bank Holiday weekend in Scotland, the total on the day of the robbery soared to £2.6 million (roughly £69 million today). I'm not saying I condone illegal activity, like arson is dead bad, for example, but what type of daft arse lets a train go from Glasgow to Euston with that much cash on it? In this economy? And pre-high tech security? Wise up.

— 9TH —

1173 – In Pisa, builders begin work on a bell tower for the city's cathedral. When discussing how to create a tower that wasn't like other girls, they decided to make sure to build on weak subsoil and shallow foundations. This would make sure that the bell tower would unintentionally tilt, but no stress lads, because in about eight hundred years, pasty tourists with Year Seven backpacks will be queueing by the plenty, ready to look like they're holding up the tower for their Instagram pics. I'm sure the original builders are so happy to know that that is their legacy.

August

— 10TH —

1792 – The French monarchy is on its knees, but not in a fun way. Louis XVI, his wife Marie Antoinette and their children flee for their lives as the revolutionaries make moves through Paris. Although Marie Antoinette was falsely credited with saying, 'Let them eat cake,' maybe if her husband hadn't waited seven years to eat hers, they might not have ended up in this mess. Louis preferred playing with clocks (and no, there wasn't an accidental 'l' added to that), instead of sticking it in her. Having no heir for a solid chunk of time wasn't exactly a good look, as it made the monarchy seem a bit unstable. This wouldn't have been the definitive reason for overthrowing the monarchy, but it didn't help Marie Antoinette's reputation one bit. Peasants called her 'the Austrian Bitch', to which she responded, 'Can you even spell that? Get off your high horse and go back to singing "One Day More".' She was also called 'Madame Deficit', as she was being blamed for France's financial crisis.

Top 5 Quotes From History

5. 'Let them eat cake!' – Marie Antoinette. This one only reaches number 5, mainly down to the fact that it isn't true at all, and was only attributed to her to show that she was more out of touch than those who ski. The quote can be linked to Enlightenment philosopher Jean-Jacques Rousseau in 1767, when Marie Antoinette would've been twelve, but he just attributed it to 'a great princess'.

4. 'Haha, you up?' – Albert Einstein to his cousin, Elsa. Although married to super-bright physicist and mathematician Mileva Marić, he largely saw her as someone to iron his shirts and cook his meals. He clearly yearned for someone to help keep those family reunions small, so he divorced Mileva and wedded Elsa, to whom he remained married until her death, but he still cheated on her, too. With absolutely anyone and everyone.

3. 'The only thing we have to fear is fear itself' – FDR, 1933. Franklin D. Roosevelt said this during the Great Depression (1929–39), so unfortunately this is only number 3, as when a lad who just won the presidency and has done quite well for himself is telling people living on 'coffee soup' and 'dandelion salad' that they're doing just fine, he probably isn't reading the room. FDR was known for his radio 'fireside chats', in which he'd explain politics in simple terms to the public, to provide reassurance.

◆• August •◆

> **2.** 'There's only two types of people in the world / The ones that entertain, and the ones that observe' – Britney Spears, 'Circus', 2008.
>
> **1.** 'I just proper love impaling' – Vlad the Impaler. Vlad was Voivode (prince) of Wallachia (now in Romania) three times before his death, c. 1476.

— 11TH —

1660 – Henrietta Maria Wentworth, an English courtier, is born. She caught the eye of King Charles II's illegitimate son, the Duke of Monmouth. Despite being married and implicated in a plot to kill his father, he had that irresistible bad-boy charm. Blowing his strawberry-watermelon vape smoke into her face really sealed the deal, and off they fucked to Holland in exile. When his uncle claimed the throne in 1685, the Duke launched a rebellion financed by Lady Wentworth's jewellery. Honestly, why was he so bothered about rebellion? He wasn't even part of the official bloodline. Maybe if his dad hadn't been busy sticking it in every tart and had actually married one, he would've had a better claim to the throne.

— 12TH —

30 BC – Cleopatra ends her own life. After her lover Caesar Salad was assassinated, Rome fell into civil war and she turned to Roman general Mark Antony. When on the pull for Mark Antony, she dressed up as Venus, the Roman goddess of love. Mark thought this was class and all, if not slightly cringe, but went along with it anyway, as the poon was life-changing. Said poon unfortunately did cause a bit of shit, including a war with Caesar's heir, Octavian. Antony was actually married to Octavian's sister, Octavia, but he thought she was dead craic, so made sure to let everyone know that he was banging Cleopatra by posting their relationship status for everyone to see. In 34 BC, Antony shocked Rome by publicly recognizing Cleopatra's son, Caesarion, as the son of Caesar and giving him the title 'King of Kings'. Since Caesar had only adopted Octavian, recognizing Caesarion as his biological son threatened Octavian's political position. The final nail in the coffin was when Mark Antony called Octavia a bint and divorced her, which led to Octavian declaring war on Cleopatra. Sadly, Mark and Cleo lost, and she had no choice but to end her own life to avoid being captured. But we don't know for definite if Cleopatra was actually bitten by a snake!

— 13TH —

1964 – The last execution in the UK is performed. At 8 a.m., Peter Anthony Allen and Gwynne Owen Evans had the dubious honour of being the last people executed in the UK. The public was growing tired of state-sanctioned executions – too messy and depressy. They preferred a nice, relaxing evening in front of the telly. Meanwhile, their great-grandparents scoffed, 'Back in my day, a good hanging was the highlight of the week! I worry for this generation, entertainment's really lost its edge.' Some historians and criminologists reckon that if the lads had just managed to delay things by a few weeks, they might have dodged capital punishment altogether. Just their luck to be punctual for once in their lives.

❖• August •❖

— 14TH —

1739 – King George II puts his royal seal on the charter for the Foundling Hospital, founded by Thomas Coram to take care of abandoned children. If you'd been spawned out of wedlock, then this was what life had in store for you. To avoid shame, mothers could leave their baby at the Foundling Hospital with a token, which the children would be given after they left. They'd be taught sewing, shoemaking and reading, and be shipped off at fourteen to become apprentices. They were also given new names, to distance them from their backgrounds, which was deemed to have made them the scum of the earth, and to try and deter them from the same path.

— 15TH —

1248 – Archbishop Konrad von Hochstanden lays the foundation stone of Cologne's cathedral. This became one of Germany's most famous landmarks. The archbishop didn't bother building with the rest of the stones, because that's a job for the overworked and underpaid, and instead returned to the comfort of his chambers, whereupon the real work began for those not blessed with the luxury of avoiding calluses.

— 16TH —

1896 – Gold is discovered in the Klondike region of Canada's Yukon Territory, sparking the Klondike Gold Rush. Suddenly, every man with a pickaxe and a dream of easy riches decided that freezing their chebs off in the middle of nowhere was a good shout. Out of a hundred thousand people, only about four thousand became rich, with them absolutely decimating wildlife and having a severe impact on the native Hän peoples. And although many didn't find gold, maybe what mattered more were the friends they made along the way – those being dysentery and frostbite.

— 17TH —

1998 – US President Bill Clinton finally remembers that he done diddled Monica Lewinsky and admits it to a grand jury after denying it numerous times. Maybe he just forgot? He was getting on a bit. Or maybe, just maybe, he purposefully tried to skew the narrative and happily pushed a woman in her early twenties in front of the bus instead.

— 18TH —

1963 – James Meredith, the pioneering African American who dared to grace the halls of the University of Mississippi, finally escapes with a degree. This accomplishment was much to the dismay of the elite chads at Sigma Mega Alpha Delta Lotta Blow frat house, who notoriously chanted, 'People of colour shouldn't be allowed to study here; it'll lower the tone,' in between bites of the fraternity vomlet during their initiations.

August

— 19TH —

1883 – Coco Chanel is born. Working as a seamstress in her late teens, she then decided to open up her own millinery shop, with her practical designs attracting many influential women to abandon stifling corsets and petticoats.

In between doing collabs with the Nazis, she created perfume too. If you were blindfolded and asked to differentiate between Chanel No. 5 and an elderly person who'd pissed themselves and hadn't changed their pants for three days, you might struggle to tell the difference.

— 20TH —

c. AD 14 –It's all kicking off. Augustus dies the day before. New emperor Tiberius reaches Nola and writes to the provinces on this day. Tibby then cracks on and goes ahead and murders Augustus' exiled grandson, Agrippa Postumus. Just before getting murdered, Agrippa allegedly said, 'Can this not wait? I'm literally on bereavement leave and if you don't allow me this it will actually go against my human rights.' The dismissal of Agrippa reflected the regime's insecurity and its awareness that, even in AD 14, Tiberius faced numerous opponents eager to support an alternative emperor. So, even if Tiberius thought Agrippa was a top fellow, the survival of the regime necessitated Agrippa's demise, irrespective of what he thought of him.

— 21ST —

1911 – *Mona Lisa* is stolen from the Louvre. Vincenzo Peruggia, this Italian handyman bloke, sneaked into work early, probably to avoid the boss or something. He swanned in, dressed in his white smock like he was off to a fancy-dress party as a painter, grabbed the *Mona Lisa*, tucked it under his arm, and fucked off. No one batted an eyelid, probably because everyone else was too busy going, 'Bonjour, je suis à la croissant civ voo play' to each other.

He kept the Mony-Lee in his gaff for two years. The French were too engrossed in pickpocketing American tourists in berets to have realized it had been stolen, until a visitor asked where it had gone. The French papers went mental, people queued up to see the empty space where she used to hang, and the police made a token visit to Peruggia's place. He told them he was working elsewhere that day, and they went, 'Fair enough, mate, carry on,' and didn't even bother looking in the trunk where he had hidden the *Mona Lisa*.

Eventually, Peruggia reckoned he was actually a bit of a patriot and wanted to take the painting back to Italy. But, let's be honest, he was probably thinking he could make a few quid, too. He took it to a local gallery owner in Florence, thinking he was gonna be minted. But the gallery owner was like, 'Are you actually dense, do you really think no one is going to notice if I have this hanging about in my gallery?' So the police were called A$AP Rocky and Peruggia was chucked in prison for a bit.

The *Mona Lisa* was carted back to Paris, and suddenly she was the most famous painting in the world. Before that, she was just another picture by Leonardo DiCaprio, and hardly anyone knew her. Now she's a global superstar, thanks to Vincenzo Peruggia and his little French holiday.

— 22ND —

AD 565 – St Columba, this Irish abbot who fancies himself a bit of a missionary and scholar, decides to cross a river in Scotland. He stumbled upon a group of Picts doing a proper burial for their mate who'd been mauled by some 'water beast' in the river. Columba, being the type to chat shit, waltzed up to Loch Ness like, 'Did you murk this lad?' The Loch Ness monster, or Lochy-N as the locals probably didn't call him, denied it. St Columba then replied, 'He is dead and that's really hurt his feelings so don't piss me about, or I'll make sure your old tweets from ten years ago resurface, and that'll be the end of your career, sunshine.' Lochy-N then said, 'I'm proper sorry, it's all love.' And that is the 100 per cent true story of how St Colomba managed to scare the shit out of the Loch Ness monster, and we know about this because of St Adomnán's book *The Life of Saint Columba*. But who knows if Adomnán was chatting absolute bollocks or not.

— 23RD —

1572 – Thousands of Huguenots are killed in the St Bartholomew's Day Massacre. Some said Catherine de' Medici, the Queen Mother of France, was behind it, but that's just an awks mix-up, like starting a sentence with 'You guys' and instantly locking eyes with the blue-haired person. Sure, she didn't like Protestants – who did? – but she wasn't trying to wipe them out. She was just planning a big royal wedding between her daughter Marguerite and the Protestant Henry of Navarre, reasoning, 'What could go wrong?' The answer was, everything. Someone tried to knock out the Huguenot leader Admiral Gaspard de Coligny. Catherine sent her doctor to help him out. Next thing you know, Paris turned into a medieval bloodbath.

— 24TH —

1875 – Swimmer Captain Matthew Webb is in search of a personality, and as everyone else hitting a quarter-life crisis has already chosen to run marathons, he makes it his mission to be the first person to swim the English Channel. He'd started his attempt from Dover, reaching Calais, France at 10.40 a.m. the following day. He'd been in the water for twenty-two hours. Imagine how wrinkly his bollocks were from being in the water for that long.

— 25TH —

1530 – The birthday of Russian ruler Ivan the Terrible. Bless him, imagine being nicknamed 'the Terrible' – surely a knock to the lad's confidence. But back in the sixteenth century, this meant 'powerful'. After a rather tragic childhood – both parents dying, with him and his brother being neglected and used as political pawns – Ivan made it his mission to provide the blueprint for incels by plucking feathers from live birds and chucking cats out of windows. After a few years of labelling himself a nice guy, then calling women fugly for not putting out, he gained full power at sixteen. He married, but his wife, Anastasia, died. He wanted to abdicate but only agreed to return if he could off his enemies at will. His execution methods were quite the spectacle, featuring boiling alive, impalement, roasting over open fires, and good old limb-tearing.

Post-Anastasia, Ivan developed a penchant for accumulating wives, even setting his sights on Elizabeth I. Considering a few of his spouses met mysterious ends, it's probably for the best for the ginger ninja that she wasn't added to his collection.

— 26TH —

Happy National Toilet Paper Day – hurray. This leads to the age-old question of what did people used to use to wipe their arses? Well, if we go back to the Ancient Greeks, the answer is shards of pottery. Must be pretty rank for archaeologists thinking they've dug up something monumental and it ends up having traces of shit on it. For the Romans, we've got the classic sharing with the boys of Spongebob on a stick. But don't worry about sharing ass germs, as it was dipped in vinegar between wipes, so it was still no homo. Throughout the ages, you could use whatever you had – fur, fruit skins, seashells, rags, or your hand, if you're really at one with your body. In the 1850s, toilet paper was first commercially marketed and sold as 'medicated paper' by New York's Joseph Gayetty. If you squeezed out one big chungus, though, you were done for, as the paper was quite thin. And the added risk of getting a splinter also wasn't great.

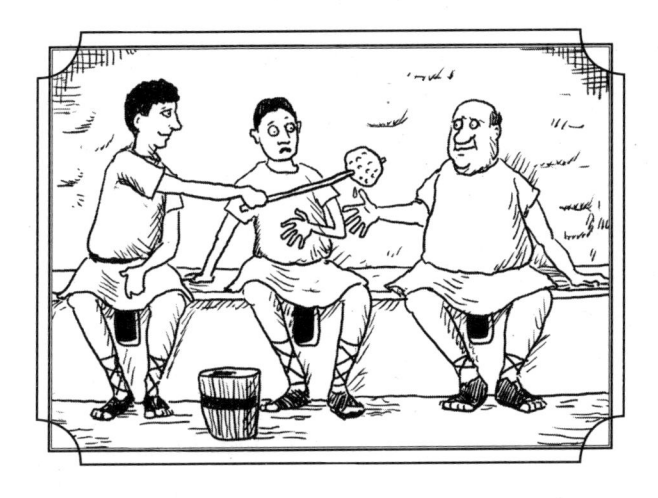

— 27TH —

1955 – The *Guinness Book of World Records* is bound. It included quite wholesome records, such as the biggest baby (9.13 kg/ 20 lbs 2 oz), but unfortunately does not include the stretchiest foof next to it. Now, people go absolutely off on one trying to get in this book, including the likes of 'fastest marathon on a swing', 'furthest throw of a washing machine' and 'most candy canes in a beard'.

— 28TH —

1828 – Birthday of Leo Tolstoy, Russian novelist. He churned out corkers such as *Anna Karenina* and *War and Peace*, which is nearly 1,500 pages long. Not to shit on his rainbows and clouds and that, but who has that much to say? And who has the time to read all of that in this economic state? Did he throw in the kitchen sink for good measure?

— 29TH —

1842 – The Treaty of Nanking is signed in China, marking the end of the First Opium War. This opened up five treaty ports for British trade, along with handing over Hong Kong as a British colony. Essentially, it was a 'Thank you for letting us invade and peddle our drugs. 420 blaze it for real and all that; so here's your consolation prize.'

— 30TH —

1797 – Mary Shelley (née Godwin) exits British philosopher Mary Wollstonecraft. She's best known for walking so emos could run, having come up with the idea for *Frankenstein* at just eighteen years old. Others of her escapades include doing a pump pump squirt and losing her V-card on her mother's grave with her future husband, Percy Bysshe Shelley. She told her dad that she wanted to go on a walk with him around the grave to discuss important intellectual thoughts but, alas, she was instead getting bent over with her bloomers around her ankles.

— 31ST —

1854 – Turns out giving Tiny Tim floater water and telling him to 'See it off' isn't the move, and cholera proceeds to break out in London. Anaesthetist John Snow discovered that the outbreak likely came from a pump in Broad Street, with eighty-nine people dying in the area within the week. Even the Brita filter wasn't saving Tiny Tim at this point.

Beauty Tips for the Modern Flapper

You'll be the talk of the town, or maybe the A&E.

Glow From the Inside (Thanks to Radium!)
Spice up that mud mask with some radium-based Kemolite mud. It may result in a glowing complexion ... or a premature visit to the cemetery. But at least your husband will notice how much you glow.

Petroleum Wash: A Hair Wash, but Not Really!
When the salon doesn't have hot or cold running water, just let Becky with her BTEC Level 1 in Hair and Beauty douse your hair in petrol instead. It loves it! Just ask Helenora Elphinstone-Dalrymple, who died tragically after a Harrods hair treatment in 1909. Some say it was an accident; others claim it was the price of looking fabulous. Either way, remember: beauty has always been worth dying for.

X-Ray Hair Removal: Because Shaving is for Amateurs
Why bother with razors or tweezers when you can zap pesky hairs off with X-rays? You might lose a few layers of skin, but at least you won't have to worry about regrowth.

Cold Cream for Every Occasion
Have a skin problem? Cold cream. Bad mood? Cold cream. Husband threatening to leave you for his secretary? Cold cream.

And lastly — Never, Ever Age!

Did **F. Scott Fitzgerald** secretly collab with his wife, and who banned slut drops on the **Mayflower**?

September

Back to the grindstone, as the factory doors swing open and the streets fill with the sounds of industry. The school year begins, and with it teachers who are a bit too keen to go S&M non-consensual mode and use those whips on the kiddies. You come to the realization that education is just a futile attempt to rise above your station and that you'll never escape the allegations of your mother being the village bike. The weather cools, but so do your spirits, as the fleeting joys of summer have been replaced by the dreary monotony of daily life.

— 1ST —

1715 – After livin' for thou nyash and dyin' for thou nyash, Louis XIV succumbs to gangrene, four days before his seventy-seventh birthday. Frightened by prolonged civil rebellions against his family in his youth, Louis XIV moved away from Paris and transformed Versailles, which had originally been used as a hunting lodge by Louis XIII, into a lavish palace. But, alas, devouring many a pie and poon takes its toll. He suffered from gout and diabetes, before an infection in his leg turned gangrenous and put an end to the party.

— 2ND —

1666 – The sun is shining, the tinnies are coming out and there is a faint smell of toast in the air. It was summer. You were lying on your deck chair and, apart from the sound of your neighbours keeling over from the plague for attention, life was pretty solid. But not for long, because there was going to be a fuck-off massive fire, and it started in Thomas Farriner's bakery on Pudding Lane. In 1666, people didn't realize the huge dangers of having tightly packed-together timber buildings, covered in a flammable substance called pitch, and roofed with thatch. They were just here for a good time, and clearly not a long time. After the fire broke out it quickly spread across London. There was no organized fire brigade, because their mentality was, 'Can you not just blow it out?' They had leather buckets and some BB water guns, but, unfortunately, those didn't do a lot. Instead of water, the navy decided to just blow up some houses instead, which they thought would stop the fire from spreading from house to house. By 5th September, the fire was mostly under control, but a lot of London had to be reconstructed afterward.

September

— 3RD —

1752 – Eleven days go missing in Great Britain. People were wondering how the day after Wednesday 2nd September 1752 instantly became Thursday 14th September 1752. Sadly, this wasn't due to time travelling. The 'new style' Gregorian calendar had come into effect, and eleven days were cut in the switch to amend an error in the old Julian calendar.

— 4TH —

1998 – Google is formally incorporated by its founders, Larry Page and Sergey Brin, in California. The two Stanford University students were tinkering away in their friend's garage in Menlo Park, and wanted to google a fun Buzzfeed quiz to take, such as 'Sarumann or Gandalf: Which Tolkien Character Should We Send Back in Time to Outshine Christ?' But sadly, there was no way to google such joyous quizzes as Google didn't exist yet. So, after fannying about doing neeky tech stuff and developing an algorithm called PageRank, they eventually came up with the Google we have today.

— 5TH —

2016 – Anti-women's rights activist Phyllis Schlafly passes away. In the 1970s, she campaigned against the Equal Rights Amendment, arguing it was a gateway for all hell to break loose, with the hell being things like gays. After working in a munitions factory in World War Two to pay for her tuition at Harvard University and running for Congress, Phyllis recoiled at the thought of women being able to have equal rights. She was very outspoken about her opposition of the Equal Rights Amendment as she thought this would mean drafting women to war. In 1983, Schlafly famously sent fifty-three senators homemade quiches, accompanied by a note that said, 'Real Men Do Not Draft Women.'

While also vocalizing that men shouldn't take it up the arse, her son was simultaneously doing exactly that, and after he came out as gay she insisted he agreed with her views.

— 6TH —

1901 – President William McKinley decided that a handshake tour at the Pan-American Exposition in Buffalo was the perfect way to win hearts. Unfortunately anarchist and now president-murderer Leon Czolgosz had other plans and gave him two bullet points on why that was a bad idea, and thus boom-boom-powed him into the grave.

— 7TH —

1533 – Elizabeth I was born, a disappointment to both her parents, not only because she was ginger but also because she was a woman. A truly sad day. She'd go on to be a powerful ruler, defeating the Spanish, establishing a secure Church of England, famously declaring that she never wanted to get taken to pound town and boasting nuclear breath, as she only brushed her teeth with sugar paste. After battling smallpox, Lizzie was also a lover of mercury-based white foundation, resulting in grey, shrivelled skin and in everyone going, 'Wow, Liz, your inside beauty is really shining today.'

— 8TH —

1504 – Michelangelo's *David* is installed in Florence. The colossal statue, the first of its kind since classical antiquity, had men everywhere feeling seen and celebrated. Finally, a hero in the popular culture with a small penis. A chode without the girth, if you will. But in ancient times, a small prick meant you were intellectual and kept your urges under control.

September

— 9TH —

1947 – There's a bug in a Harvard University computer. No, literally, a moth was trapped in the hardware. Contrary to popular stories, this hasn't got anything to do with our word for computer glitches. That kind of 'bug', referring to an engineering problem, can be traced back to the Victorian era, and Thomas Edison also refers to a literal bug in one of his telephone apparatuses, according to his letter dated 3rd March 1878.

— 10TH —

1897 – London taxi-driver George Smith is the first person to be charged with drink driving. He reportedly 'swerved from one side of the road to the other, and ran across the footway into 165 New Bond Street'. When the authorities showed up, they didn't need a breathalyser – he stank of booze. But, to keep up appearances, they asked George to walk a straight line. George, ever the innovator, responded, 'Would a drunk person do this?' and proceeded to re-enact the *High School Musical* dance routine he learned at seven and forced his parents to watch. He was fined twenty shillings.

— 11TH —

1850 – Swedish soprano opera singer Jenny Lind performs her first concert at New York's Castle Garden. Lind was dubbed the 'Swedish Nightingale', and her fans screamed and cried as she graced the stage, debating with each other what her surprise song would be, or if she'd announce another rerecording (Jenny's Version). She became the first Professor of Singing at the Royal College of Music. But it was her tour of America that really took everyone by storm, raking in about $10 million in today's money. Instead of starting a skincare line that would give you mild acne, Jenny decided to give away her fortune to charities and scholarships.

— 12TH —

1940 – Four teenage boys in France are larking about and accidently discover the Palaeolithic (really old, like definitely more than ten years ago and probs over a million) Lascaux cave paintings. The majority of the paintings show animals in detailed colour. What do they mean? Who knows! Recent research points to them being related to animal life cycles due to the markings next to the paintings referencing a calendar, rather than recording speech. But the people who made them are dead now, so we can't really ask them.

— 13TH —

1916 – Roald Dahl is born in Cardiff. After fighting in the RAF, he became a bestselling children's author, known for the likes of *Charlie and the Chocolate Factory*, *Matilda* and *The Witches*. His books have sold over 300 million copies worldwide. Children clearly love the thinly veiled threats of doom that Dahl expertly wove into his stories. After all, nothing says 'bedtime story' quite like drowning in chocolate rivers. In 2023, Penguin announced they'd be cutting out offensive language in his books. So instead of Mr Twit being called 'ugly and beastly' he'd just be called 'beastly'. But if he's fuggers then he's fuggers? Just say it with your chest, no shame in it.

— 14TH —

1837 – The first Tiffany store opens its doors in New York City. Originally called Tiffany, Young and Ellis – because Charles Lewis Tiffany and John B. Young were feeling really imaginative that day – the shop offered a delightful assortment of stationery and fancy goods. Because no one really cared about ballpoint pens, in their first three days of business they recorded a whopping $4.98

in sales. But once they realized there was a market for $10,000 sterling-silver balls of yarn, they were good to go.

— 15TH —

1922 – The end of straw-hat season in New York. Straw hats were customarily worn from 15th May to 15th September, when men could smash their straw hats on the floor and everyone would swap theirs out for felt hats.

In 1922, however, riots broke out over eight days surrounding 15th. Groups of men and boys fought each other, smashing and trampling hats in the streets. The *New York Times* reported on 16th 'gangs of young hoodlums' around the city.

— 16TH —

1620 – The *Mayflower* ship sails from Plymouth to America, carrying the anti-banter brigade: the Pilgrim Fathers. These Puritan Separatists, a boatload of people so determined to avoid fun that they crossed an ocean for it, fled the Church of England in 1620 to establish the first permanent New England colony. They were the kind of lads who thought a good time meant months of seasickness and near starvation, all for the chance to build a society where doing slut drops on the dancefloor was considered a gateway to sin.

— 17TH —

1976 – The Sex Pistols perform a concert at Chelmsford top-security prison. The Pistols that had sex in them imagined they'd go down in history for being edgelords. But in reality, overdubs had to be made on the recording because the prisoners were actually indifferent to their performance. There were even reports of booing, with some prisoners allegedly saying they'd rather knife their XL bully again than have to listen to any more.

— 18TH —

1714 – George I lands in Britain to be crowned after Queen Anne dies. As a Hanoverian, he wasn't really a fan of England, couldn't be arsed to learn the language, and didn't understand why we all gagged over mushy peas. He left the politics to his government, meaning the Whigs dominated parliament. He also gave his son daddy issues by imprisoning his mother for getting on her knees for everyone.

— 19TH —

1879 – Crowds are razzle-dazzled by Blackpool's new illuminations. Blackpool was a holiday hotspot for Victorians – the deprivation must've really appealed to them or something. But Blackpool wanted to stand out from other fierce competition, such as Hartlepool, the tyre-nicking capital of the world. The council managed to scrape together a sum of £5,000 for an experiment with electric lighting. They grandly dubbed it 'artificial sunlight', and amassed nearly a hundred thousand visitors. What a momentous occasion this was, inspiring northern mothers everywhere to tell their kids to 'turn off the big light, it's not Blackpool Illuminations', but at this moment in time, it in fact was Blackpool Illuminations.

— 20TH —

1973 – A tennis match ensues between twenty-nine-year-old Billie Jean King and fifty-five-year-old Bobby Riggs at the Houston Astrodome. Riggs, the self-proclaimed 'male chauvinist pig', handed her a lollipop. King handed him a piglet. Great. Despite Riggs's boasts that women were no good at tennis, and his previous victory over Margaret Court, King hammered him 6–4, 6–3, 6–3. The only thing Riggs truly conquered that day was his ego, whereas King, who was also the first prominent female athlete to come out the closet, took home $100,000 and free drinks at every lesbian bar.

— 21ST —

1915 – Cecil Chubb pays £6,600 (equivalent to £680,000 today) to buy Stonehenge at an auction. It was said that his wife, Lady Mary, was fucked off because she'd wanted a set of curtains, not a set of rocks. That October, Cecil passed Stonehenge into public ownership and asked that we shouldn't pay 'a sum exceeding one shilling' per visit. It's currently £37 for one adult ticket.

— 22ND —

1792 – The National Convention is established, meaning France is declared a republic. This basically stripped King Louis XVI of his powers. Louis was gutted that he could no longer swan about in his powdered wigs and high heels in a bid to appear as a judge on *Drag Race*. At their first meeting, the Convention decided to try King Louis XVI for treason, and found him guilty. Versailles proceeded to get turned into a Wetherspoons and Louis was executed on 21 January 1793.

— 23RD —

1387 – King Richard II hosts a massive banquet. Unlike today, where we usually have savoury dishes followed by sweet, in the Middle Ages they were all mixed. Solteties, or food sculptures that were not meant to be eaten, were also served. These showed the wealth and power of the hosts, and could convey various political and religious messages. Then, to eat, they just served up any meat they could find – chicken, rabbit, pigeon, partridge, swans, pigs – some of which were mixed up with fruits, custards, porridges, pastries and honey. No quinoa and spinach for these hard lads, they wanted real food. And gout, by the sounds of it.

— 24TH —

1896 – F. Scott Fitzgerald's birthday. He's best known for writing *The Great Gatsby*, a tale where Leonardo DiCaprio pines over a woman over twenty-five, which can help us to identify that this book is, in fact, fiction. In this tale of lost loves and living in the past, F. Scott Fitz dropped a surprise collab with his wife, Zelda, on a few lines. This was such a surprise that Zelda didn't even know, as he'd nicked some pages out of her diary to write about his character Daisy Buchanan. But when Daisy says that if she has a daughter, 'I hope she'll be a fool – that's the best thing a girl can be in this world, a beautiful little fool,' it's a bit obvious that men, famously known to scratch and sniff their balls in public, wouldn't have pulled out a line like that.

September

— 25TH —

1690 – Boston's first newspaper is launched. *Publick Occurrences Both Forreign and Domestick* was printed by Boston resident Richard Pierce. Dyslexia sufferer or victim of pre-dictionary spelling, scholars will never know. The paper started out with good news for only the settlers, talking about the 'Christianized Indians' and their 'newly appointed day of Thanksgiving'. But people craved drama! They wanted to know who was streaking around town after too much moonshine, or if the knitting circle was a front for lasses to show each other their ankles. Editor Benjamin Harris gave in and started reporting that their kids had been abducted: 'a couple of Children belonging to a man of that Town, one of them aged about eleven, the other aged about nine years, both of them supposed to be fallen into the hands of the Indians.' The colonial authorities were not impressed by the negative vibes, shut the paper down after just one issue and threw Harris into prison. But it still paved the way for other newspapers to come, such as John Campbell's *Boston News-Letter* in 1704.

— 26TH —

1949 – Work begins to mend the 'Hollywoodland' sign in LA after it falls into disrepair. A sign of hope and stardom for so many, but the 'land' bit was dropped quicker than a thirty-year-old female actor who looked her age. Thus, the iconic 'Hollywood' sign was born.

— 27TH —

1822 – Thanks to his 100-day Duolingo streak, French scholar Jean-François Champollion announces that he has deciphered the Rosetta Stone. Egyptian hieroglyphics could finally be understood. By speaking into his phone and repeating common Egyptian phrases such as 'bird, eye, ambiguous slug', he picked up the lingo pretty quick. Champollion discovered that some signs were syllabic, some alphabetic, and some determinative. So, what did the Rosetta Stone reveal? Turns out, it was a decree from priests of a temple in Memphis (the Egyptian one, not Elvis's) pledging their support for the reign of thirteen-year-old Ptolemy V on the first anniversary of his coronation.

— 28TH —

48 BC – Pompey gets absolutely battered in Egypt by courtiers of pharaoh Ptolemy XIII. Civil war was rife and Pompey got done in by Caesar Salad in the Battle of Pharsalus, resulting in Pomp's fleeing to Egypt. Caesar, hot on his tail and now in a position of power, sailed after him. Egypt was a mess with internal strife and Rome practically owned them. Pompey had previously helped Ptolemy XII but now Ptolemy XIII's advisors were in a bind. They owed Pompey but didn't want to piss off Caesar. So, Ptolemy's regent, a eunuch named Pothinus, hatched a plan: welcome Pompey, then kill him to win Caesar's favour.

September

— 29TH —

1829 – Police take to the streets of London for the first time, ready to batter malnourished ten-year-olds for pinching loaves of bread. The Met donned a blue uniform, as opposed to the red worn by the army, so they didn't appear 'military'. Before 1829, the number of constables and watchmen varied significantly among London parishes, with wealthier ones having more men and offering better pay. The Metropolitan Police was established, in part, to create a standard approach to law enforcement across the city.

— 30TH —

2004 – The first ever photo of a live giant squid in the wild is taken. The photo was captured by a pair of Japanese researchers who had hung a lengthy line with a camera and bait from their research vessel. As the year was 2004, the squid was annoyed that they had infiltrated his selfie session for Myspace.

Why was Brigham Young a Top Shagger, and was the Prince Regent an alky?

October

Happy Halloween! It's that time of year when everything starts dying again. Leaves fall off trees, crops get harvested, and girlies are getting burned at the stake for not wanting to marry someone older than your dad, or knowing how to make herbal tea.

— 1ST —

1553 – Mary I is crowned at Westminster Abbey. She may have been past her sell-by date, but at thirty-seven, Mary I becomes the first Queen Regent. With the midlife crisis and crows feet settling in, Mary walked beneath a canopy carried by the barons of the Cinque Ports, while her chief magnates carried the sceptre, orb and crown to distract everyone from her clear missed Botox appointments.

— 2ND —

1871 – Leader of the Church of the Latter-Day Saints, aka the Mormons, Brigham Young is awarded Top Shagger award for having sixteen wives, and is also arrested for having sixteen wives. Young pleaded with authorities as he believed polygamy was essential for salvation. 'If I don't conquer all the punani of the land I'm damned forever,' he said. By the time he died on 23 August 1877, Brigham Young had married fifty-six women. Of these, ten had divorced him, nineteen had died before him, twenty-three were still alive, and four were unaccounted for.

— 3RD —

1849 – The rock 'n' roll life of writing poetry and courting hoes gets too much for Edgar Allan Poe, as he is found lying outside a polling station in Baltimore. We do not know why he was there, but he was almost unconscious and his clothes had been taken (he was instead wearing a thin suit). People believe he may have been drugged and used to commit fraud as a 'repeater', where one person would cast multiple ballots in the elections being held that day. He was taken to hospital and died four days later.

— 4TH —

1883 – The *Orient Express* sets off on its maiden voyage from Paris to Constantinople, kicking off a legendary era of luxury travel and wildly inaccurate murder mysteries. Forty passengers were crammed into a glorified tin can on rails for seven days. Passengers endured the pungent mix of cigar smoke, sweat, no personal space and a bathroom situation that would make you change your mind about adult nappies.

— 5TH —

1789 – A Parisian mob of mainly women decides to invite (force) the French royal family back to Paris. When they got there, Marie Antoinette said she would've loved to come but she wasn't so keen on the French. Besides, she'd already made plans that day. Said plans included prancing about the Trianon Estate, where a country cottage was built for her so she could culturally appropriate the malnourished folk and churn butter. As word of the march spread, the Palace guards said, 'Oh là là', and, 'J'habite dans une petite ville. J'aime jouer au football avec mon frère,' and promptly shut the gates. (Fortunately, I am not French. However, thanks to my GCSE qualification, this is the closest I can get to a translation of what they really said.) But it was too late; the mob had forced them to go to Paris and Versailles ceased to be a royal residence.

— 6TH —

2007 – Completely unprovoked, Brit Jason Lewis embarks on a world tour using nothing but human-powered modes of transport. Instead of collecting rare memorabilia or dating someone who is younger than your children, like most people who succumb to a midlife crisis, Jason wanted to one-up everyone. Starting on 12th July 1994, the circumnavigation took him twelve years to complete. This involved walking, cycling, inline skating, pedalling a boat across seas, rowing, kayaking, and swimming, over the course of 74,843 km (46,505 miles).

— 7TH —

1916 – In an American-football game that makes UK ex-prime minister Boris Johnson's infamous kid-knocking-out stunt look like a pat on the back, Georgia Tech demolishes Cumberland 222–0. When it got halfway and Georgia Tech were over a hundred points in, they asked why Cumberland were standing around like tits, but still carried on thrashing them.

— 8TH —

1582 – This day never happens, according to Pope Gregory XIII's new calendar. The Gregorian calendar was introduced in Italy, Spain, Portugal and Poland. Prior to this, everyone was stuck with the Julian calendar, a relic from Caesar's salad days. The Julian calendar had a bit of a leap-year obsession, adding an extra day every four years to overcompensate for the actual length of the solar year. As a result, by 1582, it was so out of sync that spring was arriving ten days too early. So the Pope decided to drop ten days from October to bring it back into sync. The Catholic countries snapped up the new Gregorian calendar, but the non-Catholic nations, ever the contrarians, took their sweet time. Parts of Germany finally got with the programme in 1698, and Greece, proving that they could take their time on a good thing, didn't switch until 1923.

— 9TH —

1192 – King Richard I of England leaves the Holy Land as the Third Crusade ends. The bad weather cast him ashore near Venice, where he was captured by Duke Leopold of Austria. King Richard was then handed over to German emperor Henry VI, who held him to ransom.

— 10TH —

1731 – Henry Cavendish is born in France. He was known for inventing the world's biggest scales and weighing the Earth. He found that the Earth's average density is 5.48 times greater than water, but had to phrase this in a body-positive way so as to not offend anyone.

— 11TH —

1919 – The Handley Page Transport plane is on its way from London to Paris. You were never one for violence against children but the yelping toddler kicking the back of your seat was really testing things. But all was not lost, as the very first inflight meal was served: a pre-packed lunchbox containing sandwiches and fruit.

What Would Ar Vicky Do?

You decide how Queen Victoria would handle the most pressing of modern dilemmas!

The Self-Checkout Showdown
Victoria's at Tesco, and the self-checkout keeps hounding her about an 'unexpected item in the bagging area'. She's about to scrap someone. What would Ar Vicky do?

a) Demand the manager and insist that self-checkouts are an affront to the royal family, henceforth banning them from all UK stores.

b) Sigh deeply, throw her bags on the floor, and declare the machine is obviously part of a republican conspiracy.

c) Smash the screen, blame it on the Irish, and storm out carrying England's best oxymoron: a selection from the 'Tesco Finest' range.

The Snap-Streaks Obsession
Victoria's on a Snap streak with her favourite lady-in-waiting and is refusing to let it end. Even during a crucial diplomatic meeting, she's sneaking photos under the table to keep the streak alive. Should she get a grip? What would Ar Vicky do?

a) Continue the streak at all costs, even if it means taking a peace-and-pout selfie mid-convo with the prime minister. Argue that being Snapchat streak queen and posing for selfies with captions like 'nrs, cousin won't rail me:/' are more important than international politics.

b) Have her personal assistant take photos of her beside world leaders to send on Snap, cleverly keeping the streak alive while also maintaining her royal duties.

c) Announce that the British Empire's true strength lies in its consistency – especially in Snap streaks – and therefore hers must continue for the good of the nation.

The Argos Christmas Catalogue Conundrum

It's that time of year again and the Argos Christmas catalogue has arrived. Victoria's ready to pick out some festive gifts for the bairns, but she's dismayed to find it's full of shite, such as the horrors of 'Furbies'. Should she embrace the modern gift-giving era, or give the children something more refined? What would Ar Vicky do?

a) Give her grandchildren the gift of slow cognitive development by presenting them with an iPad, but include a note to the parents: 'Enjoy the impending behavioural problems! Love, the Queen.'

b) Order only classic wooden toys, then deliver a royal speech about how modern children have lost the art of simple, wholesome play and demand Argos bring back durable, simplistic gifts such as lead toy soldiers.

c) Buy an 'Elf on the Shelf' in a bid to traumatize the children when they find it looming over their bed at 3 a.m.

— 12TH —

1810 – The seeds of the first Oktoberfest are sown in Munich. Prince Regent Ludwig of Bavaria (who later became King Ludwig I), married Princess Therese of Saxe-Hildburghausen. Festivities and drinking were held in some fields, preventing any poor sod from attempting to pronounce the princess's last name, and paving the way for generations of fourteen-year-olds with their first cans of Lambrini. The wedding was marked with festivities that lasted until 17th, then there was a big horse race. The celebrations were repeated the following year and Oktoberfest was born.

— 13TH —

AD 54 – Another Roman emperor dies, gee fucking wizz. This time it was Claudius. It's generally accepted that he was poisoned and, not to victim blame, but like, if all these emperors are getting deleted why are you guys still willingly becoming emperor? Come on. But who poisoned him? And how? It was a long time ago now, so maybe people should just move on. But some think it was committed by his taster (a eunuch called Halotus) at a banquet, or by his wife Agrippina, with a mushroom. Some say he vomited up the contents of his stomach and had to be given a second dose of the poison by his doctor, who put a poisoned feather down his throat.

— 14TH —

1322 – Edward II doesn't even have time to spray his Lynx Africa, and instead legs it as they get absolutely done in by the Scots in the Battle of Old Byland in Yorkshire. Edward has to leave behind his personal belongings, so like swords, maybe more swords, and probs a medieval prozzie wench mid-negotiation of her hourly rate.

— 15TH —

1860 – Eleven-year-old girl Grace Bedell writes a letter to Abraham Lincoln, giving him some looksmaxxing advice. She wanted him to 'let [his] whiskers grow', and urged him that this was the only way for him to become white boy of the month among the youths. 'You're only a solid 7 at the moment, and this is down to your baby face. Maybe try buccal fat removal? If not, grow a beard.' Lincoln responded four days later, and although he never promised to grow his beard, photos after the letter show he did in a quest to become a smash. The first photo of Lincoln with a beard was taken in January 1861. Lincoln visited Bedell, gave her a kiss and said he had taken her advice during a trip to Washington as president-elect.

— 16TH —

1847 – Charlotte Brontë publishes her debut novel, *Jane Eyre*, under the pseudonym Currer Bell. The novel is about some sulky girl named Jane, who becomes a governess at a big posh house. She then conveniently falls in love with the equally sulky older man who owns said big posh house. But is the house haunted? Mysterious things occur, screams can be heard, random fires happen. Is it a ghost? No, just Jane's fancyman's wife, who is locked up in the attic. Phew, that was a close one, wouldn't have wanted to call out the unemploy – sorry, *paranormal* investigators or anything. Although this should've been the most obvious of red flags, Jane loves the colour red so, after the locked-up wife burns down the house, they decide to get married. If you're annoyed I've spoiled the ending, grow up.

— 17TH —

1814 – The City of London is flooded with beer. Although it sounds like every Tom, Dick and Harry went to Seshlehem, instead a tidal wave of over half a million litres of beer was unleashed onto the streets as a massive fermenting tank at Meux & Co. Horse Shoe Brewery exploded. The wave was so strong it washed away two houses and, rather tragically, nine people met their end in what could only be described as the world's most depressing pub crawl. It's probably the only time in history where you could literally say, 'London was swimming in booze.'

— 18TH —

1216 – 'Bad King John' dies of dysentery. He may have taxed you out of house and home while simultaneously smashing your lass's back doors in, but he also killed his nephew and starved his enemies to death, earning him the nickname 'Bad King John'. Our lad's motto was 'Live fast, die young' as he believed that bad girls like himself did it well, before dying in his early thirties. But in them days he was probably ready for the retirement home, anyway. Absolutely gutted he caught a case of dysentery, he consoled himself by eating peaches and drinking cider. Unsurprisingly, his stomach cramps worsened and he died.

— 19TH —

1469 – Seventeen-year-old Ferdinand and eighteen-year-old Queen Isabella, Catholic monarchs of Spain to be, rush to tie the knot, desperate to make their family tree a circle. One week after they'd met, they were married at Valladolid's Vivero Palace. Asset-rich but cash-poor, a sad reality for many rahs, they had to borrow money from their friends to pay for the wedding. The couple even had a forged document allegedly signed by Pope Pius II to get around the fact that they were so closely related, because your kids coming out scrambled and mangled shouldn't get in the way of true love.

— 20TH —

2022 – A new record as Liz Truss becomes the UK's shortest-serving prime minister. She lasted a grand total of forty-five days, took her pension and got out of there. Her term was shorter than most *Love Island* series and she was outlasted by a vegetable. On 14 October 2022, the *Daily Star* started a livestream featuring an iceberg lettuce next to a framed photo of Liz Truss. The question was simple: which would last longer, the prime minister or the lettuce? In an unexpectedly tense showdown, Truss announced her resignation before the lettuce had a chance to wilt.

— 21ST —

1958 – Baroness Swanborough – known in less posh circles as Stella Isaacs, Marchioness of Reading – makes history by becoming the first woman to barge into the all-male House of Lords. Her entrance was so audacious it was like bumping into your mum at a strip club. Before this, she'd been busy founding the Women's Voluntary Service during World War Two.

— 22ND —

1844 – The ultimate celestial surprise party delivers The Great Disappointment. Adventists, convinced that Jesus had RSVP'd for his second coming, gathered to gaze at the sky, ready for the big reveal. They had their best robes ironed and their boots polished by an overworked ten-year-old for a shilling, expecting a grand entrance. But as the day wore on and the sky remained empty, it became clear that their guest of honour had ghosted them. The crowd, clutching their confetti and harps, were left in tears as they realized the divine after-party wasn't happening after all.

— 23RD —

1814 – The birth of modern plastic surgery, as the first nose job is performed in Britain. Taking fifteen minutes, surgeon Joseph Constantine Carpue reconstructed the collapsed nose of an army officer. Said collapse was not a result of taking his nose on the slopes, but rather due to long-term mercury treatments for a liver complaint. The operation required no anaesthetic because the officer wanted the full experience. It also wasn't invented yet. Neither were antibiotics, so everyone just crossed their fingers and hoped for the best.

— 24TH —

AD 79 – Mount Vesuvius erupts in Pompeii, the city that loved to play 'the floor is lava'. While it's commonly believed that Vesuvius erupted on 24th August, a newly discovered inscription suggests that the disaster might have actually occurred in mid-October.

◆• October •◆

This has fuelled ongoing speculation that the eruption happened later than traditionally thought, especially given the presence of autumn fruits and heating braziers found among the ruins.

— 25TH —

1881 – Pablo Picasso is born in Malaga, Spain. If you went to an art gallery and played 'I could paint that', his work would be the first you'd point to. Sure, he painted and that, but he also abused many women during his lifetime. One of them was the French model Marie-Thérèse Walter, who was seventeen when they began their relationship – while he was forty-five, and married. He whipped out the Crayolas and was inspired by Year Four artwork when he drew Walter in his *Nude, Green Leaves and Bust*. Some argue that you should separate art from the artist, but can you view it quite the same way when you know that it was painted while Walter was at a summer camp for girls, and Picasso rented a cabana nearby to paint and have sex with her?

— 26TH —

1861 – The US 'Pony Express' is discontinued. Probably because people got tired of waiting for next-day delivery when their packages were still stuck on horseback. Turns out, ponies just weren't cut out for the fast-paced world of modern shipping. The service ran from 3rd April 1860 to 26th October 1861, but it looks like Amazon Prime's two-day shipping was just too much competition for a bunch of tired horses.

— 27TH —

1904 – The New York Subway opens, promising a quick and efficient way to travel nine miles from City Hall to 145th Street. It quickly became the world's largest 4D motion ride, with visuals of smackheads trying to make eye contact with you, aromas of eau de unwashed, the sounds of screaming children and the taste of regret for not just walking. The new line was a hit, connecting City Hall, Grand Central Station and Times Square.

— 28TH —

1636 – Harvard College is founded, because apparently, the world needs a place for overly ambitious seventeen-year-olds to stress about their futures. Little did anyone know, it would become the go-to institution for producing CEOs, Nobel Prize laureates and the kind of people who start sentences with, 'Well, actually ... '

— 29TH —

1618 – Sir Walter Raleigh meets his end, as introducing the potato and tobacco to Britain wasn't enough to save him. He may have been loved by the Irish and girls wearing signet rings, but after returning from his final expedition, he was accused of deliberately inciting war between Spain and England. When he got his head chopped off, it was sent to his wife, who had it embalmed and kept it in a velvet bag for the rest of her life, which was twenty-nine years.

— 30TH —

1501 – Legend has it that Cesare Borgia hosts a party with his sister, the pope and countless prozzies who danced naked. According to the diary of papal official Johann Burchard, 'chestnuts were strewn around, which the naked courtesans picked up, creeping on hands and knees between the chandeliers', all while the pope, Cesare and his sister Lucrezia 'looked on'. Prizes such as silk and tunics were given to the man who had sex the most times with one of the prostitutes. But how much of this is true? The Borgia's had a hate train of people, so maybe some events were exaggerated.

— 31ST —

Happy Halloween! In the early twentieth century, people decide to give a modern twist to the old tradition of souling and guising. Back in the day, impoverished folk would visit wealthy households, receiving tasty soul cakes in exchange for praying for the souls of the rich person's dearly departed. Fast forward to the early 1900s, and kids took over the tradition, knocking on doors not for prayers, but for ale and food – their idea of trick-or-treating, with a bit more sophistication.

In Scotland and Ireland, guising involved dressing up in costumes and performing a bit of poetry, a joke, or even a trick, before receiving treats such as fruit, coins, or nuts. By the 1920s, this charming tradition turned into a free-for-all, as rowdy youths embraced Halloween as their chance to cause a ruckus. Things quietened down during World War Two, but once the baby boomers arrived, Halloween was reinvented as a family-friendly affair, complete with organized fun and teenagers prancing about as 'sexy binmen' or 'sexy Gru from *Despicable Me*'.

Why did *Ivan the Terrible* have a menty-b, and how did *Charles Darwin* channel Destiny's Child?

November

The month of death and decay, when the last leaves fall like the hopes of a pauper. Guy Fawkes' Night offers a brief respite of fire and light, but even that is just a reminder of the futility of rebellion. Thanksgiving? What are you thankful for, your diet of gruel?

— 1ST —

1512 – The public are treated to dick pics galore as the ceiling of the Sistine Chapel is uncovered and made available for public viewing. They had to squint to see them, partly because they are tiny and also because the ceilings are so high up.

— 2ND —

1960 – At a time when lobotomies were solid but saying 'fuck' crossed the line, Penguin Books are found not guilty of obscenity for publishing D. H. Lawrence's *Lady Chatterley's Lover*. The book is about a married rich lady who travels to pound town with the groundskeeper, a simple man who unfortunately struggles to pronounce his Ts. But, like the martyr she was, Lady Chatterley persisted with the affair as her husband wasn't able to fulfil her needs after returning disabled from World War One. The 'obscenity' trial lasted six days. Witnesses spoke of the literary excellence of the book and said that banning it 'would be inimical to a free society', and they firmly believed that detailed sex scenes would pave the way for other literary masterpieces, such as *Fifty Shades of Grey*.

— 3RD —

1752 – Composer George Frederick Handel gets his eye stabbed and believes it will cure his bad eyesight. When complaining of not being able to see, he was told, 'Have you tried looking harder?' but it came to no avail. So his surgeon, William Bromfield, performed a 'couching' procedure, where a needle was poked into his eye – no painkillers, nothing, just pure vibes. The aim was to push away the cataract from the field of vision, but by the end of January he'd completely lost his sight. With the state of people in their crunchy lice-ridden wigs, he'd probably seen enough anyway.

November

— 4TH —

1879 – Dr Thomas Elkins patents improvements to the refrigerator. If one of your malnourished offspring succumbed to the consequences of chalk and plaster bread, you could at least keep their body cool until the burial. Before the invention, food was kept cool by people crossing their fingers and hoping for the best. And using boxes filled with ice. Bodies were just left out, which welcomed disease and pests, and a smell like a badger's arse.

— 5TH —

1605 – Guy Fawkes puts on his own DIY firework display in parliament. He firmly believed it was his purpose in life to create an event in which British people would pay £20 to stand in a field freezing their bollocks off to watch the most underwhelming firework displays known to man. The government didn't quite get his vision and he got really fucked off about it. It didn't help that King James I kept persecuting Roman Catholics. So, Fawkes decided to give them an example by igniting lots of gunpowder and standing back, and if King James I and his parliament accidentally got blown up, too, so be it. At least they would go out with a bang, he thought. Sadly, it didn't go quite to plan and he got arrested. 'But you didn't even give me a chance to sell you an £8.50 hotdog while you fanny about with a sparkler,' he cried. But it was too late. On 7th November, authorities tortured him to get him to spill the names of his accomplices.

— 6TH —

1931 – With nothing but Harry Potter gleggs, his pet goat for milk on the go and a dream, British newspapers rave about Gandhi's appearance at Buckingham Palace the previous day. Despite having been brought up in a wealthy Indian household and holding previous ambitions to become a 'gentleman', Gandhi interpreted the 'morning dress' code from the palace's invitation as 'showing up to the royal gaff in a loincloth, then fucking off early'. His aim was to represent the dress of millions of poor and starving Indians.

— 7TH —

1722 – Everyone is reminded that it's better to be awake when in love, as Richard Steele's play The Conscious Lovers premieres in London. However, there are moments when a little less consciousness can magically transform a 4 into a solid 6 – and, sometimes, you've got to take what you can get. The comedy is about some young people who are in love but cannot marry for a number of reasons and it initially ran for eighteen consecutive nights, because of its enormous popularity.

— 8TH —

1880 – French actress Sarah Bernhardt smashes her US debut at New York's Booth Theatre. One could compare the phenomenon to OnlyFans, in that those who were keen to pay for a peek were quick on their toes to call her a trollop. Back in the day, it didn't matter how talented or well-loved an actress was, she could never shake off the fact that she lived a public life, and was getting paid to entertain. The line between an actress and a prostitute was as thin as a wafer – no amount of talent or decency could change their minds.

— 9TH —

1907 – Edward VII is presented with the South African Cullinan diamond, the largest diamond ever found, for his sixty-sixth birthday. He was blinged out by such an ostentatious gift, after working so hard his whole life. Ed was grateful to know that his lifelong contributions, such as perfecting the art of reclining in his 'love chair', hadn't gone unnoticed. The 'love chair' was an invention to help him with his daily struggles in shagging two prozzies at once. What a trooper.

— 10TH —

1917 – Lenin bans the entire media, or any publications that disagree with him, at least. After waking up hanging out his arse from the October Revolution, Lenin questioned his life choices and felt mega regrets about the God-knows-what he posted on his socials last night. But instead of going through the hassle of deleting his posts, he thought, 'Sod it,' and just deleted the press.

— 11TH —

1880 – Average Aussie lad Ned Kelly is hanged after a bit of light murdering and outlawing. To honour his legendary pissing about, they made a cast of his head for a wax museum. He was then given to Melbourne University medical students for dissection.

— 12TH —

1935 – If she won't give you head, get her a lobotomy instead. Portuguese doctor Antonio Egas Moniz performed his first lobotomy on a sixty-three-year-old woman with depression, anxiety, hallucinations, insomnia and paranoia. Evaluations of the woman two months later showed her anxiety had decreased. But if I also no longer knew my arse from my elbow, I'd probably be super chilled, too. He was awarded a Nobel Prize in 1949.

— 13TH —

1646 – Lincolnshire peasants are desperate for a bit of mental stimulation to distract them from the inevitable – catching leprosy. Since flicking through a book wasn't an option – because let's face it, those povos couldn't read – they opted for a 'bull run' instead. Today marks the earliest full recording of this annual event. Shops were boarded up, streets barricaded and by late morning a bull was let loose, chased down to the Bull-meadow or into the river, where it was caught, killed and butchered. Meat was then given out to the people as a treat.

— 14TH —

1666 – Sick of fires and the plague, diarist Samuel Pepys wets himself with excitement watching a blood transfusion between two dogs. Pepys thought it was a cracking day out, watching one dog's blood let out until it died, and then 'into the body of another on one side, while all his own run out on the other side'. His diary entry is the first recorded blood transfusion.

— 15TH —

1904 – You can now pull up on her landing strip as the Gillette razor blade is patented. However, shaving for women didn't kick off on a large scale until the 1920s, when shorter dresses came into fashion, so the only thing you'd have been shaving off was that pedo 'stache.

— 16TH —

1938 – LSD is accidentally synthesized by Dr Albert Hofmann in Switzerland. It was a few years later, when riding his bike, that he found out the effects of the drug and had the first ever acid trip. Although he wasn't overly impressed, the nittys found in sticky-carpet club corners certainly were.

— 17TH —

1558 – Elizabeth I hears about the death of her half-sister, Mary and becomes queen. Legend has it that she said, 'Am I meant to be sad or something, because no offence, but I'm not her mate no more. The poxy slag locked me in the Tower of London and put me under house arrest, so I've taken her off my close friends list and she's not coming to my birthday party. Not that she can, because she's six feet under now.'

— 18TH —

1477 – The first book to be printed in England with a date is published. *The dictes and sayings of the philosophers translated by Anthony Woodville, Lord Rivers* was full of life-changing sayings from the big dicks of philosophy. Such quotes included:

> *When in doubt, mumble. No one will know if you're wrong. If thou chatteth shit, thou deserves to get banged. Love thy neighbour. But don't go so far as to fist thy sister.*

— 19TH —

1581 – Ivan the Terrible, the first Tsar of Russia, has a midlife crisis. He felt he was falling off, worried he couldn't keep up with his namesake. But instead of being average terrible and buying a BMW, he went against the grain and one step further by murdering his son. Many have argued about why he killed his son and heir, Tsarevich Ivan Ivanovich, but one Italian Jesuit claims Ivan did the deed after he came across his son's wife dressed only in her underwear, found it skanky and began to hit her. His son stepped in to defend his pregnant wife and his father hit him on the head.

— 20TH —

1995 – Dirty laundry is aired, secrets are spilled and jaws are dropped and no, I don't mean Camilla's when she's with Charles. Princess Diana got messy as her *Panorama* interview was broadcast on the BBC. She spoke about Charles smashing Camilla's batty in and how that made her dead upset and there was absolutely nothing that could console her. Apart from her bit on the side, James Hewitt, of course. The interview was watched by 23 million people.

— 21ST —

1953 – Some smartarse is exposed for trying to mug everyone off. In 1912, archaeologist Charles Dawson claimed to have found a skull that was the 'missing link' between apes and humans, that would have put humans on Earth around five hundred thousand years ago. The fragments found came from two different species – a human and an ape – and the remains were only fifty thousand years old. Scratches on the teeth showed that they had been filed down to look human.

How to Poison your Husband – Renaissance Italy-style

Giulia Tofana transformed her seventeenth-century make-up business into a poison empire in Italy, secretly selling a lethal potion known as 'Aqua Tofana', which was responsible for the deaths of hundreds of men. Here's a step-by-step guide to using it to your advantage:

Step 1: Pop to the 1630s Apothecary
Pop in to Ye Olde Boots and ask for Aqua Tofana, the poison that's colourless, slow and undetectable.

Step 2: Hide in Plain Sight
Disguised as holy water or as a beauty product, Aqua Tofana blends seamlessly into daily life. Add a few drops to your husband's shepherd's pie. He'll think it's indigestion, while you nod sympathetically and say, 'Oh dear, I am like dead sad for you.'

Step 3: Play the Concerned Wife
Aqua Tofana is the slow-burner of poisons – it works best over time. He'll start to feel under the weather, but offer him a blanket and a Hobnob and murmur about 'a nasty bug going round'. After another dose or two he'll be vomiting, but after the fourth dose he won't be, and that's because he'll be dead.

Step 4: Enjoy Your Freedom
Unless you get caught, of course.

— 22ND —

1718 – Blackbeard meets his end on his ship *Queen Anne's Revenge*. The pirate is known for his infamous beard that was black, but little else is known about him, pre-Johnny Depp cosplay. He could read and write, which suggests he was from a wealthy family. Legend says he'd turn on his own crew members and set his lengthy beard alight. Although his career was short, he captured over forty-five vessels. 1689–1718 was the golden age of piracy, so it was a good time if you wanted an illegal DVD copy of *Shark Tale* recorded on a shaky pixelated camera in the cinema. But even the many 'You wouldn't steal a car. Piracy. It's a crime' adverts didn't scare Blackbeard. He continued until the very end, when the Royal Marines slashed off his head.

— 23RD —

1407 – John the Fearless (Taylor's Version), Duke of Burgundy, decides to take the lyrics a bit too literally as he drags his political rival, Louis, Duke of Orleans, 'head first, fearless'. As Louis rode home on his horse, John's lads gave him a medieval makeover: head split like a ripe melon, brain splattered across the road, and, just for good measure, they lobbed off his hand. The opponents were both dukes in France, which was basically a collection of tiny kingdoms where 'peaceful diplomacy' meant seeing who could decapitate the other first. John clearly won this argument.

— 24TH —

1859 – Charles Darwin's newest bestseller, *On the Origin of Species*, explains why your uncle is hairier than Harambe. The book, which claims that all living things are related, caused a stir among Victorians.

Darwin, who seemed to believe that humans might have more in common with monkeys than angels, suggested that species evolve over time through a process called 'natural selection', and pointed readers to Destiny's Child's 'Survivor' if they were still not getting it. According to Darwin, it's not just the strongest that survive, but the ones most willing to change, adapt and grow opposable thumbs.

Critics were divided on the work. Some praised Darwin for his groundbreaking ideas, while others raised highly important questions such as, 'If we're all related to monkeys, how long will it take for the ones in the zoo to turn into humans?'

— 25TH —

1984 – Pop stars gather in London to form Band Aid and record a charity single in an attempt to vaguely help victims of the Ethiopian famine. They sang about how there were no rivers that flowed and the greatest gift Africans would get that year was life. Zuri from Limpopo sat in silence while listening to the lyrics 'Do they know it's Christmastime at all?' 'I mean, I think so. We've just put the tree up and Dad said Santa is bringing me a Cabbage Patch Kid,' she mutters. The single raised around £8 million for the humanitarian relief.

— 26TH —

1651 – Nepo baby Henry Ireton dies of fever. He was Oliver Cromwell's son-in-law, signed Charles I's death warrant, and commanded an army or two. After accompanying Cromwell to Ireland, he remained in charge when Cromwell left. But, sadly, nepotism can only get you so far, and clearly not far enough to get you a bottle of Calpol Six Plus, as Henry died from fever.

— 27TH —

1810 – Theodore Hook pulls off the ultimate prank by turning 54 Berners Street into London's most chaotic address. Hook arranged for an endless stream of services and deliveries – from chimney sweeps to pianos, wedding cakes, dentists, the Mayor of London, you name it – to show up at the house of well-to-do widow Mrs Tottenham. He made a bet with his mate for one guinea to make a random house the talk of the town, and won.

— 28TH —

1893 – In a shocking turn of events, women in New Zealand vote in a parliamentary election for the first time. Despite doomsday predictions that the nation would descend into chaos if women were given the vote, nothing exploded, no one fainted, and the sun didn't fall out of the sky. The day turned out to be, as one newspaper put it, a 'gay garden party', which sounds like a good day for the queer community, too.

November

— 29TH —

1935 – Erwin Schrödinger, an Austrian-Irish physicist, publishes his famous thought experiment, Schrödinger's Cat. The theory brilliantly demonstrated that a cat in a box could be both alive and dead at the same time, giving pet owners everywhere a convenient excuse for never knowing where their cats are or what they're up to. This left the world's cats feeling deeply misunderstood and quantum physicists wondering if they should've chosen a less murderous hobby. It also provided the perfect alibi for people who wanted to avoid responsibility: 'I did the dishes, but also didn't do the dishes. Thanks, quantum theory!'

— 30TH —

1936 – Londoners are treated to the most spectacular bonfire party, as the Crystal Palace goes up in flames. Caused either by an electrical fault or a cigarette end, the fire destroyed the iconic glass and cast-iron marvel originally built to house the Great Exhibition of 1851, which featured hundreds of displays about culture and industry.

Why was **Queen Victoria's** face like a slapped arse, and how did *paper crowns* become all the rage in the 1400s?

December

Ah, December, the month of forced merriment and hollow cheer. Christmas is a time for giving, sure – but really, it's just a time for the wealthy to flaunt their excess and ostentatiously signal their virtues, then ignore Tiny Tim in the street. The yule log burns bright, but so does your resentment, as you endure yet another year spent envying anyone with more than one pair of shoes.

— 1ST —

1955 – Rosa Parks refuses to give up her seat on the bus. Already knee-deep in activism, she'd been the recording secretary for the National Association for the Advancement of Colored People (the NAACP) for almost fifteen years before she decided she wasn't moving for anyone. The bus driver demanded she stand and said to her, 'Why aren't you moving seats – do you think you're hard or something?' After she replied, 'Why are you so offended about where I sit? You fucking snowflake,' she was arrested. The Montgomery Improvement Association organized a boycott of the city's bus system, which crippled them through lost revenue.

— 2ND —

1908 – Two-year-old Pu Yi becomes the last emperor of China. He demanded people respect him, despite his age. Disagree with him? When you were on nappy duty he'd make sure he'd shat all the way up his back for you to clean. Want to take away iPad time? He'd be honking up his food all over the floor. Enjoy cleaning that up, bitch. During the Chinese Revolution of 1911–12 he was pensioned off, and then installed as a puppet ruler of Manchuria by the Japanese in 1932.

— 3RD —

1779 – Actress Mary Robinson tries her best not to catch a case. After seeing Mary perform in *A Winter's Tale* as Perdita, the seventeen-year-old Prince of Wales was titmatized. What was a girl to do? There wasn't exactly a nonce patrol kicking about in the 1700s. He offered her £20,000, so while Mary's moral compass closed, her legs opened. Four years later, the prince had bored of Miss Cougar and refused to pay the £20k, until she threatened to publish their letters. King George III, his dad, then gave her

£5,000 to get him out of the situation. Mary became a feminist writer and poet.

— 4TH —

1872 – An American merchant ship known as the *Mary Celeste* is found floating about, Billy No-Mates, without a crew on board. So, Captain Morehouse and his crew approached the ship, pretty buzzing because they thought this was a class way to get on an episode of *Most Haunted*. Only a few weeks previously, both ships had been in New York Harbour, so where was everyone? As the crew were trying to communicate with ghosts, going, 'If you're here, just tap the fucking table,' they found the ship was in tidy condition, with six months of food supply left. There were no signs of any fighting that had taken place, nor of a fire, or any other disaster. None of the crew of the *Mary Celeste* were to be seen again.

— 5TH —

1484 – Pope Innocent VIII issues a papal bull, or official document, that condemns witchcraft. He was like, 'Listen, shaggers, if you're clarting about putting broomsticks in between your legs, then pack it in. My ninety-eight-year-old nan just died really suddenly and I think the only thing I can pin it down to is sorceresses and people with bad vibes.' Witchcraft was considered an act of treason, as it was seen to be an offence committed against God.

— 6TH —

1421 – Henry VI, the only son and heir of Henry V of England, is born. No, Henry V didn't respawn, they just couldn't think of any other names. Little Henry succeeded to the English and French thrones before his first birthday, after his father Henry and grandfather Charles VI of France died within months of each other. The royal court had transformed into a Monty Python sketch – whenever you'd shout, 'Henry,' half the room turned around.

— 7TH —

1507 – The first named reference of a non-translucent Tudor, John Blanke, is made. John was a royal trumpeter and the first Black person whose image survives from Tudor England. Many were shocked at the possibility of someone who didn't look anaemic, but a number of Black people served in European royal courts, and a document shows that John was paid twenty shillings for working every day of this month.

— 8TH —

1983 – Television cameras are allowed into the House of Lords after a vote of peers, with 74 in favour and 24 against. MPs continued to block moves to televise the House of Commons' debates, fearing politicians might play up to the cameras and bring it into disrepute. Meanwhile, over in the Lords, barons started staging elaborate scandals for ratings, Lord Geraldational Wealth started lipsing his mate's wife in the hideaway and Viscount Tomkin Advantage of the Workingclassington was caught telling a girl, 'Haha, yeah, sure your drink is meant to fizz like that.' But not all of the Lords were like that. While they all did go to private school, not all participated in spitting on the cleaners.

— 9TH —

1960 – At 7 p.m., over 3 million people tuned in to the first episode of *Coronation Street*. Staring at their black and white TVs, people were hooked to plot lines such as 'This bairn accidentally swallowed ecstasy, thinking it was paracetamol, but it was OK, we just dropped her at a rave and she danced it off'. But why's it called a soap opera? Soap operas first appeared on American radio in the 1930s, sponsored by companies selling soap or other household items. Frequently produced by advertising agencies rather than broadcasters, they became popular among their predominantly female audiences, but were often dismissed by those who considered themselves to have more refined tastes.

— 10TH —

1541 – Catherine Howard's alleged shawty, Thomas Culpeper, is executed for adultery. Catherine had probably popped that cherry before marrying Henry VIII, and the lad was not pleased. The incriminating evidence to prove that Culpeper done diddled her was a letter Catherine wrote to him, ending the note with: 'Yours for as long as your life endures'.

However, during this time, it was actually common to write soppy shite like that to sign off your letters. When Howard married, many people who knew her as a teenager were given positions at court, and this may have been to buy their silence.

Culpeper was likely very ambitious; he'd learned about of Catherine's sexual past, and he was trying to exploit this, and could have been trying to blackmail her. So it's probably the case that Catherine was just trying to suck up to him.

— 11TH —

1282 – The last prince of an independent Wales is killed. Llywelyn ap Gruffyd was enjoying the simple pleasures of life, such as entering the anal canals of sheep, while campaigning in the Builth region. But suddenly, he was involved in a minor scrap with the English and his head was later sent to be put on public display in London.

— 12TH —

1915 – American singer Frank Sinatra is born in New Jersey to Italian immigrants. At six months, he was already looking middle aged and his first words were 'New York'. An actor and a singer, he also managed to pull a few worldies. Married four times, he was busy in the bedroom, too, having three kids with Nancy Barbato.

— 13TH —

1989 – Taylor Swift arrives into the world. It was alleged that, just after she exited the foof, she was raised into the air while the 'Circle of Life' played, to commemorate that a star had been born. She's broken so many records, including the most number-one albums by any woman ever. She's also made history with the Eras Tour, most memorably causing millions of girls and gays everywhere to question their sexuality during her infamous 'Vigilante Shit' chair dance.

— 14TH —

1861 – Queen Victoria's cousin-husband, or cusband, Prince Albert, dies at forty-two. Vicky thought giving her kids mummy issues would be a great form of character building, so proceeded to blame Albert's death on her son, Bertie. Albert had originally gone to Cambridge to bollock Bertie for being a communal dick and sleeping with an Irish actress. Albert apparently said, 'Listen, shagger, it's not a good image to be fannying about with a lass whose culture is potatoes and sliding down rainbows. Mixing with that will only get you the clap.' It was supposed that he picked up typhoid fever after this and died not too long after. But Albert had always been a sickly bugger. The queen noted how she worried about his upset stomach, and from childhood Albert had always reacted badly to the common cold and feverish chills. His death sent Queen Victoria into a lifetime of black clothes and the face of a slapped arse.

— 15TH —

1791 – The US Bill of Rights is ratified in Congress. This comprised the first ten amendments to the United States Constitution, giving Americans the right to have Freedom of Speech and to be able to chatteth as much shite as they wanted without being oppressed. The Second Amendment also gave them the right to bear arms, which did cause some upset among the armless communities.

— 16TH —

1773 – Boston hosts a tea party. But instead of different genres of Tarquins asking each other which school they went to, it turned into a massive scrap. The Tea Act had just been introduced, giving the East India Company a monopoly over the tea trade. This pissed off Americans, who were already fuming about higher taxes and little representation in parliament. Though the act didn't slap on any new taxes, it was seen as another attempt by the British to show Americans that they had a bigger schlong. With tempers flaring, the crowd surged towards the harbour. That evening, dozens of men, some disguised as Native Americans, boarded tea ships, unloaded hundreds of chests of tea, and chucked them into Boston Harbour. Back in England, authorities were shocked. Yeah, they could probs go without PG Tips for a while, but the cultural appropriation of dressing up as Native Americans? Unforgivable. The yanks were forced to make an apology video and were subject to cancellation.

The History Gossip

— 17TH —

497 BC – Romans celebrate the first Saturnalia. Basically Christmas for those called Claudius, Saturnalia was originally an agricultural festival to celebrate the god Saturn for doing them a solid one and providing the Earth and grass and that. Over time, people started exchanging gifts. Some would even partake in a 'secret Saturn' at work. Although there was a budget of five silver coins, many would have to pretend to be pleased with their clearly recycled Tescoeth wine from the back of the cupboard. Slaves would wear their masters' clothes, and there were even occasions on which women would take part in gladiator games, with the celebrations becoming a three-day affair.

— 18TH —

1892 – The *Nutcracker* ballet premieres at the Mariinsky Theatre in St Petersburg, Russia. This dazzling performance was the first of many Christmas outings to see people in fancy outfits, a girl with a chronic sugar addiction and inevitable on-set diabetes, and a bunch of mice who enjoy giving each other a left, right, goodnight.

December

— 19TH —

1820 – Mary Ashton Livermore, a temperance worker, women's rights activist, lecturer and writer is born. She founded her own suffrage paper, *The Agitator*, in 1869. The newspaper was dedicated to telling men why they were wrong and projected hopes for future equality. Men thought this was a great chance to also write about their feelings and hopes for the future. They then came up with their own newspaper called *Get Back in the Kitchen You Daft Slag*.

— 20TH —

1803 – The United States pulled off the ultimate land grab by buying 828,000 square miles (2.1 million square km) from France for a measly $15 million in the Louisiana Purchase – proving once again that America is always down for a bargain, especially when it involves doubling in size overnight. Napoleon must've been having a clearance sale on empires, and Thomas Jefferson was just thrilled to pass this on to his ancestors to eventually achieve the American Dream that is strip malls.

— 21ST —

1937 – Walt Disney's *Snow White and the Seven Dwarfs* is screened for the first time in Los Angeles. Although the film was designed to give children a complex about eating fruit, *Snow White* also warned the masses about the horrors of not getting preventative Botox. The film cost over $1.4 million to make and took two hundred separate paintings to complete. Hitherto, full-length animated feature films weren't a thing, so this was a major artistic and technical advancement. Celebrities in the audience, such as Clark Gable, laughed and cried at the animation and had to be reminded, 'Love, it's not real, stop getting so emosh.'

— 22ND —

1877 – *Scientific American* newspaper publishes an article about Thomas Edison coming into the office earlier in the month and playing a phonograph, a device which recorded and played back sounds. The music played was Edison's rendition of 'Mary had a Little Lamb'. The editors asked if he was able to play like any noughties club bangers or if he'd used up all of his free skips for the day, as that song was a bit dead.

— 23RD —

1888 – Famous scranner of yellow paint and hater of ears, Vincent Van Gogh, cuts off the lower part of his lugs in France. He then proceeded to present the bits to a young woman at the local brothel, to which she replied, 'That's so nice, thank you, but it's a shilling for a motorboat, and we only take cash or card.' The lucky recipient was an eighteen-year-old called Gabby. She was too young to work as a prozzie, but was working as a maid to pay back mounting medical bills resulting from a bite by a rabid dog.

— 24TH —

1777 – James Cook encounters Christmas Island, also known as Kiritimati Atoll. Kiritimati, which is just the Gilbertese way of spelling Christmas, seemed fitting for his festive adventure. In order to spread Christmas cheer, Cook graciously decided not to

✦• December •✦

colonize it, leaving that to the Americans in 1856. The scurvy was enough of a present this year.

— 25TH —

1233 – The first Christmas nativity is put on, in Italy. Crowds gathered to watch the local primary school put on a show, crafted by St Francis of Assisi. Little Timoteo, cast as a shepherd, stood centre stage, oblivious to the fact that he was supposed to be acting. Halfway through the carol, he decided it was the perfect time to embark on a thorough nasal excavation, much to the delight of himself and the mortification of his teacher. Meanwhile, the popular girl had of course been graced with the role of Mary. She gracefully entered the stage, after being ridden onto it by the neeks dressed as the front and back end of the donkey. In her mind, she was not just playing Mary; she *was* Mary, divinely chosen and far superior to her mere classmates. And to top it all off, the important other observers of the nativity that were in Bethlehem that faithful night were in the background, such as the narwhals and lobsters, all singing 'Silent Night' in some sort of unison.

How Would You Solve a National Crisis?

Just Hide in a Tree (Charles II, 1651)

When the country's gone to shit and the entire parliament is after you, sometimes the best solution is ... to hide in a tree? After his dad (Charles I) lost his head, Charles II fled and spent a day hiding up a tree.

Pros:

- It's surprisingly effective! No one expects the king to climb trees.
- Great story for later: 'I climbed that tree just like I climbed your mum.'

Cons:

- You're stuck in a tree.
- It doesn't actually solve the constitutional crisis – just delays it.

Throw Yourself Out a Window (Defenestration of Prague, 1618)

Facing opposition? Why not just literally throw your enemies out of a window? That's what happened in Prague when three Catholic officials were chucked from a castle window, solving the problem – at least for a few minutes.

Pros:

- Nothing says 'I'm done with this debate' like launching your enemies out of the nearest window.
- Quick, decisive, and guaranteed to make a scene.

Cons:

- You might spark a massive European war that lasts thirty years.

Marry Off Your Children for Peace
When all else fails, just marry your kids off to the rival family! Medieval royals loved this strategy. Sure, your daughter's only twelve, but if her marriage can end a war, it's worth the awkward teenage wedding.

Pros:

- Peace is restored, and all you had to do was shuffle around some teenagers!
- You get to enjoy a big, fancy wedding while pretending everything's totally fine.

Cons:

- There's a chance the marriage won't work out and the war will start all over again.
- Your kid might not be thrilled about being used as a political bargaining chip, but that's their problem.

— 26TH —

1606 – Shakespeare's *King Lear* is performed for King James I. Jimmy's arse was embedded in the sofa, having binged all the Quality Streeteth. King Lear then came on, but unfortunately, he couldn't switch it off, as there was only one channel and that was the live stage. Although lines such as 'Blow winds and crack your cheeks! Rage, blow, You cataracts and hurricanoes' are great and all, he'd rather have just watched the *Gavin and Stacey* Christmas special. There's no direct evidence on when the play was first performed and written, but Shakespeare's audience would already have been familiar with the story through a combination of myth and history.

— 27TH —

1901 – Marlene Dietrich, the androgynous Old Hollywood actress, is born in Berlin. After leaving Germany for Hollywood, she went on to perform in various films, then renounced her German citizenship in 1939. It was an open industry secret that Dietrich was bisexual and she had many affairs. Her American debut, *Morocco*, starred Dietrich as a cabaret performer who flirted with everyone and everything. The film features the iconic scene where she dons a tuxedo and top hat, and kisses a woman on the lips. The scandal. Women were confused and appalled – 'Has she mistaken her for her husband?', with the men adding, 'Oh, I usually skip this part.'

— 28TH —

1612 – Italian astronomer Galileo Galilei first observes what turned out to be the planet Neptune. For centuries, it was believed he mistook it for a star and shrugged it off. Recently, however, this narrative has been challenged, suggesting Galileo may have been onto something but decided to keep it to himself, possibly because he was distracted by the drama of inventing modern science, or figuring out how to avoid getting excommunicated for saying the Earth orbits the sun.

— 29TH —

1940 – London experienced its most flamboyant fireworks display, courtesy of the Germans. Hundreds of fires from the firebombs illuminated the city in a way no Christmas lights ever could. The next day, a photo of St Paul's Cathedral standing tall amid the carnage hit the newspapers, which showed London was harder than lads who do shots of apple sours.

— 30TH —

1460 – Richard of York's head gets a post-mortem makeover with a paper crown. In the Battle of Wakefield, as many as two and a half thousand men bit the dust, including Richard of York, his son Edmund, and his brother-in-law, the Earl of Salisbury. Instead of a respectful moment of silence for the fallen, the Duke of Somerset decided to turn the city of York's western gate into a macabre fashion show. He had the heads of the three barons mounted above Micklegate Bar, with Richard of York's noggin getting a special accessory: a paper crown.

— 31ST —

It's New Year's Eve! A risky time for those who dread oral herpes, many choose to go out and force themselves to have a good time by getting wankered. Gifts used to be exchanged on New Year's Eve, but from the 1840s, that moved back to Christmas, after it became massively more important to the Victorians.

How to Pull – 1700s-Style

Receding hairline giving you no choice but to settle down? No fear, here are some tips from the 1799 edition of the 'New Academy of Compliments', on how to pull before all the rare gems (girlies without syphilis) get snatched up.

1. Send some mixed messages. Call her a minger before saying you enjoy the fuggers girls:
'I am as lantern-jaw'd as you are platter-fac'd; but yet perhaps we may have lovely babes when we come together, if we can but tell how to get them.'

2. Lay it on thick. Tell her you'd scramble her eggs:
'Madam, as you are fair and beauteous, be generous and merciful to him that is your slave.' After you buy this loade of absolute shite, your husband proceeds to UNO reverse, thrusting a mop in your face and making you the unpaid slave-labourer.

3. Don't try to catch her out by asking if she frequents the local dogging spots:
'When a young gentleman has found a conqueress of his affection, let him not rudely accost her if she be a virgin, lest his good meaning be taken in evil part.'

But what if you don't want to go by the book and fancy a bit of freestyling? Maybe try sending a lock of your nitty hair, or maybe confess your love in the most delicate way, through the art of letter writing.

Letters were a way of detailing various sentiments that would be too embarrassing to say in person, like expressing their fondness toward someone. Love letters were carried around on a person, read over and over again and could be used in court as physical evidence of commitment. Examples that could inspire your romantic prose could be something along the lines of the following:

Dearest Big Batty gal,

I hope this letter finds you in the most splendiferous of spirits. Ever since Miss sat us together in double science, my thoughts are consumed by your charm. I am in awe at the way you conduct yourself. The way you so elegantly remove yourself from the classroom after your bold and daring confrontation with the school mistress was most pleasing. A girl in whomst speaks her mind, is, excuse my forwardness, a rare gem these days.

Let me know if one wants to link up, as together I believe we can make all kinds of waves among the ton.

Until then, bless up.

Yours Faithfully,
Mr M2Drippy

Glossary

Hey there! Congratulations on making it this far, unless you've come here while reading due to your confusement. Welcome to the glossary.

So, you might be wondering why, as a historian, I throw around words like 'minger' to describe Anne of Cleves (no offence, Anne, for real rip). Well, history doesn't have to be all buttoned-up and dull. Sprinkling in some Northeast and general British slang and cheeky expressions makes the past feel a bit more … alive, don't you think?

Language is a wild thing – it changes, evolves and sometimes takes the mickey out of the so-called 'proper' way of speaking. Using non-standard words isn't just for laughs; it's a way to shake up the status quo. Let's be honest, sticking strictly to 'correct' language often props up old power structures that could do with a good shake. By tossing in some regional slang from my ends, we're not just having a bit of fun – we're giving a nod to voices that don't always get heard.

Plus, let's face it: calling someone a 'minger' is a lot more vivid than saying they're 'less than aesthetically pleasing'. It adds colour, humour and a bit of that generational spice. What gets a laugh from one group might leave another scratching their heads, and that's part of the charm. Mixing UK and US English, throwing in regional dialects – it all adds to the rich tapestry of our language.

This glossary is here to help you navigate the quirky twists and turns of history, told with a dash of Geordie flair and a wink of irreverence. After all, learning about the past should be as entertaining as it is enlightening.

Enjoy the ride!

A rah: A stereotypical affluent person. To achieve such status, one must have generational wealth and a second home in Cornwall.

A smash: Someone who is an absolute stunner. Henceforth, someone you would want to smash.

A$AP Rocky: As soon as poss!

Ar Di: People sometimes refer to Princess Diana as 'Ar Di' as an affectionate and familiar way of saying 'our Di'. Using 'Ar Di' conveys a sense of personal connection and endearment toward Princess Diana. It reflects how many people in the UK – and around the world – felt a strong bond with her, seeing her not just as a royal figure but as someone relatable and close to their hearts.

Arsey cow: A term for someone (usually a woman) who's being particularly difficult or bad-tempered. That friend who's always in a mood and ready to argue over the slightest thing.

Aye, that's solid: An enthusiastic way of agreeing with someone. It's like saying, 'Yes, that's great!' but with a bit of Northern flair.

Backshots: Doggy style. Not with actual dogs.

Bairns: Another way of saying 'children', mainly used by the downstairs people in *Downton Abbey* and the likes.

Billy Big Bollocks: A playful nickname for someone who is overly confident or boastful. Imagine a person who thinks they're the bee's knees because they won a local talent show.

Bint: A slightly cheeky term for a woman, sometimes used jokingly among friends. It's akin to calling someone a 'lass' but with a bit more sass.

Blindly rinsed out of a couple of grand: Being swindled or spending a large amount of money without realizing it. Picture buying a 'designer' watch that turns out to be a cheap knockoff.

Glossary

Blinged out: Adorned with lots of flashy jewellery or accessories. Someone who sparkles so much they could be mistaken for a disco ball.

Boris Johnson's infamous kid-knocking-out stunt: Refers to when Boris Johnson, playing rugby with children, accidentally knocked one over.

Bottles of Prime: A popular energy drink that's all the rage. Everyone wants a bottle as if it's the elixir of life, or at least the key to social-media fame.

Bust a nut: Hanky panky solo-times. Wanking. Masturbating.

She'd resemble a butcher's bin: A colourful way to say someone's lady parts looks dishevelled or messy, perhaps after being thrown around in the bedroom.

Butters: Someone who is unattractive. Derived from 'butt ugly'.

Central Cee: A British rapper known for his catchy tunes and sharp lyrics. If you're into UK hip-hop, you've likely bobbed your head to his tracks.

Chads: A term for stereotypically confident, popular guys. High-school jocks who are good at sports and maybe a bit full of themselves.

Chatting balls: Talking nonsense or saying things that aren't true. Like when your mate claims he can run a marathon without any training.

Chebs: Boobies.

Chode or choad: A penis that is short and wide.

Chungus: A fun word popularized by internet memes, usually describing something large and endearing – like a chunky rabbit. Or a massive shit.

Clarting about: Messing around or wasting time. If you're supposed to be studying but end up getting sent out of class for throwing pens at people, you're clarting about.

Club bangers: Songs that are guaranteed to get everyone dancing in a club. The DJ's secret weapons to fill the dance floor.

Coffin-dodgers: A cheeky term for elderly people. It's like calling them 'old-timers'.

Chat shit get banged: Said by someone who doesn't tolerate nonsense and is quick to confront those who talk badly. They believe if you speak ill, you should be prepared for the consequences. Of getting smacked.

Corsa: A popular compact car in the UK, often the first car for new drivers. Known for being economical and, well, not exactly a luxury vehicle.

Craic: An Irish term meaning fun, entertainment, or enjoyable conversation. If someone asks, 'What's the craic?' then they want to know what's happening.

Daft arse: A playful insult for someone acting foolishly. Similar to calling someone a 'silly goose'.

Darlo finger: To put up your only pointing finger when posing for photos. This is commonly done by nineteen-year-old boys with Adidas tracksuits and skin fades. Sort of like dabbing, for chavs.

Dead bad: Really bad or severe. 'I had a dead bad headache after that concert.'

Dead upset: Extremely upset. 'She was dead upset when her team lost the match.'

Devo: Short for devastated. 'I'm devo that the concert got cancelled.'

Glossary

Doing a pump-pump-squirt: The type of sex that is so unbelievably underwhelming and lasts about three seconds.

Doing an Austin Butler impression: Speaking in a deep, sultry voice or adopting a cool demeanour, mimicking actor Austin Butler in character as Elvis.

Doing a solid: Doing someone a favour. 'Thanks for lending me your umbrella – you really did me a solid.'

Done diddled: Got tricked or swindled. 'I paid for a genuine jersey online, but it was a fake; I got done diddled!' Can also be used to describe someone having sex: 'Marc absolutely done diddled me. Was so average.'

Edgelords: People who make controversial or provocative statements mainly to shock others, often online. They live on the 'edge' of acceptable behaviour.

Emosh: Emotional. 'That movie was so sad, I'm feeling emosh.'

Facey-b: A colloquial term for Facebook. 'I'll send you the event details on Facey-b.'

Fanny: A vagina. Also used to refer to someone who's being silly or ineffective.

Fannying about: Wasting time or not getting to the point. 'Stop fannying about and help me with this!'

Feeding a Tic Tac to a whale: otherwise known as 'throwing hot dogs in hallways'. A woman's inner sanctum is not cosy and snug. Or maybe the man has a pencil for a penis.

Finger blasting: A term for intimate activity involving hands. Perhaps best left unexplored in polite company.

Fleeced: Being overcharged or ripped off. 'They charged me double for that drink; I got fleeced!'

Foof: A term for female genitalia. Sometimes used to avoid more explicit language.

Free skips: In music apps, skipping songs without limits.

Fru-fru: Describes something overly fancy or elaborate. 'He showed up in some fru-fru outfit with feathers and sequins.' Also can describe a vagina. Context. Is. Everything.

Fugly: A blend of two words meaning 'terribly ugly'.

Fun sponge: A person who dampens the mood or spoils the fun. 'Don't invite him; he's such a fun sponge.'

Garms: Short for garments; slang for clothes. 'Check out his new garms – looking sharp!'

Gallagher special: Referring to the Gallagher brothers from Oasis and their infamous falling out.

Get her pasty smashed: Engaging in intimate relations. Such as sex.

Get taken to pound town: Sex.

Getting emosh: Becoming emotional. 'She started getting emosh during the wedding speeches.'

Getting wankered: Getting extremely drunk. 'They went out and got absolutely wankered last night.'

Ghostface vibes: Giving off mysterious or eerie feelings, possibly referencing the masked character from the *Scream* movies.

Gleggs: Glasses or spectacles. 'I can't read the menu without my gleggs.'

Harambe: A gorilla who became an internet sensation in 2016. Mentioned in memes and jokes, often nostalgically.

Glossary

Hard lad: A tough guy or someone who portrays themselves as strong and unyielding. 'Watch out for him; he's a hard lad.'

Honk: To vomit. 'That dodgy kebab made me honk.'

Honking up: The act of vomiting. 'He's been honking up all morning after that party.'

Honks: Something that smells bad. 'What's that smell? It absolutely honks!'

Hoyed: Threw something with force. 'He hoyed the ball right over the fence!'

I'm such a Rachel!: Referring to Rachel Green from *Friends*, suggesting one relates to her character – perhaps in fashion or romantic mishaps.

International cock and ball: A beautiful game played by many lads on university socials or nights out. The game consists of 'International cock or ball / Is it a cock? / Or is it a ball?' Whoever was sung at has to show either a bit of cock, or a bit of ball and everyone else has to guess.

Jizz in pantaloons: To cum in ones panties.

John the Fearless (Taylor's Version): A blend of historical figure John the Fearless and a nod to Taylor Swift's re-recorded albums.

Keeping it lemon/cushty: Keeping it cool.

Lairy: Behaving in a loud, excited, or slightly aggressive manner. 'The crowd got a bit lairy after the match.'

Landing strip: A term for a particular style of grooming body hair. Also used in aviation!

Lard arse: Someone who has broken the scales because of their excess weight.

Lipsing: Slang for kissing or making out. 'Caught them lipsing behind the bins.'

Looksmaxxing: Attempting to improve one's appearance to the highest degree possible. 'He's into looksmaxxing with all that grooming and fashion.'

Lord Farquaad bob: A short, blunt haircut resembling that of Lord Farquaad from *Shrek*. Not the most flattering comparison!

Lord Fauntleroy's skiddies: Soiled undergarments. In this case, Lord Fauntleroy's.

Lugs: Slang for ears. 'Get those tunes out of your lugs and listen up!'

Mandem: A group of male friends. 'Hanging out with the mandem tonight.'

Mank/manky: Something dirty or unpleasant. 'Don't touch that manky towel!'

Marbs: Short for Marbella, a glitzy holiday spot in Spain popular with Brits seeking sun and fun.

Mega lush: Extremely attractive or enjoyable. 'That dessert was mega lush!'

Mewing: A technique involving holding the tongue against the roof of the mouth to improve jawline definition. 'He's been mewing to get that chiselled look.' As perfected in Blue Steel.

Minger: A derogatory term for someone considered unattractive.

Mint: Excellent or very good. 'That new café is mint!"

Minted: Wealthy or affluent. 'She won the lottery and now she's minted.'

MLM: Multi-Level Marketing, a business model sometimes compared to pyramid schemes.

Glossary

Motorboat: To place one's face between someone's chest and making a motor sound.

Muff-diving: To perform intimate acts around the foof.

Muff: A colloquial term for female genitalia.

Munter: A derogatory term for someone perceived as unattractive.

Myspace: An early social-networking site popular in the mid-2000s, before Facebook took over. Think of it as a vintage version of social media.

Necking pints: Drinking beer quickly. 'He was necking pints like there was no tomorrow.'

Neeks: A blend of 'nerd' and 'geek'. Someone who's into niche interests, possibly in a quirky way.

Nepo baby: A term for someone who has benefited from nepotism, especially in entertainment – think celebrities' kids who become famous.

Nittys: Slang for individuals who love to take drugs.

Nonce patrol: Vigilante groups aiming to expose or confront paedophiles, particularly those committing serious offences. Not an activity endorsed by authorities.

Noncy tendencies: Behaviours that might raise suspicions of inappropriate paedo conduct.

Noshed on: Slang for receiving a certain intimate act. Alternatively, could mean eating something enthusiastically.

NWS: No worries.

Paedo 'stache: A derogatory term for that 1970s moustache style.

Peen: Penis.

Picts: An ancient people who lived in what is now Scotland during the Early Middle Ages. Known for their mysterious symbols and resistance to Roman invasion.

Pieing her off: Ignoring or dismissing someone, especially in a romantic context. 'He totally pied her off at the party.'

Pimped out: Customized extravagantly. 'He pimped out his ride with neon lights and new rims.'

Pissing about: Wasting time or not being serious. 'Stop pissing about and get to work!'

Podgy bugger: A teasing way to refer to someone who's a bit overweight.

Ploughed: Slang for being very drunk. 'He was absolutely ploughed after the festival.' Or can be used as slang for having sex.

Pony Express: Historically, a mail-delivery service using horse riders in the US. Used humorously to refer to slow or old-fashioned communication methods.

Poon: Slang term for female genitalia.

Porky pies: Cockney rhyming slang for lies. 'Don't tell me porky pies!'

Povo cosplays: When individuals mimic the appearance of those less affluent, perhaps as a fashion statement – can be seen as insensitive.

Povo: Short for poverty-stricken, referring to someone with little money.

Poxy slag: An insult combining 'poxy' or pox-ridden and 'slag' (derogatory term for a promiscuous woman).

Glossary

Prozzie: Slang for a prostitute.

Publicly munching the royal carpet: Someone openly showing affection or engaging in intimate acts, perhaps with someone of high status.

Punani: Slang for female genitalia.

Pure vibes: Great atmosphere or energy. 'That beach party was pure vibes.'

Putting out: Agreeing to engage in intimate relations. 'There's no pressure; she doesn't have to put out.'

Quality Streeth: A playful, old-timey way to refer to Quality Street, a popular assortment of chocolates in the UK, especially during Christmas.

Rawdog: Slang for engaging in intimate activities without protection.

Reem: Meaning attractive or excellent. Popularized by reality-TV shows like *The Only Way Is Essex*. 'You look reem tonight!'

Rinse you a tenner: To borrow or take ten pounds from someone, possibly without returning it. 'He rinsed me a tenner and never paid me back.'

Riizz up: Slang for charming or flirting with someone. 'Watch him riizz up that girl at the bar.'

Rounders: A British sport similar to baseball, played with a bat and ball, typically in schools. It's like baseball's cousin with a British accent.

Salad-dodger: A term for someone who avoids healthy food, often implying they're overweight.

Science shaggers / non-science shaggers: Terms distinguishing between people who study science and those who don't.

Scran: Slang for food. 'I'm starving; let's get some scran.'

Scrap: A fight or scuffle. 'Those two got into a scrap after the game.'

Sesh-head: Someone who loves to party, especially frequently. 'She's a real sesh-head on the weekends.'

Seshlehem: A playful term combining 'sesh' (session/party) and 'Bethlehem,' indicating the ultimate party spot. 'We're heading to Dave's place; it's the Seshlehem tonight!'

Seshy: Related to partying or being in a party mood. 'Feeling seshy this Friday?'

Shagging: Engaging in intimate relations. 'They've been shagging for a few months now.'

Shanked mega-style: Stabbed or attacked severely. Also used metaphorically to mean being seriously betrayed.

Shanking: The act of stabbing someone. 'In the movie, the hero avoids getting shanked.'

Shart: An unfortunate mishap where one attempts to pass gas but, well, more happens. A blend of 'shit' and 'fart'.

Shawty: An American slang term for an attractive woman. 'He was trying to get the attention of that shawty at the club.' Or a term of endearment.

Shit craic: A situation that's not fun or enjoyable. 'That party was shit craic; left early.'

Sick: In slang it means awesome or really good. 'That skateboard trick was sick!'

Skanky: Dirty or sleazy, sometimes used to describe someone perceived as unkempt or promiscuous.

Sket: A derogatory term for a promiscuous woman.

Glossary

Slut drops: A dance move where one drops into a low squat from standing, then rises again – popular in clubs.

Smash that pasty: An expression meaning to engage in sexy times.

Smashing your lass's back doors in: Sexy times.

Smirnoff Ice strawpedo: A way to drink a bottled beverage quickly by inserting a straw and chugging it – popular among partygoers.

Snowflake: Used to describe someone seen as overly sensitive or easily offended.

Soppy shite: Someone who's overly sentimental or emotional. 'He's a soppy shite when it comes to romantic movies.'

Souling and guising: Old traditions similar to modern trick-or-treating, involving dressing up and performing in exchange for food or money.

Spaff money up the wall: Wasting money on things that aren't worthwhile. 'He spaffed his bonus up the wall on gadgets he never uses.'

Spaff themselves: An expression meaning to get overly excited. 'They practically spaffed themselves when the band came on stage.'

Spaffed about: Wasted or used frivolously. 'He spaffed about all afternoon instead of working.'

Speccy git: An insult aimed at someone who wears glasses ('speccy') and is annoying ('git').

Spoons: A nickname for Wetherspoons, a chain of pubs in the UK known for affordable drinks and food.

Standing around like tits: Doing nothing productive and possibly looking foolish. 'We were just standing around like tits waiting for the bus.'

Strawberry woo woo: A fruity cocktail made with vodka, peach schnapps, and cranberry juice – sweet and popular on nights out.

Stroppy: Being bad-tempered or easily annoyed. 'Don't get stroppy with me!'

Super chilled: Very relaxed or easygoing. 'She's super chilled, nothing bothers her.'

Surprise collab: An unexpected collaboration between artists or brands. 'Did you hear about the surprise collab between those two bands?'

Tacky-chun: Short for 'tactical chunder,' meaning to vomit deliberately to feel better, usually during heavy drinking sessions.

Tap the fucking table: A phrase from Cheryl Cole's appearance on *Most Haunted*, urging any spirits to make a noise.

Tart: An old-fashioned, derogatory term for a woman perceived as promiscuous.

Tear-arsing: Moving very quickly or recklessly. 'He came tear-arsing down the street on his bike.'

Tescoeth: A playful, old-timey way to refer to Tesco.

The 'gram: Slang for Instagram. 'Post that pic on the 'gram!'

The Dome: Could refer to a well-known venue or building nicknamed 'The Dome'.

The face of a slapped arse: Looking very grumpy or displeased. 'After hearing the bad news, he had the face of a slapped arse.'

The floor is lava: A game where one imagines the floor is lava and must avoid touching it – usually played by children but fun for all ages! Not fun for those in Pompeii.

The Only Way is Essexth: A playful, old-timey way to refer to

Glossary

The Only Way is Essex, a British reality-TV show focusing on the lives of several people in Essex.

The Reef: Short for Tenerife, a sunny holiday destination in the Canary Islands.

The village bike: A derogatory term implying someone has been intimate with many people.

Tindeth: An archaic way of referring to Tinder, the dating app. 'They met on Tindeth.'

Tiny Tim: A character from Charles Dickens' *A Christmas Carol*, symbolizing innocence and hope.

Titmatized: Playfully suggesting someone is mesmerized by someone's chest.

Tits up: When something goes completely wrong or fails. 'Well, that plan went tits up.'

To bollock: To scold or reprimand someone severely. 'The boss bollocked him for being late.'

To mug everyone off: To disrespect or deceive people. 'He tried to mug everyone off with that fake story.'

To murk: Slang for defeating or outdoing someone, sometimes used in gaming or sports contexts. 'He totally murked the competition.'

To not catch a case: To avoid legal trouble or arrest for chatting to underage girls.

Top shagger / toppest of shaggers: Someone reputed to be very active in bedding people.

Tosser: An insult similar to idiot or jerk. 'Don't listen to him; he's a tosser.'

Trollied: Extremely drunk. 'They got absolutely trollied at the wedding.'

Uncultured snowflakes: A term combining 'uncultured' (lacking cultural awareness) and 'snowflakes' (people perceived as overly sensitive).

Uno reverses: A reference to the 'Reverse' card in the game Uno, used metaphorically to indicate turning the tables in a situation.

Waitrose shoppers and yummy mummies: Waitrose is an upscale UK supermarket; 'yummy mummy' refers to an attractive, fashionable mother – often seen shopping there.

Wank: A vulgar term for self-pleasure; also used to describe something as poor quality or worthless. 'That movie was absolute wank.'

Wanky: Pretentious or trying too hard to impress. 'His speech was a bit wanky, wasn't it?'

Weapons: Slang for very unattractive people. 'Did you see them? Absolute weapons!'

Who ate all the pies?: A football chant teasing someone for being overweight. 'Who ate all the pies?' sung in jest.

Wide-on: A cheeky term for female arousal, the counterpart to 'hard-on'.

Worldlies: Extremely attractive people; the best of the best. 'She's a worldie!'

Yutes: Slang for youths or young people. 'The yutes are always on their phones these days.'

Recommended Reading

Mortimer, Ian (2022), *The Time Traveller's Guide to Regency Britain: A Handbook for Visitors to 1789–1830*, New York, Pegasus Books.

Goodman, Ruth (2013), *How to Be a Victorian*, London, Penguin Books.

Worsley, Lucy (2019), *Queen Victoria: Daughter, Wife, Mother, Widow*, London, Hodder & Stoughton.

Rubenhold, Hallie (2006), *The Covent Garden Ladies: Pimp General Jack & the Extraordinary Story of Harris's List*, Stroud, Gloucestershire, Tempus Publishing Ltd.

Rubenhold, Hallie (2019). *The Five: The Untold Lives of the Women Killed by Jack the Ripper*, Boston, Houghton Mifflin Harcourt.

Jenner, Greg (2021). *Dead Famous: An Unexpected History of Celebrity from Bronze Age to Silver Screen*, London, Weidenfeld & Nicolson.

Tom Holland and Dominic Sandbrook (2023) *The Rest Is History*, London, Bloomsbury Publishing.

Sources

JANUARY
1st – 'Anne of Cleves' | Hampton Court Palace | Historic Royal Palaces. www.hrp.org.uk/hampton-court-palace/history-and-stories/anne-of-cleves/
2nd – Clark, Judith Freeman (2009), *The Gilded Age*. New York, Infobase Publishing.
3rd – Aretha Franklin, *Rock & Roll Hall of Fame*. rockhall.com/inductees/aretha-franklin/
4th – Kingsley, Sean. 'The Race to Preserve Treasures from a Legendary 17th-Century Shipwreck.' Smithsonian Magazine, 31 July 2022. www.smithsonianmag.com/history/inside-the-race-to-preserve-treasures-from-a-legendary-17th-century-shipwreck-in-the-bahamas-180980492/
'Maravillas.' Bahamas Maritime Museum. www.bahamasmaritimemuseum.com/maravillas.
5th – 'Henry VIII: January 1531, 1–15.' British History Online. www.british-history.ac.uk/letters-papers-hen8/vol5/pp10-22
6th – DeVries, Kelly (1999), *The Norwegian Invasion of England in 1066*. Suffolk, England, Boydell Press.
7th – 'Thomas Rowlandson | Departure of Blanchard and Jeffries' Balloon from Dover, January 7, 1785.' The Metropolitan Museum of Art. www.metmuseum.org/art/collection/search/788180
'Blanchard! Where Are Your Trousers? The First Crossing of the English Channel in a Balloon.' British Library, Untold lives blog, 7 January 2019. blogs.bl.uk/untoldlives/2019/01/blanchard-where-are-your-trousers-the-first-crossing-of-the-english-channel-in-a-balloon.html
8th – There's video evidence, but it's gross.

Sources

9th – 'Apple Reinvents the Phone with iPhone.' Apple Newsroom, 9 January 2007. www.apple.com/uk/newsroom/2007/01/09Apple-Reinvents-the-Phone-with-iPhone/
10th – 'A Brief History of the Underground.' Transport for London, 2023. tfl.gov.uk/corporate/about-tfl/culture-and-heritage/londons-transport-a-history/london-underground/a-brief-history-of-the-underground
11th – 'It Could Be Ye: England's First Lottery – the History Press.' The History Press, 28 June 2024. thehistorypress.co.uk/article/it-could-be-ye-englands-first-lottery/
12th – 'Campus Hijinks at Davidson Involved X-Rays, 1896.' North Carolina Department of Natural and Cultural Resources, 12 January 2016. www.dncr.nc.gov/blog/2016/01/12/campus-hijinks-davidson-involved-x-rays-1896
13th – 'Alchemy and The Act Against Multipliers.' Library of Congress blogs, 20 January 2023. blogs.loc.gov/law/2023/01/alchemy-and-the-act-against-multipliers/
14th – Blumberg, Jess. 'A Brief History of the Salem Witch Trials.' Smithsonian.com, 24 October 2022. www.smithsonianmag.com/history/a-brief-history-of-the-salem-witch-trials-175162489/
15th – 'The First Top Hat Causes a Commotion.' British Newspaper Archive, 15 January 2014. blog.britishnewspaperarchive.co.uk/2014/01/15/the-first-top-hat-causes-a-commotion/
16th – Levick, Barbara (2010), *Augustus: Image and Substance*. Oxfordshire, UK, Taylor & Francis.
17th – 'Antarctic Anniversaries: Captains James Cook and Robert Scott.' British Library, Untold lives blog, 17 January 2016. blogs.bl.uk/untoldlives/2016/01/cook-and-scott-antarctic-anniversaries.html
18th – Jameson, J. Franklin (ed.). 'Original Narratives of Early American History.' Winthrop's Journal, 1630–1649, Volume II. salempl.org/wp-content/uploads/2022/06/Original-Narratives-of-Early-American-History-Winthrops-Journal-vol.-2.pdf
19th – Scarisbrick, J. J. (1997), *Henry VIII* (2nd ed.). New Haven, Connecticut, Yale University Press.
20th – 'The Trial of Charles I.' UK Parliament. www.parliament.uk/about/living-heritage/building/palace/westminsterhall/government-and-administration/trial-of-charlesi/
21st – 'NO PUBLIC SMOKING by WOMEN NOW; the Sullivan Ordinance, to Be Passed by the Aldermen Today, Makes It Illegal. WILL the LADIES REBEL as the Ladies of New Amsterdam Did When Peter Stuyvesant Ordered Them to Wear Broad Flounces?' *New York Times*, 21 January 1908. www.nytimes.com/1908/01/21/archives/no-public-smoking-by-women-now-the-sullivan-ordinance-to-be-passed.html
22nd – 'Victoria (r. 1837–1901).' Royal UK. www.royal.uk/encyclopedia/victoria-r-1837-1901

23rd – 'CHAPTER VI, NARCOTIC DRUGS AND PSYCHOTROPIC SUBSTANCES, 2. International Opium Convention, The Hague, 23 January 1912.' United Nations Treaty Collection. treaties.un.org/Pages/ViewDetailsIV.aspx?src=TREATY&mtdsg_no=VI-2&chapter=6&Temp=mtdsg4&clang=_en

24th – 'On January 24, 1972, Sergeant Shoichi Yokoi Was Found by Two Chamoru.' Guam Museum Foundation, 28 June 2022. www.guammuseumfoundation.org/2022/06/28/on-january-24-1972-sergeant-shoichi-yokoi-was-found-by-two-chamoru/

25th – Currie, James (1824), *The Works of Robert Burns*. Glasgow, Blackie and Son.

26th – 'The First Public Demonstration of Television | 26 January 1926.' Baird Television. www.bairdtelevision.com/firstdemo.html

27th – 'Lewis Carrol.' Poetry *Foundation*, 2018. www.poetryfoundation.org/poets/lewis-carroll.

28th – 'The First Speeding Fine – for Travelling at 8 Mph.' The British Newspaper Archive blog, 28 January 2014. blog.britishnewspaperarchive.co.uk/2014/01/28/the-first-speeding-fine-for-travelling-at-8-mph/

29th – Philp, Mark. 'Thomas Paine.' Stanford Encyclopedia of Philosophy, 18 July 2013. plato.stanford.edu/entries/paine/

30th – 'The Restoration – the Stuart Successions Project.' University of Exeter. stuarts.exeter.ac.uk/education/moments/the-restoration/

31st – Brammer, Robert, '"I'll Be Damned If I Don't Do It!": The Failed Assassination Attempt on President Andrew Jackson | in Custodia Legis: Law Librarians of Congress.' Library of Congress blogs, 16 January 2014. blogs.loc.gov/law/2014/01/ill-be-damned-if-i-dont-do-it-the-failed-assassination-attempt-on-president-andrew-jackson/

FEBRUARY

1st – Wanamaker, Marc and Nudelman, Robert W. (2007), *Early Hollywood*. Charleston, South Carolina, Arcadia Publishing Incorporated.

2nd – 'The Death of Queen Victoria – Archive, 1901.' *Guardian*, 23 January 1901. www.theguardian.com/uk/1901/jan/23/monarchy.fromthearchive

3rd – Embrechts, Paul, Hofert, Marius, and Chavez-Demoulin, Valérie (2024), 'The Black Tulip and February 3, 1637' in *Risk Revealed: Cautionary Tales, Understanding and Communication*. Cambridge, Cambridge University Press, pp. 337–344.

4th – 'On This Day – 4 Feb 2004: The Launch of Facebook.' BBC Sounds, 4 February 2023. www.bbc.co.uk/sounds/play/p0dz8plp

5th – Conley, John J. 'Marie de Rabutin-Chantal, Marquise de Sévigné (1626—1696).' Internet Encyclopedia of Philosophy. iep.utm.edu/sevigne-marquise-de-marie-de-rabutin-chantal/

❖❖ Sources ❖❖

6th – 'Queen Elizabeth II's Accession and Coronation.' Royal UK. www.royal.uk/queen-elizabeth-iis-accession-and-coronation#:~:text=On%206%20February%201952%2C%20King,came%20with%20her%20new%20title
7th – 'Amphora; Vessel (Closed); Cameo.' British Museum. www.britishmuseum.org/collection/object/G_1945-0927-1
8th – 'The life, death, and legacy of Mary, Queen of Scots.' National Museums Scotland. www.nms.ac.uk/discover-catalogue/the-life-death-and-legacy-of-mary-queen-of-scots#:~:text=After%2019%20years%20as%20a
9th – Foster, Ellen. 'Saint Apollonia.' The Lady Apollonia West Country Mysteries, 18 November 2018. blogs.valpo.edu/ellenfoster/2022/11/18/saint-apollonia/
10th – Brockliss, L.W.B. (2016), *The University of Oxford: A History*. Oxford, Oxford University Press.
11th – Brown, G. (2006), *Literary Sociability and Literary Property in France, 1775–1793*. Farnham, Surrey, Ashgate Publications.
12th – 'Our History.' NAACP (National Association for the Advancement of Colored People). naacp.org/about/our-history
13th – 'Catherine Howard'| Hampton Court Palace | Historic Royal Palaces. www.hrp.org.uk/hampton-court-palace/history-and-stories/catherine-howard/#gs.fgamen
14th – Little, Becky. 'Nothing Says 'I Hate You' like a 'Vinegar Valentine.' Smithsonian Magazine, 10 February 2017. www.smithsonianmag.com/history/nothing-says-i-hate-you-vinegar-valentine-180962109/
15th – 'On this day – Feb. 15, 1804, New Jersey Passes Law Delaying End of Slavery for Decades.' The Equal Justice Initiative. calendar.eji.org/racial-injustice/feb/15#:~:text=Using%20the%20language%20of%20bondage.
16th – '100th Anniversary of British Archaeologist Howard Carter Opening the Sealed Doorway to Tutankhamen's Tomb in Thebes, Egypt.' University of Birmingham, Cultural Calendar, 16 February 2023. blog.bham.ac.uk/culturalcalendar/2023/02/16/100th-anniversary-of-british-archaeologist-howard-carter-opening-the-sealed-doorway-to-tutankhamens-tomb-in-thebes-egypt
17th – Patrick, Kevin (2017), *The Phantom Unmasked*. University of Iowa Press.
18th – Lewis, Matt. 'What Led to George, Duke of Clarence's Execution by Wine?' History Hit, 26 June 2023. www.historyhit.com/what-led-to-george-duke-of-clarences-execution-by-wine/#:~:text=On%2018%20February%201478%2C%20aged
19th – Thouret J.-C., Juvigné E., Gourgaud A., Boivin P., Dávila J., 'Reconstruction of the AD 1600 Huaynaputina eruption based on the correlation of geologic evidence with early Spanish chronicles', 11 Data Repository at www.elsevier.com/locate/jvolgeores, see 'Electronic Supplements', *Journal of Volcanology and Geothermal Research*, Volume 115, Issues 3–4, 2002, pp. 529–570

20th – 'William Buckland (1784–1856) – Notice on the Megalosaurus or Great Fossil Lizard of Stonesfield with Observations on the South-Western Coal District of England. (Reprinted from Transactions of the Geological Society of London, 1824).' www.rct.uk/collection/1090881/notice-on-the-megalosaurus-or-great-fossil-lizard-of-stonesfield-with

21st – 'Richard Trevithick's Steam Locomotive.' National Museum Wales, 15 December 2008. museum.wales/articles/1012/Richard-Trevithickrsquos-steam-locomotive/

22nd – 'Little Colonel Movie.' Pewee Valley Historical Society, 2015. www.peweevalleyhistory.org/little-colonel-movie.html#:~:text=%22The%20Little%20Colonel%22%20with%20Shirley

23rd – '4 Stories about Pitt's Vaccine Legacy, 68 Years after the First Public Polio Shots.' University of Pittsburgh, 23 February 2022. www.pitt.edu/pittwire/features-articles/jonas-salk-polio-vaccine-anniversary#:~:text=On%20Feb

24th – 'Prince Charles and Lady Di to Marry.' BBC, On This Day, 24 February 1981. news.bbc.co.uk/onthisday/hi/dates/stories/february/24/newsid_2516000/2516759.stm

25th – Clark, Heather. 'Like Fury: Sylvia Plath and Ted Hughes at Cambridge.' *Ted Hughes Society Journal*, vol. 6, no. 2, 21 Nov. 2017, pp. 40–57. pure.hud.ac.uk/en/publications/like-fury-sylvia-plath-and-ted-hughes-at-cambridge

26th – Maison Victor Hugo Besançon. maisonvictorhugo.besancon.fr/en/

27th – Stearns, Bertha-Monica, 'The First English Periodical for Women.' *Modern Philology*, vol. 28, no. 1, 1930, pp. 45–59. www.jstor.org/stable/433233

28th – 'New Blue Plaque Recognises Contribution of Rosalind Franklin to DNA Breakthrough.' Corpus Christi College, University of Cambridge. www.corpus.cam.ac.uk/articles/new-blue-plaque-recognises-contribution-rosalind-franklin-dna-breakthrough

29th - 'Everything You Need to Know about Leap Years.' www.bbc.co.uk/programmes/articles/16vV1jB2VCLPrkypwV749Jh/everything-you-need-to-know-about-leap-years

MARCH

1st – 'St David: The Greatest Figure in the Welsh Age of Saints.' VisitWales. www.visitwales.com/info/history-heritage-and-traditions/st-david-five-facts#:~:text=He%20performed%20miracles

2nd – Murphy, Paul Thomas (2012), *Shooting Victoria: Madness, Mayhem and the Rebirth of the British Monarchy*. London, Head of Zeus.

3rd – 'Second Draft: In 1875, at the First Indoor Hockey Game, Guess What Broke Out?' Montreal Gazette. montrealgazette.com/opinion/columnists/second-draft-in-1875-at-the-first-indoor-hockey-game-guess-what-broke-out

Sources

'Daily British Whig (1850), 5 Mar 1875, p. 2.' Digital Kingston, Vitacollections. vitacollections.ca/digital-kingston/2795817/page/2?q=hockey&docid=OOI.2795817

4th – Sullivan, Mark. '"More Popular Than Jesus": The Beatles and the Religious Far Right.' *Popular Music* 6, no. 3 (1987): 313–26. www.jstor.org/stable/853191

5th – '2 Yankees Disclose Exchange.' *New York Times*, 6 March 1973. www.nytimes.com/1973/03/06/archives/2-yankees-disclose-family-exchange-peterson-and-kekich-give-details.html

6th – U.S. Patent 2,370,990, *The Naval Aviation Physical Training Manuals: Gymnastics and Tumbling* The United States Naval Institute 1944 – issued by Aviation Training Division of U.S. Navy

7th – Codex Justinanus 3:12:2 (Rordorf, Sabbat et Dimanche, no. 111)

8th – 'Diary Entries from March 1669 (the Diary of Samuel Pepys).' www.pepysdiary.com/diary/1669/03/

9th – 'Barbie Timeline.' Mattel. www.barbiemedia.com/timeline.html

10th – 'Ahoy! Alexander Graham Bell and the First Telephone Call.' Science Museum, 19 October 2018. www.sciencemuseum.org.uk/objects-and-stories/ahoy-alexander-graham-bell-and-first-telephone-call

Zagorsky, Jay L. 'Rise and Fall of the Landline: 143 Years of Telephones Becoming More Accessible – and Smart.' The Conversation, 14 March 2019. theconversation.com/rise-and-fall-of-the-landline-143-years-of-telephones-becoming-more-accessible-and-smart-113295

11th – 'FAQs'. UK Parliament Archives. archives.parliament.uk/help/faqs/#:~:text=While%20the%20Monarch%20has%20the,is%20regarded%20as%20a%20formality

'The Scottish Parliament and Law Making.' The Open University. www.open.edu/openlearn/mod/oucontent/view.php?id=69024§ion=2.2

12th – 'Mrs Beeton.' BBC History. www.bbc.co.uk/history/historic_figures/beeton_mrs.shtml#:~:text=Mrs%20Beeton%20(1836%20%2D%201865)&text=Isabella%20Mayson%20was%20born%20on

13th – 'Uranus: Exploration - NASA Science.' science.nasa.gov/uranus/exploration/

14th – 'Ten Most Wanted Fugitives 60th Anniversary, 1950–2010.' Federal Bureau of Investigation. www.fbi.gov/file-repository/ten_most_wanted_60th_anniversary.pdf/view

15th – 'Julius Caesar.' Oxford Reference. www.oxfordreference.com/display/10.1093/oi/authority.20110803095541196#:~:text=Hostility%20to%20Caesar's%20autocracy%20culminated,led%20by%20Brutus%20and%20Cassius

16th – Cronholm, Neander Nicolas (1902), *A History of Sweden from the Earliest Times to the Present Day*. Hungerford, Legare Street Press (Reprint 2022).

17th – 'Electronic Irish Statute Book (EISB).' Irish Statute Book, Office of the Attorney General. www.irishstatutebook.ie/eli/1927/act/15/enacted/en/print#sec2

18th – Chambers, Robert (1864), *Chambers Book of Days*. London and Edinburgh, Chambers.

19th – 'King Gustav III 1771–1792.' The Royal Palaces (Sweden). www.kungligaslotten.se/english/archives/swedish-regents/2018-03-05-king-gustav-iii-1771-1792.html

20th – Barr, Justin, et al. 'Surgeons in the Time of Plague: Guy de Chauliac in Fourteenth-Century France.' *Journal of Vascular Surgery Cases and Innovative Techniques*, vol. 6, no. 4, 27 July 2020, pp. 657–658. www.ncbi.nlm.nih.gov/pmc/articles/PMC7384400/, doi.org/10.1016/j.jvscit.2020.07.006

21st – 'Thomas Cranmer.' BBC History. www.bbc.co.uk/history/historic_figures/cranmer_thomas.shtml

22nd – Inglis, Simon (1998), *The Official Centenary History of the Football League, 1888–1988: League Football and the men who made it*. London, Willow Books.

23rd – Metcalf, Allan (2012) *OK: The Improbable Story of America's Greatest Word*. Oxford, Oxford University Press, p. 28.

24th – McMillen, Laura. 'What Was the Loveday and Why Did It Fail?' History Hit, 22 November 2022. www.historyhit.com/how-did-king-henry-vi-attempt-to-reconcile-the-warring-roses/#:~:text=The%20

25th – 'Tichborne Dole.' Oxford Reference. www.oxfordreference.com/display/10.1093/oi/authority.20110803104604558#:~:text=Quick%20Reference,Lady%20Day%20(25%20March)

26th – Roberts Stephen. 'Henley Regatta Celebrates Its 180 Year Anniversary This Year.' Great British Life, 17 June 2019. www.greatbritishlife.co.uk/magazines/cotswold/22575560.henley-regatta-celebrates-180-year-anniversary-year/

27th – 'Typhoid Mary's Life Sentence in Quarantine.' University of Michigan. deepblue.lib.umich.edu/bitstream/handle/2027.42/109695/TyphoidMary.pdf;sequence=1

28th – '*The True American. [volume]* (New Orleans [La.]), 29 March 1837.' Chronicling America: Historic American Newspapers, Library of Congress. chroniclingamerica.loc.gov/lccn/sn83016527/1837-03-29/ed-1/seq-1/

29th – 'Niagara Falls Runs dry.' The Exchange Museum. nfexchange.ca/museum/discover-our-history/history-notes/when-niagara-falls-ran-dry

30th – 'Assassination Attempt.' Ronald Reagan Library. www.reaganlibrary.gov/permanent-exhibits/assassination-attempt

31st – 'Origins and Construction of the Eiffel Tower.' La Tour Eiffel, 1 October 2018. www.toureiffel.paris/en/the-monument/history

APRIL

1st – 'Three Jane Austen Letters Are Shown Together for the First Time.'

Sources

University of Cambridge, 28 March 2017. www.cam.ac.uk/news/three-jane-austen-letters-are-shown-together-for-the-first-time#:~:text=The%20last%20of%20the%20letters

2nd – Lotzof, Kerry. 'Maria Sibylla Merian: Metamorphosis Unmasked by Art and Science.' Natural History Museum. www.nhm.ac.uk/discover/maria-sibylla-merian-metamorphosis-art-and-science.html

3rd – '1954: Oxford Wins 100th Boat Race.' BBC, On This Day, 3 April 1954. news.bbc.co.uk/onthisday/hi/dates/stories/april/3/newsid_2889000/2889013.stm

4th – 'Timeline.' Microsoft Corporation. www.microsoft.com/en-gb/about/timeline/

5th – 'Pocahontas.' National Women's History Museum, 2015. www.womenshistory.org/education-resources/biographies/pocahontas#:~:text=During%20this%20event%2C%20Pocahontas%20told

6th – Ontiou Dasylva. 'This Week in Olympic Sports History: April 1–7, Athens 1896 – the First Modern Games.' International Olympic Committee, April 2024. olympics.com/en/news/this-week-olympic-sports-history-april-1-7-athens-1896-first-modern-games

7th – Lochun, Kev. 'The Extraordinary Legend of Highwayman Dick Turpin.' History Extra, 1 March 2024. www.historyextra.com/period/georgian/dick-turpin-highwayman-crimes-death/

8th – 'Buddha's Birthday.' The Pluralism Project, Harvard University. hwpi.harvard.edu/files/pluralism/files/buddhas_birthday.pdf

9th – 'Winston Churchill's Citizen of the United States Speech.' America's National Churchill Museum www.nationalchurchillmuseum.org/citizen-of-the-united-states.html

10th – 'London's 391 Years of Going Bananas for Bananas.' BBC News, 10 April 2024. www.bbc.co.uk/news/uk-england-london-68770149

11th – Hojinacki, Nathaniel J. and Larsen, Jeff. (2009), 'Treaty Signed Between the Allied Powers and His Majest the Emperor Napoleon.' https://via.library.depaul.edu/napoleon/5

12th – Aitken, George A. (1899), *The Tatler*, Volume 1 of 4. Project Gutenberg. www.gutenberg.org/files/13645/13645-h/13645-h.htm#:~:text=According%20to%20the%20first%20number

13th – 'History of the Museum.' The Metropolitan Museum of Art. www.metmuseum.org/about-the-met/history#:~:text=On%20April%2013%2C%201870%2C%20The

14th – Kellogg, John Harvey. 'US558393A – Flaked Cereals and Process of Preparing Same.' Patented 14 April 1896. patents.google.com/patent/US558393A/en

15th – '"Liner Collides with Iceberg. Passengers Safe": The Titanic, in Our Newspapers.' British Newspaper Archive blog, 14 April 2016. blog.

britishnewspaperarchive.co.uk/2016/04/14/liner-collides-with-iceberg-passengers-safe-the-titanic-in-our-newspapers/

16th – Bates, Kath. 'Sir Isaac Newton I Oxford Open Learning.' Homeschooling, 26 March 2018, www.oxfordhomeschooling.co.uk/science/sir-isaac-newton/

17th – 'The Discovery of New York.' Castello Di Verrazzano | Greve in Chianti. www.verrazzano.com/en/la-scoperta-di-new-york/

18th – 'About CliffsNotes.' CliffsNotes, 2015. www.cliffsnotes.com/discover-about

19th – 'Author Attempts to Jump-Start Town with Fictional UFO Story.' Texas State Historical Association. www.tshaonline.org/texas-day-by-day/entry/118

20th – Collins, Dick. 'The Devil and Daniel Farson: How Did Bram Stoker Die?' *Journal of Dracula Studies*, vol. 10, 2008. research.library.kutztown.edu/cgi/viewcontent.cgi?article=1057&context=dracula-studies

21st – Borman, Tracy, 'Long Live the King: St George's Day and the Accession of Henry VIII.' Historic Royal Palaces, 22 April 2020. www.hrp.org.uk/blog/st-georges-day-and-the-accession-of-henry-viii/#gs.fgjqvs

22nd – Johnson, Ben. '1945 and the End of World War Two – Timeline of Events in 1945.' Historic UK. www.historic-uk.com/HistoryUK/HistoryofBritain/World-War-2-Timeline-1945/

23rd – 'When Was Shakespeare Born?' Shakespeare Birthplace Trust. https://www.shakespeare.org.uk/explore-shakespeare/shakespedia/william-shakespeare/when-was-shakespeare-born/#:~:text=The%20Birth%20of%20William%20Shakespeare&text=William%20Shakespeare%20was%20born%20in

24th – 'Life and deathline of Mary, Queen of Scots.' National Museums Scotland. www.nms.ac.uk/discover-catalogue/life-and-deathline-of-mary-queen-of-scots

'Mary, Queen of Scots (r.1542–1567).' Royal UK. www.royal.uk/mary-queen-scots-r1542-1567#:~:text=Tall%2C%20graceful%20and%20quick%2Dwitted,an%20ear%20infection%20in%201560

25th – Abbott, Geoffrey (2007), *What a Way to Go: The Guillotine, the Pendulum, the Thousand Cuts, the Spanish Donkey, and 66 Other Ways of Putting Someone to Death*. New York, St. Martin's Griffin (reprint edition).

26th – 'Pazzi Conspiracy' Victoria and Albert Museum. collections.vam.ac.uk/item/O349106/pazzi-conspiracy-medal-unknown/

Martines, Lauro (2004), *April Blood: Florence and the Plot Against the Medici*. Oxford, Oxford University Press.

27th – Heppenstall, Janice. 'Spinsters.' 21st April 2020. TitBits Magazine (1889) – English Ancestors. englishancestors.blog/tag/titbits-magazine-1889/

28th – 'Harper Lee Biography.' Chicago Public Library, 31 October 2001. www.chipublib.org/harper-lee-biography/

Sources

29th – 'Cook's Journal, April 1770.' National Museum of Australia. www.nma.gov.au/exhibitions/endeavour-voyage/cooks-journal/april-1770
30th – 'Online Exhibition: Charles Dickens at 200 | Smith College Libraries.' www.smith.edu/libraries/libs/rarebook/exhibitions/dickens/11-tale-of-two-cities.htm

MAY

1st – 'Elvis Ties Knot with Priscilla.' Newspapers.com, 2 May 1967. www.newspapers.com/article/the-times-elvis-ties-knot-with-priscilla/50481413/
2nd – 'Anne Boleyn.' | Tower of London | Historic Royal Palaces. www.hrp.org.uk/tower-of-london/history-and-stories/anne-boleyn/#gs.ezkibe
3rd – Davis, Anita (2014), *The Margaret Mitchell Encyclopedia*. Jefferson, North Carolina, McFarland Publishers.
4th – 'War Ration Book One / Ration Coupons on the Home Front, 1942–1945.' Duke Digital Repository. repository.duke.edu/dc/hfc/hfccp01025
'Rationing.' The National WWII Museum, New Orleans. www.nationalww2museum.org/war/articles/rationing-during-wwii#:~:text=The%20government%20began%20rationing%20certain
5th – Norwood, Arlisha and Brandman, Mariana. 'Nellie Bly (1864–1922).' National Women's History Museum, 2022. www.womenshistory.org/education-resources/biographies/nellie-bly-0
6th – 'Penny Black.' Stanley Gibbons. www.stanleygibbons.com/shop/great-britain/penny-black#
'Historic Sales Summary – Grosvenor Philatelic Auctions.' Grosvenor Philatelic Auctions, 27 March 2020. www.grosvenorauctions.com/auctions/historic-summary?gb_cat=1840+One+Penny+Black+and+Two+Pence+Blue&Sale_no=53&histgbcat=yes
7th – 'Ludwig van Beethoven (1770–1827) Symphony No. 9 in D minor, Opus 125, "Choral" (1824) 65 minutes.' Fort Worth Symphony Orchestra. fwsymphony.org/program-notes/beethoven-ludwig-van-symphony-no-9-in-d-minor-opus-125-choral#:~:text=The%20premiere%20of%20Beethoven
8th – 'Julian of Norwich – A Saint for Our Times.' York Minster. Julian-of-Norwich-080520.pdf (yorkminster.org)
9th – 'The King, the Crown and the Colonel.' The National Archives. www.nationalarchives.gov.uk/education/resources/the-king-the-crown-the-colonel/
10th – Perez-Selsky, Elisa (2013), 'Policing Privilege and Disciplining Bodies: Victoria C. Woodhull, Anthony Comstock, and the Platform for Social Engineering.' *Voces Novae:* Vol. 5, Article 6. https://digitalcommons.chapman.edu/vocesnovae/vol5/iss1/6
11th – 'Jules Hardouin-Mansart.' Palace of Versailles, 2 November 2016. en.chateauversailles.fr/discover/history/great-characters/jules-hardouin-mansart

Sturgis, Russell, and Davis, Francis A. (2013), *Sturgis' Illustrated Dictionary of Architecture and Building*, Courier Corporation. New York, Dover Publications.

Da Vinha, M. (2009), *Louis XIV and Versailles*. Art Lys.

Slaud, J. (2012), *Ils ont Donne L'eau a Versailles*. Éditions Onde.

Vigarello, G. (2013), *Concepts of Cleanliness: Changing Attitudes in France since the Middle Ages*. Past and Present Publications, Cambridge, Cambridge University Press.

12th – Alexander, Kerri Lee. 'Florence Nightingale.' National Women's History Museum, 2019. www.womenshistory.org/education-resources/biographies/florence-nightingale

13th – 'Ronald Ross: The Nobel Prize in Physiology or Medicine 1902.' The Nobel Prize. www.nobelprize.org/prizes/medicine/1902/ross/facts/

14th – 'Durham: Bishops.' British History Online. www.british-history.ac.uk/fasti-ecclesiae/1066-1300/vol2/pp29-32

'Gateshead and District, 1855.' Co-Curate. co-curate.ncl.ac.uk/gateshead-and-district-1855/

15th – Ridgway, Claire. 'The final days of Anne Boleyn: why did she die?.' History Extra, 19 May 2021. www.historyextra.com/period/tudor/anne-boleyn-death-execution-where-buried-how-die/

16th – 'The 1st Academy Awards | 1929.' Academy of Motion Picture Arts and Sciences. www.oscars.org/oscars/ceremonies/1929

17th – 'Lord Byron (George Gordon).' Poetry Foundation. www.poetryfoundation.org/poets/lord-byron

18th – Daly, Lawrence J., (1970) 'A Mandarin of Late Antiquity: The Political Life and Thought of Themistius.' Dissertations. 1019. ecommons.luc.edu/luc_diss/1019

19th – Staveley-Wadham, Rose. 'The "Sensational" Trial of Oscar Wilde – Reports of Ignominy, Shame and Tragedy.' British Newspaper Archive blog, 9 June 2020. blog.britishnewspaperarchive.co.uk/2020/06/09/trial-of-oscar-wilde/

20th – 'Amelia Earhart Departs on Solo Flight across Atlantic, May 20, 1932.' National Air and Space Museum, 2014. airandspace.si.edu/multimedia-gallery/amelia-earhart-departs-solo-flight-across-atlantic-may-20-1932

21st – Roach, Levi. 'Emperor Otto III and the End of Time.' Transactions of the Royal Historical Society, 19 November 2013, 23:75-102. doi:10.1017/S0080440113000042

22nd – 'A Guide to the United States.' History of Recognition, Diplomatic, and Consular Relations, by Country, since 1776: Korea.' Office of the Historian, Foreign Service Institute, United States Department of State. history.state.gov/countries/korea#:~:text=The%20United%20States%20and%20the

Sources

23rd – Harpham, David, 'The Case of Captain William Kidd – a 300 Year Old Miscarriage of Justice?' New Histories, vol. 3, issue 7, University of Sheffield. newhistories.sites.sheffield.ac.uk/volumes/2011-12/volume-3/issue-7-open-theme/the-case-of-captain-william-kidd-a-300-year-old-miscarriage-of-justice
24th – 'Napoleonic Prisoners of War at Dartmoor Prison.' Dartmoor Prison Museum, 18 May 2024. www.dartmoor-prison.co.uk/dartmoor-prison-museum-news-detail.php?relID=79&pageNum_rsSummaries=0
25th – 'London Zoo Seeks Memories and Memorabilia to Mark 200th Anniversary.' BBC News, 29 April 2024. www.bbc.co.uk/news/uk-england-london-68911505
 'Don Juan, Comte de Montizón (1822–87) – Obaysch, the Hippopotamus, London Zoo.' Royal Collection Trust. www.rct.uk/collection/2905524/obaysch-the-hippopotamus-london-zoo
26th – 'Witchcraft in Bermuda – Women & the American Story.' New-York Historical Society Museum and Library: Women & the American Story, February 2024. wams.nyhistory.org/early-encounters/english-colonies/witchcraft-in-bermuda/#:~:text=The%20jury%20found%20her%20guilty
27th – Sherwood, Roy. 'Oliver Cromwell, Kingship and the Humble Petition and Advice.' The Cromwell Association, 1999. www.olivercromwell.org/wordpress/articles/oliver-cromwell-kingship-and-the-humble-petition-and-advice/
28th – 'Ian Fleming.' www.ianfleming.com/ian-fleming/
29th – 'Charles II's Restoration, May 1660.' The National Archives blog, 29 May 2020. blog.nationalarchives.gov.uk/charles-ii-restoration-may1660/
30th – 'First Lady.' Royal Society, 8 March 2024. royalsociety.org/blog/2024/03/first-lady/
31st – 'Monday 31 May 1669.' The Diary of Samuel Pepys. www.pepysdiary.com/diary/1669/05/31/#:~:text=And%20so%20I%20betake%20myself

JUNE

1st – 'Blenheim: Blenheim Palace.' British History Online. www.british-history.ac.uk/vch/oxon/vol12/pp448-460
2nd – 'The Coronation of Queen Elizabeth II.' www.bbc.com/historyofthebbc/anniversaries/june/coronation-of-queen-elizabeth-ii/
3rd – 'The Marriage of the Duke and Duchess of Windsor – 3 June 1937.' The British Newspaper Archive blog, 2 June 2013. blog.britishnewspaperarchive.co.uk/2013/06/02/the-marriage-of-the-duke-and-duchess-of-windsor-3-june-1937/
4th – ' Emily Davison and the 1913 Epsom Derby.' The National Archives blog, 4 June 2013. blog.nationalarchives.gov.uk/emily-davison-and-the-1913-epsom-derby/

5th – '1944: Celebrations as Rome Is Liberated.' BBC, On This Day, 5 June 1944. news.bbc.co.uk/onthisday/hi/dates/stories/june/5/newsid_3547000/3547329.stm#:~:text=Early%20this%20morning%20it%20was

6th – Wilkie, G. (1818) *The Tablet of Memory*. Longman, London, p. 64.

7th – 'James Young Simpson.' Royal College of Physicians of Edinburgh, 9 February 2017. www.rcpe.ac.uk/heritage/james-young-simpson

8th – 'June 8, 1929 Margaret Bondfield is appointed Minister of Labour.' *The Sunday Post* (Dundee), PressReader.com. www.pressreader.com/uk/the-sunday-post-dundee/20220605/282535842010514?srsltid=AfmBOorc8A94xYncbaNkeXa1ylAMLEI2All4rHJV3nb5q2-hUO_GnWRw

9th – Ally Pally, 'Spectacle and the Opening of the Theatre.' Alexandra Palace, 25 April 2018. www.alexandrapalace.com/blog/spectacle-and-the-opening-of-the-theatre/#:~:text=On%209th%20June%201873%20fire

10th – Marr, John S., and Calisher, Charles H. 'Alexander the Great and West Nile Virus Encephalitis.' *Emerging Infectious Diseases*, vol. 9, no. 12, 1 Dec. 2003, pp. 1599–1603. www.ncbi.nlm.nih.gov/pmc/articles/PMC3034319/, doi.org/10.3201/eid0912.030288

11th – 'Katherine of Aragon.' | Hampton Court Palace | Historic Royal Palaces. www.hrp.org.uk/hampton-court-palace/history-and-stories/katherine-of-aragon/#gs.ezxr2j

12th – 'The Complete Works of Anne Frank.' Anne Frank House, 15 October 2018. www.annefrank.org/en/anne-frank/diary/complete-works-anne-frank/

13th – Keefe, Simon P. 'Wolfgang Amadeus Mozart the Child Performer–Composer.' Oxford University Press EBooks, 8 September 2016, pp. 550–575. doi.org/10.1093/acprof:oso/9780199685851.003.0024

14th – 'Norway Gives Women Partial Suffrage.' Oxford University Press blog, 14 June 2012. blog.oup.com/2012/06/norway-gives-women-partial-suffrage/

15th – Mitchell, Leslie, 'The Man Who Stopped Time.' Stanford Magazine, June 2001. stanfordmag.org/contents/the-man-who-stopped-time

16th – '1963: Soviets Launch First Woman into Space.' BBC, On This Day, 16 June 1963. news.bbc.co.uk/onthisday/hi/dates/stories/june/16/newsid_2685000/2685283.stm

17th – Calabria, Michael D. (2022), *The Language of the Taj Mahal: Islam, Prayer, and the Religion of Shah Jahan*. London, New York, I.B. Tauris.

18th – 'Anointed with oil: The coronation ampulla of Charles I.' National Museums Scotland. www.nms.ac.uk/discover-catalogue/anointed-with-oil-the-coronation-ampulla-of-charles-i#:~:text=When%20Charles%20I%20ascended%20to

Bergeron, David M, 'Charles I's Edinburgh Pageant (1633).' *Renaissance Studies*, vol. 6, no. 2, June 1992, pp. 173–184. doi.org/10.1111/j.1477-4658.1992.tb00261.x

◆• Sources •◆

19th – Malloch, Russell, 'The Centenary of the Creation of the House of Windsor.' The Gazette, 2017, www.thegazette.co.uk/all-notices/content/101228
20th – 'Queen Victoria' | Kensington Palace | Historic Royal Palaces. www.hrp.org.uk/kensington-palace/history-and-stories/queen-victoria/#gs.ezyo8m
21st – Davies, C. S. L., and Edwards, John. 'Katherine [Catalina, Catherine, Katherine of Aragon] (1485–1536), queen of England, first consort of Henry VIII.' Oxford Dictionary of National Biography, 19 May 2011. Oxford, Oxford University Press.
22nd – 'The Somerset v Stewart Case.' English Heritage. www.english-heritage.org.uk/visit/places/kenwood/history-stories-kenwood/somerset-case/
23rd – 'Alan Turing: Centenary Lectures.' University of Oxford Podcasts. podcasts.ox.ac.uk/series/alan-turing-centenary-lectures
24th – Walck, Pamela E. (2020), 'Mutiny at Bamber Bridge: How the World War II Press Reported Racial Unrest among U.S. Troops and Why It Remains in British Memory.' *American Journalism* 37 (3): 346–71. doi:10.1080/08821 127.2020.1790849
25th – Foreman, Paul (2015), *The Cambridge Book of Magic*. Lulu.com
Harding, Vanessa (2008), 'Cheapside: commerce and commemoration.' *Huntington Library Quarterly* 71 (1), pp. 77–96
26th – 'George IV.' BBC, History. www.bbc.co.uk/history/historic_figures/george_iv_king.shtml
27th – Michals, Debra (ed.), 'Helen Keller.' National Women's History Museum, 2015. www.womenshistory.org/education-resources/biographies/helen-keller
28th – 'The Treaty of Versailles.' The National Archives. beta.nationalarchives.gov.uk/explore-the-collection/stories/the-treaty-of-versailles/
29th – Ellery, Eloise. 'Mussolini Decrees Nine-Hour Working Day.' *Current History (1916–1940)*, vol. 24, no. 5, 1926, pp. 803–06. *JSTOR*, www.jstor.org/stable/45335745
30th – Cajori, Florian (1916), *William Oughtred : a great seventeenth-century teacher of mathematics* Chicago, London: The Open Court Publishing Co.

JULY
1st – 'The Life of Diana, Princess of Wales.' BBC, 2021. www.bbc.co.uk/news/special/politics97/diana/ob-child.html
2nd – '1964: President Johnson Signs Civil Rights Bill.' BBC, On This Day, 2 July 1964. news.bbc.co.uk/onthisday/hi/dates/stories/july/2/newsid_3787000/3787809.stm
3rd – 'Assassinating Queen Victoria: The Men Who Attempted to Murder the Monarch.' History Extra, 11 April 2023. www.historyextra.com/period/victorian/queen-victoria-assassination-attempts/

4th – 'Declaration of Independence (1776).' The National Archives, 8 April 2021. www.archives.gov/milestone-documents/declaration-of-independence#:~:text=The%20Continental%20Congress%20adopted%20the

5th – 'Birth of the NHS 1948'. The National Archives. www.nationalarchives.gov.uk/education/resources/significant-events/birth-of-the-nhs-1948/

'The Birth of the NHS.' BBC Archive. www.bbc.co.uk/archive/the-birth-of-the-nhs/zhjtd6f

6th – 'Who Killed the Princes in the Tower?' Historic Royal Palaces. www.hrp.org.uk/media/2997/richard-iii-and-the-princes-in-the-tower.pdf

7th – Pernoud, Regine (2007), *The Retrial of Joan of Arc*. San Francisco, Ignatius Press.

8th – Robertson, Craig, 'Document', The Passport in America: The History of a Document (New York, 2012; online edn, Oxford Academic, 16 March 2015). doi.org/10.1093/acprof:osobl/9780199927579.003.0002

9th – Lowish, T. L. (2021). 'Catherine the Great and the Development of a Modern Russian Sovereignty, 1762–1796.' University of California, Berkeley. escholarship.org/uc/item/6fc7r596

10th – 'Lady Jane Grey'| Tower of London | Historic Royal Palaces. www.hrp.org.uk/tower-of-london/history-and-stories/lady-jane-grey/#gs.f00m1k

11th – 'Second Statement of the Regulations for the Duel between Alexander Hamilton and Aaron Burr, July 11, 1804, Recto.' New York Historical Society, Digital Collections. digitalcollections.nyhistory.org/islandora/object/nyhs%3A236255

12th – 'Katherine Parr' | Hampton Court Palace | Historic Royal Palaces. www.hrp.org.uk/hampton-court-palace/history-and-stories/katherine-parr/#gs.f00qhy

13th – 'The Assassination of Jean-Paul Marat by Charlotte Corday – 13 July 1793.' The British Newspaper Archive blog, 12 July 2013. blog.britishnewspaperarchive.co.uk/2013/07/12/the-assassination-of-jean-paul-marat-by-charlotte-corday-13-july-1793/

14th – Hendy, David. 'Early Experiments: 1924–1929.' BBC, History of the BBC, The Birth of TV, 1972. www.bbc.com/historyofthebbc/100-voices/birth-of-tv/early-experiments#:~:text=On%20the%20afternoon%20of%20Monday

15th – 'Peldon, John Ball and the Peasants' Revolt.' Mersea Museum, 2017. www.merseamuseum.org.uk/mmresdetails.php?pid=PH01_PRV&ba=mmpeldon.php&rhit=88

'St Albans Blue Plaque Unveiled for Peasants' Revolt Leader.' BBC News, 25 February 2022. www.bbc.co.uk/news/uk-england-beds-bucks-herts-60529029

16th – 'Emily Stowe, MD.' Canadian Medical Hall of Fame, 2018. www.cdnmedhall.ca/laureates/emilystowe#:~:text=Stowe%20became%20the%20first%20woman

Sources

17th – 'Disneyland Opens in Anaheim, Calif.' United Press International Archives. www.upi.com/Archives/1955/07/18/Kids-are-delighted-with-Disneyland/1081500086844/

18th – 'Adolf Hitler Publishes "Mein Kampf".' Anne Frank House. www.annefrank.org/en/timeline/6/adolf-hitler-publishes-mein-kampf/

19th – 'Lizzie Borden.' Newspapers.com, 17 August 2018. www.newspapers.com/topics/famous-people/lizzie-borden/

20th – '"Man Walks On The Moon" – 10 Front Pages From 21 July 1969.' British Newspaper Archive blog, 27 July 2022. blog.britishnewspaperarchive.co.uk/tag/20-july-1969/

21st – Kang, Tricia. '160 Years of Central Park: A Brief History.' Central Park Conservancy, 1 June 2017. www.centralparknyc.org/articles/central-park-history

22nd – 'Joan (1210—1238) queen of Scots, consort of Alexander II.' Oxford Reference. www.oxfordreference.com/display/10.1093/oi/authority.20110803100021957?p=emailAmr1.WJpnUspY&d=/10.1093/oi/authority.20110803100021957

23rd – 'Jacobite Rising of 1745.' The National Archives. www.nationalarchives.gov.uk/education/resources/Jacobite-1745/

24th – 'Window Tax.' UK Parliament, 2019. www.parliament.uk/about/living-heritage/transformingsociety/towncountry/towns/tyne-and-wear-case-study/about-the-group/housing/window-tax/

Great Britain, *The Monthly Official Directory of the Aldershot Division*, 1876. W. Sheldrake.

25th – 'Nelson Wounded at Tenerife, 24 July 1797.' Royal Museums Greenwich. www.rmg.co.uk/collections/objects/rmgc-object-11990#:~:text=During%20his%20attempt%20to%20land

Bosanquet, H. T. A. (1952). 'LORD NELSON AND THE LOSS OF HIS ARM.' *The Mariner's Mirror*, 38(3), pp. 184–194.

26th – Perrottet, Tony. 'Who Was Casanova?' Smithsonian Magazine, April 2012. www.smithsonianmag.com/travel/who-was-casanova-160003650/

Vinovrški, Nicola. 'Casanova: A Case Study of Celebrity in 18th Century Europe.' *Historical Social Research / Historische Sozialforschung. Supplement*, no. 32, 2019, pp. 99–120. *JSTOR*, www.jstor.org/stable/26836213

27th – Pacheco, Diego. 'Xavier and Tanegashima.' *Monumenta Nipponica*, vol. 29, no. 4, 1974, pp. 477–80. *JSTOR*, doi.org/10.2307/2383897

28th – 'Catherine Howard' | Hampton Court Palace | Historic Royal Palaces. www.hrp.org.uk/hampton-court-palace/history-and-stories/catherine-howard/#:~:text=The%20King's%20Fifth%20Wife%3A%20Catherine,Queen%20at%20Hampton%20Court%20Palace

29th – Barber, Nicholas. 'Clara Bow: The Original "It Girl."' BBC, 29 December 2014. www.bbc.com/culture/article/20141222-who-was-the-original-it-girl

30th – Brownson, Siobhan Craft. 'Emily Brontë.' Poetry Foundation, 2019. www.poetryfoundation.org/poets/emily-bronte

31st – Takayanagi, M., (2020) 'Astor the Fairy Godmother: The Intoxicating Liquor Act 1923', Open Library of Humanities 6(2), 13. doi: https://doi.org/10.16995/olh.567

AUGUST

1st – Swallow, Bea. 'Joseph Priestley Mural to Mark Anniversary of Oxygen Discovery.' BBC News, 28 April 2024. www.bbc.co.uk/news/articles/c2levg9kge7o

2nd – 'Opinion: John Tyndall – the Forgotten Co-Discoverer of Climate Science.' University College London News, 31 July 2020. www.ucl.ac.uk/news/2020/jul/opinion-john-tyndall-forgotten-co-discoverer-climate-science

3rd – 'An English Expedition to America in 1527: Biggar, H. P. (Henry Percival,) 1872–1938'. Internet Archive, 2014. archive.org/details/anenglishexpedit00biggrich

4th – 'World War I.' British Newspaper Archive blog, 1 January 2018. blog.britishnewspaperarchive.co.uk/tag/world-war-i/

5th – '5 August 1962 Marilyn Monroe Death.' Newspapers.com, 6 August 1962. www.newspapers.com/article/tucson-daily-citizen-5-august-1962-maril/330720/?locale=en-GB

6th – 'Historic Figures: Jack the Ripper (?).' BBC, History, 2014. www.bbc.co.uk/history/historic_figures/ripper_jack_the.shtml

7th – 'Chimney Sweepers and Chimneys Regulation Act, 1840.' Electronic Irish Statute Book (EISB), Office of the Attorney General. www.irishstatutebook.ie/eli/1840/act/85/enacted/en/print.html

8th – Pearce, Simon. 'Heists Making Headlines: The Great Train Robbery (1963).' Newspapers.com, 13 May 2024. blog.newspapers.com/heists-making-headlines-the-great-train-robbery-1963/

9th – Potts, David M, and Lidija Zdravković (2001), *Finite Element Analysis in Geotechnical Engineering*. London, Thomas Telford.

10th – Whaley, Leigh. 'Political Factions and the Second Revolution: The Insurrection of 10 August 1792.' *French History*, vol. 7, no. 2, 1993, pp. 205–224, doi.org/10.1093/fh/7.2.205

11th – Clifton, Robin. 'Wentworth, Henrietta Maria, *suo jure* Baroness Wentworth (1660–1686), royal mistress.' Oxford Dictionary of National Biography. doi.org/10.1093/ref:odnb/29048

Smith, J. F. and Howitt, William (1873), *John Cassell's Illustrated History of England. The Text, to the Reign of Edward I by J.F. Smith; and from That Period by W. Howitt*. London, Cassell Ltd.

12th – Grout, James. 'Cleopatra's Death.' Encyclopaedia Romana. penelope.uchicago.edu/~grout/encyclopaedia_romana/miscellanea/cleopatra/rixens.html

Sources

Hamer, Mary. 'Who Was Cleopatra?' History Extra, 10 May 2023. www.historyextra.com/period/ancient-egypt/cleopatra-facts-ancient-egypt-beauty-life-death-egyptian-roman-caesar/

13th – Leatherdale, Duncan. 'Gwynne Evans and Peter Allen: The Last Men to Be Hanged.' BBC News, 13 August 2014. www.bbc.co.uk/news/uk-england-cumbria-28687221

14th – Inglis, Lucy (2014), *Georgian London: Into the Streets*. London, New York Penguin Books.

15th – Fabbri, Patrizia and Schlafke, Jacob (2019), *Cologne*. Casa Editrice Bonechi, Florence, Italy.

16th – Hammond, Trevor. 'Klondike Gold Rush Begins: August 16, 1896.' Fishwrap, the Official blog of Newspapers.com, 1 August 2015. blog.newspapers.com/klondike-gold-rush-begins-august-16-1896/

17th – 'Transcript: President Bill Clinton – Aug. 17, 1998.' CNN. edition.cnn.com/ALLPOLITICS/1998/08/17/speech/transcript.html

18th – 'Aug. 18, 1963 | James Meredith Graduates from Mississippi.' The Learning Network, 18 August 2011. archive.nytimes.com/learning.blogs.nytimes.com/2011/08/18/aug-18-1963-james-meredith-graduates-from-mississippi

19th – '1883, Birth of Gabrielle Chanel.' Chanel. www.chanel.com/gb/about-chanel/the-history/1883/

James, Caryn. 'The Truth about Coco Chanel and the Nazis.' BBC, 20 February 2024. www.bbc.com/culture/article/20240220-the-truth-about-coco-chanel-and-the-nazis

20th – Pettinger, Andrew (2012), *The Republic in Danger: Drusus Libo and the Succession of Tiberius*. Oxford, Oxford University Press.

21st – Saelee, Mike. 'Research Guides: Theft of Mona Lisa: Topics in Chronicling America: Introduction.' Library of Congress, 29 July 2019. *Guides.loc.gov*, guides.loc.gov/chronicling-america-theft-mona-lisa

22nd – Adomnán of Iona and Sharpe, Richard (trans.) (1995), *Life of St Columba*. Penguin UK.

23rd – 'St Bartholomew's Day Massacre.' BBC Radio 4, *In Our Time*, 27 November 2003. www.bbc.co.uk/programmes/p005493t

Williams, Emma Slattery. 'The Huguenots vs France: Who Were the Huguenots and What Did They Believe?' History Extra, 4 December 2020. www.historyextra.com/period/medieval/huguenot-rebellion-calvinist-edict-nantes-fontainebleau-st-bartholomews-day-massacre/

24th – 'Captain Matthew Webb Swims the Channel – 24 and 25 August 1875.' The British Newspaper Archive blog, 23 August 2013. blog.britishnewspaperarchive.co.uk/2013/08/23/captain-matthew-webb-swims-the-channel-24-and-25-august-1875/

25th - Isabel De Madariaga. *Ivan the Terrible*. New Haven Yale University Press, 2006.

26th – de Madariaga, Isabel (1942), *Ivan the Terrible*. New Haven, Yale University Press, (reprint, 2006).
27th – 'Guinness Record Book Collecting.' Guinness Book of Records. guinness.book-of-records.info/1950s.html
28th – 'Leo Tolstoy'. Tate. www.tate.org.uk/art/artists/leo-tolstoy-19796
29th – Perdue, Peter C. 'The First Opium War: The Anglo-Chinese War of 1839–1842: 1st Unequal Treaty.' MIT Visualizing Cultures, 2011. *Mit.edu*, 2011, visualizingcultures.mit.edu/opium_wars_01/ow1_essay04.html
30th – 'Mary Shelley' British Library, 31 July 2018. www.britishlibrary.cn/en/authors/mary-shelley/
31st – Snow, Stephanie J. 'Commentary: Sutherland, Snow and Water: The Transmission of Cholera in the Nineteenth Century.' *International Journal of Epidemiology*, vol. 31, no. 5, Oct. 2002, pp. 908–911, doi.org/10.1093/ije/31.5.908

SEPTEMBER

1st – 'Death of Louis XIV, 1715.' Palace of Versailles, 23 November 2016. en.chateauversailles.fr/discover/history/key-dates/death-louis-xiv-1715
2nd – 'The Great Fire of London.' London Fire Brigade, 2003. www.london-fire.gov.uk/museum/history-and-stories/the-great-fire-of-london/
3rd – 'Change in Calendar – Dates in the Old Parish Registers' National Records of Scotland, 31 May 2013. www.nrscotland.gov.uk/research/record-guides/old-parish-registers/change-in-calendar
4th – Fitzpatrick, Alex. 'Google Used to Be the Company That Did "Nothing But Search"' *Time*, 4 September 2014. time.com/3250807/google-anniversary/
5th – Johnson, Arbora. 'Phyllis Schlafly.' National Women's History Museum, 2022. www.womenshistory.org/education-resources/biographies/phyllis-schlafly
6th – 'President McKinley Shot: September 6, 1901.' Newspapers.com blog, 1 September 2014. blog.newspapers.com/president-mckinley-shot-september-6-1901/
7th – 'Elizabeth I (R.1558–1603).' Royal UK. www.royal.uk/elizabeth-i#:~:text=Elizabeth%20I%20%2D%20the%20last%20Tudor.
8th – 'Michelangelo's David.' Galleria dell'Accademia di Firenze, 17 November 2021. www.galleriaaccademiafirenze.it/en/artworks/david-michelangelo/
9th – Wills, Matthew. 'The Bug in the Computer Bug Story.' JSTOR Daily, 3 May 2022. daily.jstor.org/the-bug-in-the-computer-bug-story/
10th – 'London Cabbie George Smith Arrested for Drunk Driving in 1897.' The British Newspaper Archive blog, 9 September 2014. blog.britishnewspaperarchive.co.uk/2014/09/09/london-cabbie-george-smith-arrested-for-drunk-driving-in-1897/

Sources

11th – 'First Appearance of Jenny Lind in America, at Castle Garden, September 11th, 1850.' The Metropolitan Museum of Art. www.metmuseum.org/art/collection/search/380765

12th – 'Lascaux Cave | The Four Discoverers.' Archéologie.culture.gouv.fr. archeologie.culture.gouv.fr/lascaux/en/four-discoverers

13th – Howard, Philip. 'Roald Dahl.' Oxford Dictionary of National Biography, 23 September 2004. www.oxforddnb.com/display/10.1093/ref:odnb/9780198614128.001.0001/odnb-9780198614128-e-39827?docPos=2

14th – 'The Tiffany & Co. Timeline.' Tiffany & Co. www.tiffany.co.uk/world-of-tiffany/the-world-of-tiffany-timeline/

'Tiffany Celebrates 175th Anniversary.' ABC News, 2020. abcnews.go.com/blogs/headlines/2012/09/tiffany-celebrates-175th-anniversary

15th – McBride, Carrie. '100 Years Ago Men and Boys Fought on the Streets of New York Over Wearing Straw Hats Past Summer.' The New York Public Library, 23 September 2022. www.nypl.org/blog/2022/09/23/straw-hat-riots-nyc

16th – 'What Is the Mayflower and Why Is It Celebrated 400 Years Later?' BBC Newsround, 16 September 2020. www.bbc.co.uk/newsround/54152197

17th – Smith, Peter (2018), *Sex Pistols: The Pride of Punk*. Lanham, Maryland, Rowman & Littlefield.

18th – William Francis Collier (1892), *History of the British Empire*. Edinburgh, T. Nelson and Sons.

19th – Storey, Neil R. (2012), *The Little Book of Great Britain*. Cheltenham, The History Press.

20th – 'Battle of the Sexes.' Billie Jean King Enterprises, 2017. www.billiejeanking.com/battle-of-the-sexes/

21st – 'Stonehenge Sold for £6,600 a Hundred Years Ago Today.' English Heritage, 21 September 2015. www.english-heritage.org.uk/about-us/search-news/stonehenge-sold-100-years-ago/

22nd – 'Paris: Capital of the 19th Century.' Brown University Library Center for Digital Scholarship. library.brown.edu/cds/paris/chronology1.html

23rd – Byrd, Melanie Hollar and Dunn, John P. (2020), *Cooking through History*. Westport, Connecticut, Greenwood Publishing Group.

24th – 'A Brief Life of Fitzgerald.' University of South Carolina, 2018. sc.edu/about/offices_and_divisions/university_libraries/browse/irvin_dept_special_collections/collections/matthew_arlyn_bruccoli_collection_of_f_scott_fitzgerald/life_of_fitzgerald/index.php

Fitzgerald, Scott and Fitzgerald, Zelda (2003), *Dear Scott, Dearest Zelda : The Love Letters of F. Scott and Zelda Fitzgerald*. New York, London, Simon & Schuster.

25th – 'Publick Occurrences (Boston [Mass]) 1690–1690.' Library of Public Congress. www.loc.gov/item/sn85038269/

26th – 'The Hollywood Sign's Transformation: A Historic Moment in 1949.'

The Hollywood Sign, 2019. www.hollywoodsign.org/news-updates/september-2019#:~:text=On%20September%2026%2C%201949%2C%20the
27th – Meier, Allison C. 'Jean-François Champollion Deciphers the Rosetta Stone.' JSTOR Daily, 26 September 2022. daily.jstor.org/jean-francois-champollion-deciphers-the-rosetta-stone/
28th – 'Why Was Pompey the Great Assassinated?' History Hit, 8 August 2023. www.historyhit.com/why-was-pompey-the-great-assassinated/
29th – 'Metropolitan Police Take to the Streets.' British Library blog, 2015. blogs.bl.uk/untoldlives/2015/09/metropolitan-police-take-to-the-streets.html
30th – Staedter, Tracy. 'Live Giant Squid Photographed for First Time.' Scientific American, 29 September 2005. www.scientificamerican.com/article/live-giant-squid-photogra/

OCTOBER

1st – Hunt, Alice (2008), *The Drama of Coronation: Medieval Ceremony in Early Modern England*. Cambridge, Cambridge University Press.
  'Mary I (r.1553-1558)' Royal UK. www.royal.uk/mary-i
2nd – 'Brigham Young arrested for polygamy...' Timothy Hughes Rare and Early Newspapers. https://www.rarenewspapers.com/view/215057
3rd – Quinn, Arthur Hobson (1941), *Edgar Allan Poe: A Critical Biography*. London and New York, D. Appleton-Century Company.
4th – Orient Express. www.orient-express.com
5th – 'Departure of the King, 1789.' Palace of Versailles. en.chateauversailles.fr/discover/history/key-dates/departure-king-1789
6th – 'First individual circumnavigation of the globe using human power.' Guinness World Records. guinnessworldrecords.com/world-records/first-individual-circumnavigation-of-the-globe-using-human-power
  Expedition 360 | Around the World by Human Power. www.expedition360.com
7th – Grasso, John (2013), *Historical Dictionary of Football*. Lanham, Maryland, Scarecrow Press, Inc., Rowman & Littlefield.
8th – 'Julian/Gregorian Calendars.' The University of Nottingham, Manuscripts and Special Collections. www.nottingham.ac.uk/ManuscriptsandSpecialCollections/researchguidance/datingdocuments/juliangregorian.aspx
9th – Bennett, Steven (2021), Elite Participation in the Third Crusade. Suffolk, The Boydell Press.
10th – 'Henry Cavendish (1731–1810).' www.chatsworth.org/visit-chatsworth/chatsworth-estate/history-of-chatsworth/meet-the-devonshire-family/extended-family/henry-cavendish-1731-1810/
11th – 'First inflight meal.' Guinness World Records. guinnessworldrecords.com/world-records/498705-first-inflight-meal

Sources

12th – Corti, Count and Stamper, Evelyn B. Graham (trans.) (1943), *Ludwig I of Bavaria*. Eyre and Spottiswoode.

'The history of Oktoberfest: Historical foray through the history of the Wiesn.' Oktoberfest, München. www.oktoberfest.de/en/magazine/tradition/the-history-of-oktoberfest

13th – Suetonius (AD 121), Graves, Robert (trans.), *The Lives of the Twelve Caesars*. London, Penguin Books, 2007.

Levick, Barbara (2020), *Claudius*. Oxford, New York, Routledge.

Osgood, Josiah (2011), *Claudius Caesar: Image and Power in the Early Roman Empire*. Cambridge, Cambridge University Press.

14th – 'Sutton Bank: Memorial marks 700th anniversary of Battle of Byland.' BBC News, 14 October 2022. www.bbc.co.uk/news/uk-england-york-north-yorkshire-63245951

15th – Collected Works of Abraham Lincoln. Volume 4 [Mar. 5, 1860-Oct. 24, 1861]. University of Michigan Library Digital Collections. quod.lib.umich.edu/l/lincoln/lincoln4/1:21?rgn=div1;view=fulltext

'With Malice Toward None: The Abraham Lincoln Bicentennial Exhibition.' Library of Congress, Exhibitions. https://www.loc.gov/exhibits/lincoln/candidate-lincoln.html

16th – Brontë, Charlotte (1847), *Jane Eyre*. London, Penguin Books (reprint 2006).

17th – Oliver, Garrett (ed.) (2011), *The Oxford Companion to Beer*. Oxford University Press USA.

18th – 'John.' Westminster Abbey. www.westminster-abbey.org/abbey-commemorations/royals/john/

'How Did Magna Carta Come About?' UK Parliament. www.parliament.uk/about/living-heritage/evolutionofparliament/originsofparliament/birthofparliament/overview/magnacarta/magnacartahow/

19th – Lockett, Charles J. 'Ferdinand and Isabella: The Marriage That Unified Spain.' The Collector, 31 May 2022. www.thecollector.com/marriage-of-ferdinand-and-isabella/

Knepp-Holt, Constance M. (2021), *Monarch's Gambit: Tudors versus Spain*. Pennsylvania, Dorrance Publishing.

20th – 'Liz Truss: A quick guide to the UK's shortest-serving PM.' BBC News, 5 July 2024. https://www.bbc.co.uk/news/uk-62750866

21st – 'Baroness Swanborough takes the oath in the House of Lords.' www.parliament.uk/about/living-heritage/evolutionofparliament/houseoflords/house-of-lords-reform/from-the-collections/from-the-parliamentary-collections-lords-reform/accomodating-women-peers/baroness-swanborough-takes-the-oath-in-the-house-of-lords-21-october-1958/

22nd – White, Arthur L. (1985), *Ellen G. White the Early Years: 1827–1862 (Volume 1)*. Hagerstown, Maryland, Review & Herald Publishing Association.

'Seventh-day Adventists.' Oxford Reference.

www.oxfordreference.com/display/10.1093/oi/
authority.20110803100457323?p=emailAoIdTwBtB59Ew&d=/10.1093/oi/
authority.20110803100457323

23rd – Freshwater, M. Felix. 'Joseph Constantine Carpue and the Bicentennial of the Birth of Modern Plastic Surgery.' Aesthet Surg J. 2015 Aug;35(6):748-58. doi: 10.1093/asj/sju157. Epub 2015 Mar 19. PMID: 25795909; PMCID: PMC4520582.

24th – 'Pompeii: Vesuvius Eruption May Have Been Later than Thought.' *BBC News*, 16 Oct. 2018, www.bbc.co.uk/news/world-europe-45874858.

Lapatin, Kenneth. 'When Did Vesuvius Erupt? The Evidence for and against August 24.' Www.getty.edu, 23 Aug. 2019, www.getty.edu/news/when-did-vesuvius-erupt-august-october-24/.

25th – 'Picasso's Childhood.' *Musée Picasso Paris*, www.museepicassoparis.fr/en/picassos-childhood.

'Marie-Thérèse Walter Biography.' Masterworksfineart.com, 2018, www.masterworksfineart.com/bio/marie-therese-walter?srsltid=AfmBOooYxwC6QshgWtLOQ1JR5WdjQ3tLxm6RxPQoyD6pXjFBPo78suAt. Accessed 16 Oct. 2024.

26th – Frajola, Richard; Kramer, George; and Walske, Steven (2005), *The Pony Express, A Postal History*. Philatelic Foundation, New York

27th – 'SUBWAY OPENING TO-DAY WITH SIMPLE CEREMONY; Exercises at One o'Clock; Public to be Admitted at Seven. JOHN HAY MAY BE PRESENT Expected to Represent the Federal Government -- President Roosevelt Sends Letter of Regret.' New York Times, 27 October 1904. www.nytimes.com/1904/10/27/archives/subway-opening-today-with-simple-ceremony-exercises-at-one-oclock.html

28th – Harvard University. 'The History of Harvard.' Harvard University, 2023, www.harvard.edu/about/history/.

29th – Historic Royal Palaces. (2019). *Sir Walter Raleigh*. [online] Available at: https://www.hrp.org.uk/tower-of-london/history-and-stories/sir-walter-raleigh/#gs.g7jwzt [Accessed 16 Oct. 2024].

30th – Licence, Amy. *The Sixteenth Century in 100 Women*. Pen and Sword History, 2023.

Amir Adhamy. 'Your Guide to the Borgias.' *HistoryExtra*, 6 Oct. 2020, www.historyextra.com/period/renaissance/the-borgias-reputation-scandal-cesare-rodrigo-banquet-chestnuts/. Accessed 16 Oct. 2024.

31st – Thomas, H. (2021). *The Origins of Halloween Traditions | Headlines and Heroes*. [online] blogs.loc.gov. Available at: https://blogs.loc.gov/headlinesandheroes/2021/10/the-origins-of-halloween-traditions/.

NOVEMBER
1st – Pietrangeli, Carlo (1986), *The Sistine Chapel: The Art, the History and the Restoration*. New York, Harmony Books.
2nd – C. H. Rolph (ed.) (1990), *The Trial of Lady Chatterley: Regina v. Penguin Books Limited*. Penguin Books.
3rd – Jackson, David M. (1968), 'Bach, Handel, and the Chevalier Taylor.' Published online by Cambridge University Press, 16 August 2012. www.cambridge.org/core/services/aop-cambridge-core/content/view/AD989BB77DFC361A042E99AC2F0E1921/S002572730001365Xa.pdf/bach-handel-and-the-chevalier-taylor.pdf
4th – Elkins, Thomas. 'Improvement in refrigerating apparatus.' Patented 4 November 1879. patents.google.com/patent/US221222A/en
5th – Sharpe, James (2005), *Remember, Remember the Fifth of November: Guy Fawkes and the Gunpowder Plot*. London, Profile Books.
'Guy Fawkes.' UK Parliament. www.parliament.uk/about/living-heritage/evolutionofparliament/parliamentaryauthority/the-gunpowder-plot-of-1605/overview/people-behind-the-plot/guy-fawkes-/
6th – 'Gandhi.' The British Newspaper Archive. www.britishnewspaperarchive.co.uk/search/results/1931-11-06/1931-11-06?basicsearch=%22gandhi%22&phrasesearch=gandhi
7th – 'London Stage Event: 07 November 1722 at Drury Lane Theatre.' London Stage Database. londonstagedatabase.uoregon.edu/event.php?id=9444
8th – Izzard, Forrest (1915), *Heroines of the Modern Stage*. Sturgis and Walton Company, New York. Project Gutenberg. www.gutenberg.org/cache/epub/57611/pg57611-images.html#Footnote_30
Davis, Tracy C. (1991), *Actresses as Working Women*. Oxford, New York, Routledge. http://ndl.ethernet.edu.et/bitstream/123456789/17075/1/6.pdf
9th – Lee, Sir Sidney (2004), *King Edward VII: A Biography, Volume II*. Whitefish, Montana, Kessinger Publishing Co.
'The Cullinan Diamond Centennial: A History and Gemological Analysis Of Cullinans I And II.' Scarratt, Kenneth and Shor, Russell. Gems & Gemology, Summer 2006, Vol. 42, No. 2, Gemological Institute of America. www.gia.edu/gems-gemology/summer-2006-cullinan-diamond-scarratt
10th – 'Decree on Press was adopted: 9 November 1917.' Presidential Library, On This Day. www.prlib.ru/en/history/619704
11th – Alex C. Castles (2005), *Ned Kelly's Last Days: Setting the Record Straight on the Death of an Outlaw*. Sydney, Allen and Unwin.
Molony, John (1989), *Ned Kelly*. Melbourne University Press.
12th – Tan S.Y., Yip A. 'António Egas Moniz (1874–1955): Lobotomy pioneer and Nobel laureate.' Singapore Med J. 2014 Apr; 55(4):175–6. doi: 10.11622/smedj.2014048. PMID: 24763831; PMCID: PMC4291941.

Gross D., Schäfer G. 'Egas Moniz (1874–1955) and the "invention" of modern psychosurgery: a historical and ethical reanalysis under special consideration of Portuguese original sources.' Neurosurg Focus. 2011 Feb;30(2):E8. doi: 10.3171/2010.10.FOCUS10214. Erratum in: Neurosurg Focus. 2011 Apr;30(4).doi: 10.3171/2011.3.FOCUS10214a. PMID: 21284454.

'Lobotomy.' Oxford Reference. www.oxfordreference.com/display/10.1093/oi/authority.20110803100111247#:~:text=1%20Surgical%20severing%20of%20one,frontal%20lobotomy%20or%20frontal%20leucotomy

13th – Butcher, Richard (1646), *The survey and antiquitie of the towne of Stamford*. archive.org/details/bim_early-english-books-1641-1700_the-survey-and-antiquiti_butcher-richard_1646

14th – Pepys, Samuel (1666), *The Diary of Samuel Pepys, November 1666*. public-library.uk/ebooks/89/74.pdf

15th – Gillette, King C. 'Safety razors with one or more blades arranged transversely to the handle involving blades with two cutting edges.' Patented 15 November 1904. patents.google.com/patent/US775134A/en

16th – Feilding, Amanda, 'The Man who Mapped LSD.' Oxford University Press blog, 12 February 2019. https://blog.oup.com/2019/02/man-mapped-lsd/

17th – Abbott, Jacob (1849), *Queen Elizabeth*. Ebook 14 June 2019, BookRix. www.google.co.uk/books/edition/Queen_Elizabeth/gNuzAwAAQBAJ?hl=en&gbpv=1&dq=elizabeth+I+becomes+queen+of+england+november+17&printsec=frontcover

18th – Woodville, Anthony, Lord Rivers (trans.) (1489) 'The dictes and sayings of the philosophers.' William Caxton, Westminster. St John's College, University of Cambridge. www.joh.cam.ac.uk/library/special_collections/early_books/caxton.htm

19th – Perrie, Maureen (2003), *Ivan the Terrible*. Oxford, New York, Routledge, pp. 192.

20th – Princess Diana Interview with Martin Bashir, *Panorama*, BBC TV, 20 November 1995. www.bbc.co.uk/programmes/p031d01q

'Panorama interview with Princess Diana, 20 November 1995.' BBC, History of the BBC, Anniversaries. www.bbc.com/historyofthebbc/anniversaries/november/diana-interview

21st – Spencer, Frank (1990), *The Piltdown Papers, 1908–1955*. Natural History Museum Publications.

'Piltdown Man.' Natural History Museum, The Library and Archives Collection. www.nhm.ac.uk/our-science/services/library/collections/piltdown-man.html

22nd – Roller, Sarah. 'Who Was Blackbeard and How Did He Become One of History's Most Notorious Pirates?' History Hit, 10 November 2021. www.historyhit.com/1718-blackbeard-hunted-killed-royal-navy/

Sources

23rd – Cavendish, Richard. 'The Duke of Orleans is Ambushed.' *History Today*, Volume 57, Issue 11, November 2007. www.historytoday.com/archive/duke-orleans-ambushed
   Vaughan, Richard (1966), *John the Fearless: the Growth of Burgundian Power*. Essex, Longman.
24th – 'Charles Darwin.' National Library of Scotland. www.nls.uk/collections/john-murray/authors/charles-darwin/
25th – 'The 20th Anniversary of Band Aid.' BBC Radio 2 Documentaries, 21 November 2004. www.bbc.co.uk/radio2/r2music/documentaries/bandaid/
26th – 'Henry Ireton.' Oxford Reference. www.oxfordreference.com/display/10.1093/oi/authority.20110810105142767
27th – *Notes and Queries: a Medium of Inter-communication for Literary Men, Artists, Antiquaries, Genealogists, Etc.* (1850, revised 1890, digitized 17 October 2023). Bell. www.google.co.uk/books/edition/Notes_and_Queries_a_Medium_of_Inter_comm/3cbRG7Xp16UC?hl=en&gbpv=0
28th – 'Women vote in first general election: 28 November 1893.' New Zealand History. nzhistory.govt.nz/page/women-vote-first-general-election
29th – Schrödinger, Erwin "Die gegenwärtige Situation in der Quantenmechanik" [The present situation in quantum mechanics]. www.bonhams.com/auction/21652/lot/142/schrodingers-cat-schrodinger-erwin-1887-1961-die-gegenwartige-situation-in-der-quantenmechanik-the-present-situation-in-quantum-mechanics-in-die-naturwissenschaften-vol-23-issues-48-november-29-49-december-6-and-50-december-13-1935-pp-807-12-823-28-844-49-berlin-julius-springer-1935/
   Trimmer, John D.' The Present Situation in Quantum Mechanics: A Translation of Schrödinger's "Cat Paradox."' personal.lse.ac.uk/robert49/teaching/partiii/pdf/SchroedingerPresentSituation1935(1980trans).pdf
30th – Howells, Katherine. 'Remembering the Crystal Palace fire of 1936.' The National Archives blog, 30 November 2022. blog.nationalarchives.gov.uk/remembering-the-crystal-palace-fire-of-1936/

DECEMBER

1st – Burke, Myles. 'Rosa Parks: The "No" That Sparked the Civil Rights Movement.' BBC, 29 November 2023. www.bbc.com/culture/article/20231128-rosa-parks-the-one-moment-that-sparked-the-civil-rights-movement
   Dwyer, Liz. 'Rosa Parks Was My Aunt. It's Time to Set the Record Straight.' Shondaland, 2 February 2018. www.shondaland.com/inspire/a16022001/rosa-parks-was-my-aunt/
2nd – Roller, Sarah. 'China's Last Emperor: Who Was Puyi and Why Did He Abdicate?' History Hit, 1 February 2022. www.historyhit.com/puyi-last-emperor-of-china/
3rd – Levy, Martin J. 'Robinson [née Darby], Mary [Perdita] (1756/1758?–

1800), author and actress.' Oxford Dictionary of National Biography, 3 January 2008. https://doi.org/10.1093/ref:odnb/23857

4th – Faiella, Graham. 'The Mary Celeste: The History of a Mystery.' The Historical Association, 3 February 2023. www.history.org.uk/publications/resource/10590/the-mary-celeste-the-history-of-a-mystery

5th – 'Medieval Sourcebook: Witchcraft Documents (15th Century).' Fordham University Internet History Sourcebooks.' origin-rh.web.fordham.edu/Halsall/source/witches1.asp

Deyrmenjian, Maral. 'Pope Innocent VIII (1484–1492) and the *Summis Desiderantes Affectibus.' Malleus Maleficarum 1*. Portland State University Library, 1 January 2020. archives.pdx.edu/ds/psu/34822

6th – 'Henry VI' | Tower of London | Historic Royal Palaces. www.hrp.org.uk/tower-of-london/history-and-stories/henry-vi/#gs.f47jpm

7th – 'John Blanke' | Tower of London | Historic Royal Palaces. www.hrp.org.uk/tower-of-london/history-and-stories/john-blanke/#gs.f47kim

8th – 'Televising Parliament.' UK Parliament. www.parliament.uk/about/living-heritage/evolutionofparliament/parliamentwork/communicating/overview/televisingparliament/

9th – Photograph of 'The Original 20! This is the cast line-up for the very first episode of Coronation Street – 9th December 1960.' Facebook. www.facebook.com/photo.php?fbid=10153541411637659&id=75373902658&set=a.100876352658&locale=en_GB

10th – O'Day, Rosemary (2012). *The Routledge Companion to the Tudor Age*. Oxford, New York, Routledge.

11th – Lewis, Matt. 'The Last Prince of Wales: The Death of Llywelyn Ap Gruffudd.' History Hit, 12 June 2023. www.historyhit.com/the-last-prince-of-wales-the-death-of-llywelyn-ap-gruffudd/

12th – 'Frank Sinatra Timeline.' Frank Sinatra, 1998. www.sinatra.com/frank-sinatra-timeline/

13th – Sullivan, Caroline (2024), *Taylor Swift: Era by Era*. London, Michael O'Mara Books.

14th – Rappaport, Helen. 'What Killed Prince Albert?' History Extra, 7 January 2020. www.historyextra.com/period/victorian/what-killed-prince-albert-how-did-he-die-death-cause-age-old-illness-health-queen-victoria-season-three/

15th – 'The Bill of Rights: A Transcription.' The National Archives, 4 November 2015. www.archives.gov/founding-docs/bill-of-rights-transcript#:~:text=Amendment%20I–

16th – '1773 to 1774 | Timeline | Documents from the Continental Congress and the Constitutional Convention, 1774–1789.' Library of Congress. www.loc.gov/collections/continental-congress-and-constitutional-convention-from-1774-to-1789/articles-and-essays/timeline/1773-to-1774/

Sources

17th – 'Saturnalia.' English Heritage. www.english-heritage.org.uk/members-area/kids/kids-christmas/saturnalia#:~:text=Saturnalia%20was%20one%20of%20many

18th – New York City Ballet, Docampo, Valeria (illus.) (2016), *The Nutcracker*. London, New York, Simon and Schuster.

19th – Stockwell, Noel. 'Mary Livermore.' U.S. National Park Service. www.nps.gov/people/mary-livermore.htm

20th – 'On This Day, the Louisiana Purchase Is Completed.' National Constitution Center, 2021. constitutioncenter.org/blog/on-this-day-the-louisiana-purchase-is-completed

'Proclamation to the Residents of the Province of Louisiana, December 20, 1803.' U.S. Capitol Visitor Center. www.visitthecapitol.gov/artifact/proclamation-residents-province-louisiana-december-20-1803

De Cesar, Wayne, and Page, Susan. 'Jefferson Buys Louisiana Territory, and the Nation Moves Westward.' The National Archives, 15 August 2016. www.archives.gov/publications/prologue/2003/spring/louisiana-purchase.html

21st – Kaufman, J B. (2012), *The Fairest One of All : [the Making of Walt Disney's Snow White and the Seven Dwarfs]*. Walt Disney Family Foundation Press, San Francisco.

22nd – 'The Talking Phonograph.' *Scientific American*, 14 [?] December 1877. edison.rutgers.edu/images/innovations/TAEBdocs/Doc1150_PhonoSciAm_linked.pdf

'History of the Cylinder Phonograph.' The Library of Congress, 2015. www.loc.gov/collections/edison-company-motion-pictures-and-sound-recordings/articles-and-essays/history-of-edison-sound-recordings/history-of-the-cylinder-phonograph/

23rd – 'Vincent's Illness and the Healing Power of Art.' Van Gogh Museum, 2023. www.vangoghmuseum.nl/en/art-and-stories/stories/vincents-illness-and-the-healing-power-of-art

Hoban, Virgie. 'What Actually Happened to Vincent van Gogh's Ear? Here Are 3 Things You Should Know.' University of California, Berkeley Library, 26 November 2019. www.lib.berkeley.edu/about/news/van-Gogh-ear

24th – Hough, Carole (2016), *The Oxford Handbook of Names and Naming*. Oxford, Oxford University Press.

Davidson, Lucy. 'How Did Australia's Christmas Island Get Its Name?' History Hit, 2020.
www.historyhit.com/1643-christmas-island-gets-name/

25th – McPherson, Amy. 'Greccio: The Italian Village That's Home to the World's First Nativity Scene.' BBC, 19 December 2023. www.bbc.com/travel/article/20231219-greccio-the-italian-village-thats-home-to-the-worlds-first-nativity-scene#:~:text=This%20is%20where%20St%20Francis

26th – 'Stage History | King Lear.' Royal Shakespeare Company. www.rsc.org.uk/king-lear/past-productions/stage-history

'King Lear by William Shakespeare.' Royal Holloway, 2022. royalholloway.ac.uk/research-and-teaching/departments-and-schools/drama-theatre-and-dance/teacherhubdrama-theatre-and-dance/king-lear/

27th – Spring, Kelly. 'Marlene Dietrich.' National Women's History Museum, 2017. www.womenshistory.org/education-resources/biographies/marlene-dietrich

28th – Jamieson, Professor David. 'Galileo's miraculous year 1609 and the revolutionary telescope.' *Australian Physics*, Volume 46, Number 3, May/June 2009, pp.72–76. www.ph.unimelb.edu.au/~dnj/AP-June-2009-Galileo-Neptune.pdf

29th – 'On This Day 29th December 1940.' Royal Signals Museum. www.royalsignalsmuseum.co.uk/on-this-day-29th-december/#:~:text=On%20the%2029th%20December%201940

30th – 'Watch London Fire Raids 29th–30th December 1940.' BFI Player. player.bfi.org.uk/free/film/watch-london-fire-raids-29th-30th-december-1940-1940-online#:~:text=The%20City%20Of%20London%20suffered

31st – Williams, Brian and Brenda (2020), *A Victorian Christmas*. London, Batsford Books.

Index

A Tale of Two Cities (C. Dickens) 75
abortion laws 23
Academy Awards/Oscars 79, 84
Act Against Multiplying (1404) 18
The Agitator 195
Agrippa Postumus 135
Albert, Prince 192
alchemy 18
alcohol banned for under 18s, UK 122
Alexander II of Scotland, King 119
Alexander the Great 97
Alexandra Palace fire 97
Alice in Wonderland (L. Carroll) 25–6
American Football 160
Andre, Peter 37
Ankhesenamun, Queen 37
Anne of Cleves 12–13, 121, 204
Anne of Great Britain, Queen 47, 66, 94, 150
Anthony, Mark 131–2
ap Gruffyd, Llywelyn 191
asylums, 19th century 80
Augustus, Emperor 20, 135
Austen, Jane 60

Baird, John Logie 25
balloon flight, first gas 15–16
bananas on show in England, first 63
Band Aid concerts 183
Barbie dolls 47
Battle of Old Byland (1322) 164

Battle of Wakefield (1460) 201
BBC TV play production, first 115–16
Bean, John William 110–11
The Beatles 44–5
beauty treatments 141
Bedell, Grace 165
beer flood, London 166
Beethoven, Ludwig van 80–1
Beeton, Isabella 48
Bell, Alexander Graham 47
Berners Street hoax 184
Bernhardt, Sarah 176
Bevan, Aneurin 111
Bill of Rights (1791), US 193
birth control 23
Black Death 51
Blackbeard 182
Blackpool Illuminations 150
Blanke, John 190
Blenheim Palace 94
Bly, Nellie 79–80
Boat Race, London 61
Boleyn, Anne 14, 78, 84
Bonaparte, Napoleon 64, 87, 195
Bondfield, Margaret 96–7
Bonnie Prince Charlie 119–20
book publication in England, first dated 179
Borden, Lizzie 117–18
Borgia, Cesare and Lucrezia 170–1
Boston Tea Party 193

Boudica 91
Bow, Clara 122
boy racers 26
British Museum 31–2
Brontë, Charlotte 165–6
Brontë, Emily 122
Brutus, Marcus Junius 49
Buckland, William 38
Buddha, birth of 63
'bugs,' engineering 147
'bull run,' Lincolnshire 178
Bunsen, Robert 57
Burchard, Johann 170
Burgundy, John the Fearless, Duke of 182
Burns, George 24–5
Burr, Vice President Aaron 114
Bush, President George H.W. 16–17
Byron, Lord 84–5

calendar replaced, Julian 145, 160–1
Caligula, Emperor 38
Camilla of Great Britain, Queen 39, 110, 180
Carnarvon, Lord 35–6
Carroll, Lewis 25
Carter, Howard 35
Casanova's arrest 121
Catherine of Aragon 14, 22, 97, 101–2
Catherine the Great 112–13
Cavendish, Henry 161
Cavendish, Margaret 89
Central Park, New York City 118–19
Chaddock, Captain John 21
Champollion, Jean-François 153–4
Chanel, Coco 135
Charles I of Great Britain, King 22–3, 27, 100, 183
Charles II of Great Britain, King 46, 81, 88, 131, 198
Charles III of Great Britain, King 39, 110
child labour 128, 133
chimney sweeps 90, 128
chloroform, invention of 96
cholera epidemic 140
Christmas Island 196–7
Christmas nativity play performed, first 197
Chrystal Palace fire 185
Chubb, Cecil 151
Churchill, Sarah 94
Churchill, Winston 63

circumnavigation, human-powered global 160
circus, P.T. Barnum and J. Baileys three-ring 55
Civil Rights Act (1964) 110
Clarence, George, Duke of 36
Clarke, Reverend James Stanier 60
Claudius, Emperor 164
Cleland, John 24
Clement VII, Pope 14
Cleopatra of Egypt, Queen 131–2
Cliff's Notes study guides 67
Clinton, Bill 134
Cologne Cathedral 133–4
Conscious Lovers (R. Steele), London premiere of 176
Constantine, Emperor 46, 85
Cook, Captain James 75, 196–7
Copenhagen Fire 96
Coram, Thomas 133
Corday, Charlotte 115
cornflakes patent issued, Kellogg' 65
Coronation Street first episode of 190–1
Coxe, Francis 104
Cranmer, Thomas 51–2
Crimean War 83
Cromwell, Oliver 27, 87–8, 183
Cullinan diamond 176
Culpeper, Thomas 191
Czolgosz, Leon 146

D-Day landings postponed 96
da Verrazzano, Giovanni 66–7
Dahl, Roald 148
the Dancing Plague 123
Dartmoor Prison 86–7
Darwin, Charles 182–3
David statue, Michelangelo's 146
Davison, Emily 95
Dawson, Charles 180
de' Medici, Catherine and Marguerite 137
de' Medici, Lorenzo and Giuliano 72
de Rabutin-Chantal, Marie 31
Declaration of Independence (1776) 111
Defenestration of Prague 198
Diana, Princess of Wales 39, 110, 180
Dickens, Charles 75
Dietrich, Marlene 200
Disney, Walt 195
Disneyland opens 117

Index

DNA structure discovered 41
drink driving charge, first 147

Earhart, Amelia 85
Edison, Thomas 147, 196
Edward II of England, King 116, 164
Edward IV of England, King 112
Edward of England, King 36
Edward the Confessor 14–15
Edward the Martyr of England, King 50
Edward VI of England, King 69, 113
Edward VII of Great Britain, King 176–7
Edward VIII of Great Britain, King 95
Eiffel Tower 57
Einstein, Albert 130
Eisenhower, President Dwight D. 96
Elfthryth, Queen 50
Elizabeth I of Great Britain, Queen 17, 32, 113, 114, 138, 146, 179
Elizabeth II of Great Britain, Queen 31, 94
Elkins, Dr Thomas 175
English Channel, first person to swim the 137
Equal Rights Amendments 145–6
executions in the UK, last 132

Facebook launched 30
Fanny Hill (J. Cleland) 24
Farriner, Thomas 144
fashion 20, 123, 135
Fawkes, Guy 175
feasts, Middle Age 151–2
Federal Bureau of Investigation (FBI) 49
Ferdinand, Archduke Franz 127
Ferdinand and Isabella of Spain, King and Queen 167
Fleming, Ian 88
football league, world's first 52–3
Founding Fathers, USA 26, 111, 114
Foundling Hospital established 133
Francis, the Dauphin of France 69
Frank, Anne 98
Frankenstein (M. Shelley) 140
Franklin, Aretha 13
French Revolution 26, 57, 115, 129, 151, 159–60
Freud, Sigmund 90

Galilei, Galileo 200–1
gambling legalisation in Nevada 50

Gandhi 37, 175–6
Gardiner, Jeane 87
Genghis Khan 90
George I of Great Britain, King 150
George II of Great Britain, King 24, 119–20, 133
George III of Great Britain, King 104, 111, 188–9
George IV of Great Britain, King 60, 104
giant squid photographed, first live 155
Gillette razor blade patent 178
Godwinson, Harold 14–15
Gone With the Wind book (M. Mitchell) 79
Google 145
government cabinet minister, first British female 96–7
grave robbers, Burke and Hare 91
the Great Depression 50, 130
the Great Disappointment 168
the Great Fire of London 144
The Great Gatsby (F. Scott Fitzgerald) 152
Great Train Robbery 128
Gregorian calendar introduced 145, 160–1
Gregory XIII, Pope 160–1
Grey, Lady Jane 113–14
guillotine, first use of the 72
Guinness Book of World Records launched 139
Gustav III of Sweden, King 49–50

Halloween 171
Hamilton, Alexander 114
Handel, George Frederick 174
Handler, Ruth 47
Harold of England, King 14–15
Harris, Benjamin 153
Harrison, President Benjamin 13
Harris's List 106–7
Harvard College, foundation of 170
Henley Royal Regatta 54
Henry IV of England, King 18
Henry V of England, King 189–90
Henry VI of England (and King of France), King 189–90
Henry VIII of England, King 12–13, 14, 22, 34, 51, 56, 68, 69, 78, 84, 97, 101–2, 114, 121–2, 126, 191
hippopotamus in London Zoo, first 87
Hitler, Adolf 68, 117
Hochstanden, Archbishop Konrad von 133–4

Hofmann, Dr Albert 178
Holbein, Hans 12–13
Hollywood 30, 153
homophobia 85, 145, 146
Hong Kong, British rule of 140
House of Lords 167–8, 190
Howard, Catherine 34, 121–2, 191
Huaynaputina volcano eruption, Peru 36
Hughes, Ted 39–40
Hugo, Victor 40
Huguenots 137

ice hockey, indoor 44
incest 33, 37, 84–5, 167
Indigenous Australians 75
inflight meals introduced 161
Innocent VIII, Pope 189
iPod Touch launch, Apple 17
Ireton, Henry 183
Ivan the Terrible 138, 180
Jack the Ripper 127
Jackson, President Andrew 27
Jacobite Rebellion 119–20
James I of Great Britain, King 175, 200
Jefferson, Thomas 195
Joan of Arc 112
Joan of England (later Queen Consort of Scotland) 119
John of England, King 119, 166–7
Johnson, President Lyndon 110
Julius Caesar, Emperor 49, 131, 132, 154, 160

Keller, Helen 104–5
Kellogg, John Harvey 65
Kelly, Ned 177
Kennedy, John F. 63, 123
Kidd, Captain William 86
King, Billie Jean 150–1
King Charles Spaniels 88–9
King Lear (W. Shakespeare) 200
Klondike Gold Rush 134
Korean and USA relations 86

Ladies' Mercury magazine launched 41
Lady Chatterley's Lover (D.H. Lawrence) 174
Las Vegas, founding of 50
Lawrence, Richard 27
Leaning Tower of Pisa 128

Lee, Harper 74
Lenin, Vladimir 177
Lennon, John 44–5
letter from North America, first English language 126
Lewinsky, Monica 134
Lewis, Jason 160
Lincoln, President Abraham 165
Lind, Jenny 147
Little Colonel film (1935) 39
Livermore, Mary Ashton 195
lobotomies 177
Loch Ness Monster 136–7
London Underground opening 17
lottery, England's first 17–18
Louis XIV of France, King 144
Louis XVI of France, King 129, 151
Louisiana Purchase 195
'Loveday' service, St Paul's Cathedral 53
Lovelace, Ada 91
LSD accidentally synthesized 178
Ludwig of Bavaria, Prince Regent 164

Maclean, Roderick 44
McDaniel, Hattie 79
MacDonald, Ramsay 97
McKinley, President William 146
malaria parasite 83
Mansart, Jules Hardouin 82
Marat, Jean-Paul 115
Marić, Mileva 130
Marie Antoinette 129, 130, 159–60
Marlborough, John Churchill, Duke of 94
Mary Celeste 189
Mary I of England, Queen 51–2, 113, 114, 158, 179
Mary, Queen of Scots 32, 69
Mayflower 149
medicine, first woman to practise 116
Medieval marriages, feud settlement and 199
Megalosaurus 38
Mein Kampf (A. Hitler) 117
Meredith, James 134
Merian, Maria Sibylla 60
Metropolitan Museum of Art, NYC 65
Metropolitan Police established 155
Michelangelo 146
Microsoft, foundation of 61
'missing link' hoax 180

Index

Mona Lisa theft 135–6
Moniz, Antonio Egas 177
Monmouth Rebellion 131
Monroe, Marilyn 127
moon landing, first 118
Mormons 158
moving pictures, world's first 99
Mozart, Wolfgang Amadeus 98
Mrs Beeton's Book of Household Management (I. Beeton) 48
multiplication ban, England 18
Mussolini, Benito 105
Muybridge, Eadweard 99

'Nae Hair O'nt' (G. Burns) 24–5
Napoleonic Wars 86–7
NASA 118
NAACP 33–4, 188
National Convention, France 151
National Health Service (NHS) established 111
Native Americans 61, 153
Nelson, Lord 120
Neptune identified as a planet 200–1
New Academy of Complements 202–3
New Year's Eve 201
New York Harbour discovered 66–7
New York Subway opens 169–70
Newton knighted, Sir Isaac 66
Niagara Falls 57
Nightingale, Florence 82–3
Nissen, George 45–6
Northumberland, Walcher, Earl of 83–4
Nuestra Señora de las Maravillas 14
Nutcracker ballet premiere, Russia 194

Octavian, Emperor 131
'OK' (the word) first published 53
Oktoberfest 164
Olympic Games, first modern 62
Opium War, First 140
Orient Express maiden voyage 159
Orleans, Louis, Duke of 182
Otto III, Emperor 86
Oughtred, William 105
oxygen, discovery of 126

Paine, Thomas 26
Palaeolithic cave paintings 148
Pankhurst, Emmeline 95

Parks, Rosa 188
Parr, Katherine 114
passport, oldest 112
Peasants' Revolt 116
Penny Black stamps 80
Pepys, Samuel 46, 89, 178
Peter III of Russia, Emperor 112–13
the Phantom comic strip released 36
phonograph, invention of the 196
Picasso, Pablo 169
Pilgrim Fathers 149
plastic surgery 168
Plath, Sylvia 39–40
Pocahontas 61
Poe, Edgar Allan 158–9
poison, 'Aqua Tofana' 181
polio vaccines 39
Pompeii 168–9
Pompey the Great 154
'Pony Express' discontinued 169
presidency, first woman to run for US 81–2
Presley, Elvis 78
Price, Katie 37
Priestley, Joseph 126
Privy Council, Royal 104
Ptolemy XIII, pharaoh 154
Publick Occurences Both Forreign and Domestick 153
Pu Yi of China, Emperor

racism 33–4, 39, 79, 103, 110, 134, 153, 188
railway journey, world's first 38–9
Raleigh, Sir Walter 170
Rasputin 90
rationing, food 79
refrigeration developments 175
Richard I of England, King 161
Richard II of England, King 151–2
Richard III of England, King 111–12
Richard of York 201
Riggs, Bobby 150–1
Robinson, Mary 188–9
Rock and Roll Hall of Fame 13
Röntgen, Wilhelm 18
Roosevelt, Franklin D. 130
Rosetta Stone 153–4
'Rough Wooing', Scotland 69
Royal Society 89

St Apollonia's Day 32–3

St Bartholomew's Day Massacre 137
St Columba 136–7
St David 44
St Francis of Assisi 197
St Patrick 50
St Scholastica Day riots 33
Salem Witch Trials 19
Sanger, Alice 13
Saturnalia festival, Ancient Roman 194
Schlafly, Phyllis 145–6
Schrödinger, Erwin 185
Scientific American magazine 196
Scott, Captain Robert 20–1
Scott Fitzgerald, F. 152
Scottish Militia Bill (1708) 47
Sex Pistols 149–50
Seymour, Jane 78
Shakespeare, William 56, 68, 200
Shelley, Mary 140
Shoichi Yokoi 24
Simpson, James 96
Simpson, Wallis 95
Sinatra, Frank 192
Sistine Chapel ceiling revealed 174
slavery 35, 79, 102
smoking ban in NYC, women's 23
Snow, John 140
Snow White and the Seven Dwarfs premiere, LA 195
Somerset, James 102
South Pole, race to the 20–1
Spears, Britney 131
Springfield riot, US 33–4
STIs/clap in Georgian period 106–7
Stoker, Bram 67–8
Stonehenge 151
Stowe, Dr Emily 116
straw hat season, New York 149
suffrage 13, 95, 98–9, 184, 195
Sunday as a day of rest 46
Swanborough, Baroness 167–8
Swift, Taylor 192

Taj Mahal, India 100
Tatler magazine launched 64
Tea Act (1773) 193
telephones, invention of 47
television, invention of the 25
Tereshkova, Valentina 99–100
Tiberius, Emperor 135

Tichborne Dole 54
Tiffany Store opening, NYC 148
Tit-Bits magazine 72–3
Titanic sinks, RMS 33
toilet paper 138–9
Tolstoy, Leo 139
trampoline patent 45–6
Treaty of Fontainebleau (1814) 64
Treaty of Versailles (1919) 105
Truss, Liz 167
Tudor insults 56
Tudor marriage, surviving a 70–1
Tulip Mania, Holland 30
Turing, Alan 102–3
Turpin, Dick 62
Tutankhamun 35–6, 37
Tyndall effect 126
'Typhoid Mary' 54–5

UFOs 21, 67
Uranus, discovery of 49

Valentine's Day 34–5
Van Gogh, Vincent 196
Versailles, Palace of 82, 144, 159–60
Vesuvius volcano, Mount 168–9
Victoria of Great Britain, Queen 30, 44, 87, 96, 101, 110–11, 127, 162–3, 192–3
Vlad the Impaler 131
Voltaire 33

Wentworth, Henrietta Maria 131
West, Kanye 37–8
wife-swapping 45
Wilcox, Harvey 30
Wilde, Oscar 85
William the Conqueror 83–4
window tax 120
witchcraft and sorcery 19, 87, 104
Woodhull, Victoria 81–2
World War One 101, 105, 127
World War Two 24, 31, 45–6, 68, 79, 96, 102–3, 145, 168, 201

X-rays 18, 141

Young, Brigham 158

Zuckerburg, Mark 30